Britain's Economic and Social Development from 1700 to 1975

Britain has a surface area of 240,000 sq km (93,000 square miles). Its inhabitants number 56 million. Among the countries of the world it ranks seventy-second in terms of land area, and twelfth in size of population. Only Japan, West Germany, Belgium and the Netherlands are more densely populated. Apart from coal, oil and natural gas Britain has few natural resources. Yet in the world trade league table Britain lies fifth. Most of her exports are manufactures, and agriculture employs only a tiny proportion (less than 3 per cent) of her working population. Nearly half her food has to be imported. Britain's continued prosperity therefore, depends upon the ingenuity, skill, and determination of her people, and upon the prosperity of those countries which buy her exports. Yet in 1700, when this history begins, most of Britain's $5\frac{1}{2}$ million inhabitants depended more-or-less directly upon the land for their living. This book explains in outline how this momentous change came about, and what consequences it had for the British people.

Britain's Economic and Social Development from 1700 to 1975

R N RUNDLE

HODDER AND STOUGHTON
LONDON SYDNEY AUCKLAND TORONTO

The cover illustration shows the City Basin, Regent's Canal, London. When this was opened in 1820, exports from the industrial north and midlands could be transported entirely by canal to the Thameside docks. (The print – in the Waterways Museum collection – is reproduced by courtesy of the British Waterways Board.)

Acknowledgments
I wish to thank J. W. Packer, headmaster of Canon Slade Grammar School, Bolton, for his encouragement and advice during the early stages of the book, and Peter Brice, who read the book in manuscript and proof form, and made many helpful suggestions and corrections to the text. I am also indebted to Geoffrey Norton for vital information on Dud Dudley's process. Finally, for Jill, my wife, I have especial thanks, not only for her understanding and help as resident critic, but for the days she spent looking at industrial remains when she would have preferred beauty spots.

R.N.R.

ISBN 0 340 11614 5

First published 1973
Second impression, with amendments, 1976

Maps drawn by Crispin Fisher
Printed in Great Britain by
Hazell Watson & Viney Ltd, Aylesbury, Bucks
for Hodder and Stoughton Educational,
a division of Hodder and Stoughton Ltd,
St Paul's House, Warwick Lane,
London EC4P 4AH

The author and publisher wish to thank the following for permission to reproduce the illustrations in this book: the Radio Times Hulton Picture Library, 3, 4, 5, 6, 45, 58, 61, 65, 67, 71–4; Leicestershire County Council, 7, 8; the British Museum, 9, 11, 13–16, 18–20, 22, 24–6, 28, 30, 31, 34–6, 41, 48, 49, 51–3, 62, 63, 69; Manchester Central Library, 27, 32, 33, 38, 40; University of Cambridge Library, 29, 50, 55; Bristol Central Library, 42; Museum of English Rural Life, University of Reading, 43, 44, 70; *The Illustrated London News*, 46, 47, 54, 56, 68; the Greater London Council Members' Library, 57; the Greater London Council's Department of Architecture and Civic Design's Graphic Unit, 59; Newport Public Library, Monmouthshire, 61; Edinburgh Central Public Library, 64; the Principal, Cheltenham Ladies' College, 66; Aerofilms Ltd, 75; Mr J. W. Ginns, 77; the United Kingdom Atomic Energy Authority, 78.

CONTENTS

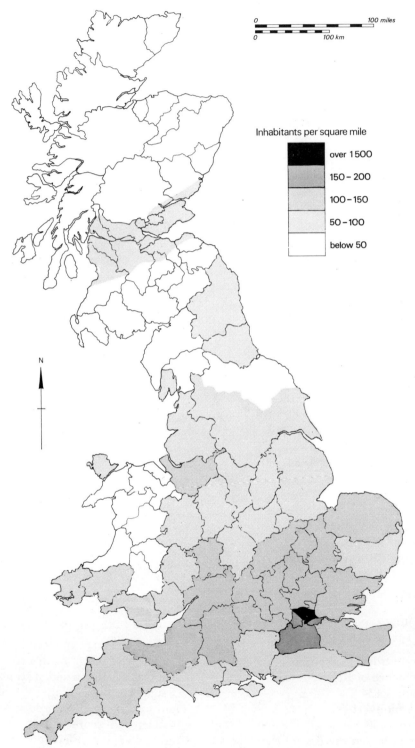

Inhabitants per square mile

over 1500

150 – 200

100 – 150

50 – 100

below 50

100 miles

100 km

N

1   *Distribution of population in Britain in the early eighteenth century*

PART I

CHAPTER 1
The Growth of Population

The astonishing rise in Britain's population, which began about the middle of the eighteenth century, and which continued until well into the nineteenth, was revolutionary in its effects. During the eighteenth century the population almost doubled, and between 1801 and 1901 it multiplied itself by three and a half times, reaching a total of 37 million. Such a rapid rate of increase not only changed the lives of the people but the very landscape itself. All these people had to be fed, housed, clothed, and provided with work, as well as governed. Thus farming, industry, transport, central and local government, education, and all kinds of public services, were transformed in order to solve the problems created, many of which in some form or other are still with us. In one very important sense therefore, this book is a commentary on that growth. The increase in population is all the more remarkable when it is realized that many educated people in the early part of the eighteenth century and even some at the end of it, thought that the population was declining.

In 1700 interest in 'political arithmetic' (or economic statistics as we should call it today) was growing. The rivalries of all the European countries caused their governments to take a closer interest in their trade and population figures, and the need for accurate statistics was increasingly evident. In England in the late seventeenth century John Graunt and Sir William Petty tried to discover the actual size of England's population. Their estimates were vague and unreliable, for they were based upon such things as returns of burials, baptisms, and marriages, and tax returns, which could be incomplete or misleading. Although Sweden and certain American Colonies held regular censuses since the middle of the eighteenth

century, the first British census was not until 1801. A census was proposed in 1753, but it was rejected on the grounds that it would lead to conscription and higher taxation, in addition to betraying England's weakness to her enemies.

The earliest accurate estimate of England's population was made in 1696 by Gregory King in his *Observations on the State of England*. He calculated the population to be about $5\frac{1}{2}$ millions. King thought that the population might well have doubled by A.D. 2300 and, should the world last so long, have redoubled by A.D. 3600.[1] Richard Price made various estimates of the population in 1759, 1767, and 1777, and reached the conclusion that it was slowly declining. Though it appears likely that little or no increase took place during the first half of the century, his conclusions were certainly wrong.

At the beginning of the century only a small proportion of the population lived in towns. London, with over 550,000 inhabitants, was already by far and away the largest town in Britain, with about 10 per cent of the country's population. Next in size came Edinburgh, Bristol, Southampton, Norwich and York with nearly 30,000 each. Perhaps another 18 towns had about 10,000 inhabitants. The average size of a 'town', according to Gregory King's figures, was about 1,000 inhabitants. Most people lived in the countryside, while the North was more sparsely populated than the South. With the exception of London there were no great urban centres. Instead, the population was spread thinly over the whole country, with no county having a density of more than 160 people to the square mile.

[1] Lists of references will be found at the end of each chapter.

The population growth was slow at first, but became very rapid during the early part of the nineteenth century, as the table below shows. Several theories have been put forward to explain this, and historians are not completely agreed upon them. One explanation is that as the Industrial Revolution developed during the eighteenth century, and England became more prosperous, more jobs were available, and men were able to earn enough money to support a family at an earlier age than before. Arthur Young (1741–1820), an agricultural journalist who travelled widely in Britain, declared that 'the increase of employment will be found to raise men like mushrooms'.[2] Early marriages were encouraged by the decline of the long apprenticeship system and by the tendency of farm labourers to have homes of their own, rather than lodgings with their employers, so that more children were born. The rising industrial towns and villages of the North and Midlands provided employment for the surplus population in the countryside; elsewhere, especially in the rural South and West of England, large-scale poor relief was made available towards the end of the century. The growth of industry, and improvements in transport and agriculture, all meant that the land could support a much greater population.

Population Table of Great Britain (in millions)
* *Estimates.*

	England and Wales	Scotland	Great Britain
*1700	5·5		
*1760	6·736		8
1801	8·892	1·608	10·5
1811	10·164	1·805	12
1821	12	2·091	14
1831	13·896	2·364	16
1841	15·914	2·630	18·5
1851	17·927	2·888	21
1861	20·066	3·062	23
1871	22·712	3·360	26
1881	25·974	3·735	30
1891	29·002	4·025	33
1901	32·527	4·472	37
1911	36·070	4·760	41
1921	37·886	4·882	43
1931	39·952	4·842	45
1951	43·744	5·096	49
1961	46·071	5·178	51
1971	48·594	5·228	53·8

The standard of living rose. During the eighteenth century some town improvement took place, and more attention was paid to personal cleanliness. The importance of fresh air, pure water, and adequate drainage, was recognized long before it was realized why they were important. With the rise of the chemical industry soap became more readily available. Cotton clothing, which had become plentiful and cheap by the end of the century, could be washed more easily than heavy woollen materials, and was a further aid to hygiene. Supplies of drinking water in towns, and sanitation, were improved. Hospitals were founded, and some of the reasons for the spread of infectious diseases were better understood.

The evil practice of drinking cheap gin, which William Hogarth portrayed in his caricature 'Gin Lane' (see page 121), declined after 1751, when Parliament taxed spirits heavily. In London, where gin drinking was most serious, burials in the 1740s had outnumbered baptisms by two to one. The environment was improved in other ways too. Transport developments enabled local food shortages to be relieved. There was more and better food. Wheaten bread became more common as the enclosure movement spread. The use of turnips as cattle food enabled more livestock to be kept through the winter, and supplies of fresh meat increased. More vegetables were grown, and scurvy among the population became less common. All these things meant better health.

Nevertheless, the average expectation of life did not lengthen very much, as the figures[3] opposite show.

The traditional explanation of the population increase – that it was due chiefly to a lowering of the death rate rather than an increase in the birth rate – has recently been modified. A distinction should be drawn between the mortality rate among adults, and the infant mortality rate. Before 1750 three-quarters of children born failed to reach the age of six years, but by 1830 improvements in

Expectation of Life (in Years)

	Early eighteenth century		c. 1824		1953	
Age	Male	Female	Male	Female	Male	Female
0	37·6	—	50·1	55·5	67·3	72·4
5	39·0	42·4	48·9	54·2	64·7	69·5
15	32·0	37·3	41·7	47·1	55·0	59·7
25	27·9	31·6	35·9	40·8	45·5	50·0
35	24·1	26·3	30·1	34·3	36·0	40·5

Thus in the eighteenth century a boy aged fifteen could expect to live until he was 47 years (i.e. a further 32 years); in 1824 the life expectancy of a boy aged fifteen was 56·7 years (i.e. he could expect to live a further 41·7 years).

midwifery and post–natal care had reduced the proportion to one-third. The lowering of the infant mortality rate, combined with the probable increase in the number of births due to earlier marriages, would go some way towards explaining the population explosion in Britain. These trends were cumulative in their effect, and were allowed to continue un-checked since the growth of industry and the available food supplies kept pace with the increasing population.

The decrease in the adult death rate was due largely to the extension of medical knowledge, and to the absence of mass killing agents such as famine, ruinous warfare, and plague. But Edward Jenner's discovery of vaccination against smallpox, which replaced the more dangerous method of inoculation, was only available after 1800, and only became free after 1840. The first operation under anaes-thetic was in 1846, and the widespread use of antiseptic surgery came as late as 1870. Indeed, admission to a hospital in the eighteenth century probably increased one's chances of dying from a contagious disease.

By 1800 the population increase was already noticeable. It does not seem likely that im-proved medical skills made such an impression upon the adult mortality rate as to have been a major cause of the increase. The reduction in the adult death rate only became an important factor in the nineteenth century, especially after 1880, when the birth rate declined. Between 1871 and 1911 the birth rate fell from

35 to 24 per thousand. After the Great War birth control was more widely practised, and large families, which had been typical of Victorian England, were uncommon. In the 1930s, when unemployment was widespread, and fears of a Second World War were growing, the birth rate fell as low as 15 per thousand.

The results of the population growth were far-reaching. The depressed state of farm labourers in the late eighteenth and early nineteenth centuries was partly due to the in-creased numbers the land had to support. Many thousands migrated to the towns where work was to be found, but those who were unwilling to leave their village, or were un-able to do so, must have been numerous. Towns sprang up like mushrooms, with their inhabitants crowded together in rows of dismal houses. The growth of Manchester was fairly typical of the new industrial towns. In 1727 Daniel Defoe declared it was 'the greatest mere village in England',[4] with a population of 9,000. By 1753 this had become 20,000. In 1790 it was 50,000, in 1801 95,000, in 1851 366,000, and in 1901 866,000. In 1786 Man-chester had only one factory chimney, that of Richard Arkwright's spinning mill. In 1801 there were fifty. In the decade 1821 to 1831 over a million persons were added to towns with over 20,000 inhabitants.

The towns were ill–prepared to receive these migrants, as suitable housing could not be easily supplied, while such improvements in drainage and sanitation which had taken place were swamped by the sheer numbers which had to be provided for. Fresh water supplies in London were polluted by over-stocked graveyards, and rivers and streams by industrial waste, so that epidemics of cholera and typhoid occurred frequently. Even the atmosphere itself was contaminated. The steam engine and the factory chimney produced the fogs that were a feature of industrial Britain. The unhealthy conditions of life in towns were not new, but as the town populations expanded they became more difficult to overcome.

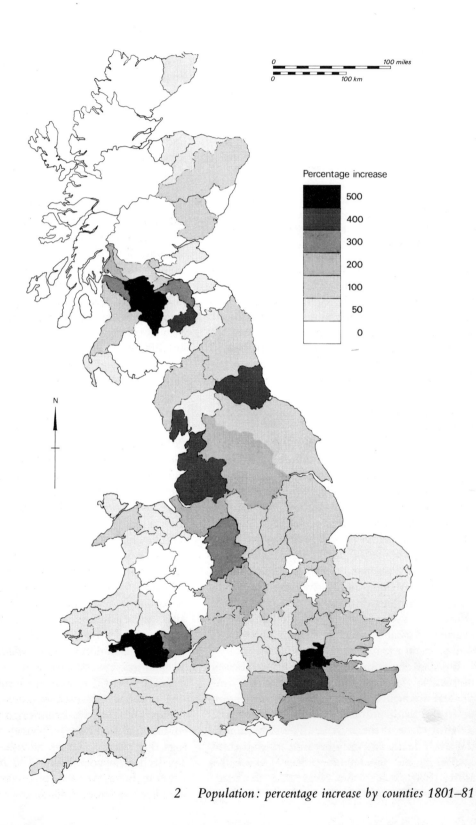

Percentage increase

500
400
300
200
100
50
0

0   100 miles
0   100 km

N

2   *Population: percentage increase by counties 1801–81*

Another important feature of the population increase was the change in its distribution. Before 1760 the most populous parts of the country were south of a line joining the mouths of the Humber and Severn. By the end of the century only Middlesex had a greater population density than South Lancashire, while South Wales, Staffordshire, Cheshire, Derbyshire, the West Riding of Yorkshire, and the Tyne valley had also become thickly populated. The increase in the North meant that the population there grew faster than in the South, not that there was large-scale migration from the South, for none of the southern counties declined in numbers. One of the key factors in the changed distribution of the population was clearly the expansion of the industries which used coal as a source of power. Apart from London, which continued its steady growth, the most densely populated parts of Britain were Clydeside, and the coalfields of the North and Midlands.

By 1800 the country had awakened to the population question, chiefly through the writings of a clergyman, the Reverend Thomas Malthus (1766–1834), and the first census took place in 1801. Malthus's vision of an island with a bulging population straining the available supplies of food was an unpleasant shock to people who had assumed that an increasing population was always desirable for a nation seeking wealth and power. In his *Essay on Population*, published in 1798, he argued that the human species tended to increase in a geometrical ratio of 1, 2, 4, 8, 16, 32, 64, 128, 256, etc., and the means of subsistence in an arithmetical ratio – 1, 2, 3, 4, 5, 6, 7, 8, 9 – so that unless checked by natural calamities, or war, population always tended to exceed the available food supplies.

Among the reasons for the rising birth rate Malthus included the Speenhamland System of poor relief, started in 1795, whereby a labourer's wage might be supplemented out of parish rates according to the cost of living and the size of his family. As a means of checking the rise in population Malthus himself preferred moral restraint, by which he meant later marriages, to the ending of outdoor relief. Nevertheless, many members of the governing classes were convinced by Malthus that the Speenhamland System encouraged improvident marriages, and large families, and in 1834 it was abolished. By the Poor Law Amendment Act of that year the destitute poor, instead of being relieved by money payments, were given no choice but to enter workhouses. (For a more detailed account of the Poor Law Amendment Act see Chapter 27.)

Malthus's arguments were also used by governments which encouraged emigration to relieve the country of its surplus population, and by industrialists and economists to develop theories of wages and prices. It was argued that wages depended upon how much capital (wealth) was available. If the population grew faster than the 'Wages Fund', wages would tend to go down. On the other hand, if the introduction of new processes and machinery led to increased production, more money would become available for paying higher wages. Similarly, the price of an article depended upon how many articles were for sale, how many people wished to buy them, and how much money they could afford to pay. Thus an increase in population, for example, without a corresponding increase in food production, would mean higher food prices.

Thomas Malthus had considerable influence in his day. Nevertheless, his more gloomy predictions did not come true. The population growth meant more workers to produce goods, and more people to buy them. This in turn encouraged farmers and manufacturers to produce more, and so make greater profits. The improvements in agriculture, such as enclosure for mixed farming, which became widespread in the eighteenth century and continued until well into the nineteenth, led to a greater output of food. When Britain became dependent upon imported food in the nineteenth century she was able to exchange manufactures for foodstuffs. In this way the Industrial Revolution ultimately resulted in a better standard of living. Yet Malthus's basic argument that population and food supplies are in a race with each other has a twentieth-century ring about it. In our time the world population explosion threatens mankind with disaster unless immediate and far-reaching steps are taken towards increasing the world's food supply and restraining population growth. It is almost certain that, had it not been for the Agrarian and Industrial Revolutions, the British, like the Irish in the nineteenth century, would have suffered from famine.

REFERENCES

1   Gregory King, *Observations on the State of England*, p. 41.
2   Arthur Young, *Six Months' Tour Through the North of England* (1770), Vol. I, p. 173.
3   From Report of Select Committee of the House of Commons on the laws respecting Friendly Societies: *Parliamentary Papers 1825*, and *Whitaker's Almanac* (1957) (quoted from *English Historical Documents*, Vol. XI, Eyre & Spottiswode (1969)).
4   Daniel Defoe, *A Tour Through the Whole Island of Great Britain* (Everyman, 1962).

CHAPTER 2
The Agrarian Revolution

To understand what the English landscape looked like two and a half centuries ago we must begin by removing nine out of every ten persons in the present population. To our eyes the countryside would have seemed curiously empty of people, towns, communications, and traffic. Movement of goods and people from place to place was on a small scale, since rivers and unsurfaced roads were the chief means of transport. Few people travelled except out of necessity and most trade was local. The countryside itself was also very different from that of today with its neat patchwork of enclosed fields, hedgerows and walls. About one-half of the arable land of England and Wales lay in open fields, where farming had altered very little for over four hundred years. In addition about one-fifth of the total area of land was waste. Upon a closer examination, however, great changes might be seen taking place, though at different rates in different parts of the country.

Under the open-field system each village usually had three or four very large arable fields, divided into strips approximately one furlong in length and twenty-two yards wide, and meadows and common pasture which merged into forest and waste. Most villagers owned scattered strips of land in each field, though some had only common grazing

3 John Cotes MP inspecting his Derbyshire estate

rights, and wood and wasteland rights. All had to farm according to the common custom of the village. One field lay fallow each year to allow it to recover its fertility. Oats or barley might be grown in one field, and wheat or rye in another, while vegetables could be grown in the villagers' gardens.

This system provided the village with nearly all its basic needs but it had serious defects. Weeds spread easily, time and labour were wasted in farming scattered strips of land, and there could be no cross ploughing. Much land was wasted by paths and balks which separated the villagers' strips from each other, and by the practice of leaving one field fallow. No winter crops could be grown when the fields were used for stubbling cattle after the harvest, and no drainage schemes could be undertaken without the consent of all the villagers. Common pasturage led not only to the over-stocking of the common, but also to the spread of cattle disease, so that the quality of livestock was low, and selective breeding impossible. The most serious objection to the open field economy however, was its resistance to change. So long as each man was forced to follow the traditional methods of cultivation, the standard of farming was bound to remain low.

The impulse towards agrarian change came from the landed nobility. The more enterprising landowners, using new, improved methods of cultivation, discovered that land, no less than trade, was a source of wealth. Farming became a fashionable occupation among the upper classes, and keeping up with the latest developments was the pastime of many great landowners. Sir Robert Walpole, the great statesman, who always dealt with the correspondence from his estates before turning to the government business of the day, was not alone in his proud boast that he personally managed his own estate. A new social class appeared during the century, that of the gentleman farmer, who regarded land not only as a mark of power and social prestige, but also as a profitable source of income.

The new farming techniques

Although farming underwent a great change during the eighteenth century, the speed of the change should not be exaggerated. As in the case of industry, it may be more correct to use the word 'evolution' rather than 'revolution'. Some parts of the country remained unchanged until the nineteenth century and, while improving landlords like Coke and Townshend rightly have an important place in any study of English agriculture during this century, it should not be forgotten that the paths they followed had been pioneered for them.

Sir Richard Weston (1591–1652) introduced four-crop rotation using flax, clover, oats and turnips on his estate in Surrey in the mid-seventeenth century. In his book *Discourse Upon Husbandry* Weston urged English farmers to copy the Dutch practice of growing root crops such as turnips, not only as winter fodder for cattle, but in order to cleanse the soil. By the late seventeenth century turnips and clover were grown extensively in Suffolk, Norfolk and elsewhere. Potato growing on a small scale was introduced into Lancashire in the same period, while peas and beans had been used as fodder for cattle since the Middle Ages.

Weston's ideas were followed by the first famous progressive farmer of the eighteenth century, Viscount Townshend (1674–1738). Lord Townshend was Secretary of State from 1721 to 1730, when he withdrew from public life after a quarrel with Walpole, and retired to his estates at Raynham in Norfolk. These consisted mostly of sandy or marshy waste which he converted into fertile land by drainage, marling, and manuring. Marling was similar to the soil mixing practised by Flemish farmers. When marl, or chalky clay, which was rich in mineral salts, was added to sandy soil, the clay particles tended to bind the soil together, thus improving its water-holding properties. Fertilizers were then retained in the soil instead of being washed down through the soil and wasted. He experimented with

4 *Jethro Tull's horse-drawn hoe was not widely used even in the*
early nineteenth century
In this picture a simple-wheeled hoe is being pushed and pulled between
rows of growing crops

different crops, and revived the Norfolk Four-Course System which became standard practice by 1850. The former system of winter corn, spring corn and fallow, was replaced by wheat, turnips, barley and clover, which were grown in rotation. This system had a number of advantages. Each field bore a useful crop instead of one-third of the arable land lying unused, and the fertility of the soil was improved. Root crops had to be hoed until their leaf development was sufficient to smother weeds, so that the soil was given a fine tilth, while the clover crop added nitrogen to the soil. More manure became available, either by folding sheep on the roots or clover, when their droppings manured the fields, or by cutting the clover for hay and using the roots as winter fodder. 'Turnip' Townshend transformed the value of his estates, and his example was followed by his neighbours. In a generation the rental value of land in Norfolk was increased tenfold.

Another gentleman farmer, Jethro Tull (1674–1741), also urged the replacement of traditional, wasteful methods by the new practices he had seen in the Netherlands and Germany. He recommended intensive cultivation, with deep ploughing and hoeing between crops. He did not believe in the value of manuring his land, however, and some of his practices would be frowned upon by modern farmers. In his book *Horse Hoeing Husbandry*, published in 1731, Tull put his theories into print, but the principles he followed on his Berkshire farm, Mount Prosperous, were not widely accepted until after his death. He advocated the sowing of seeds in straight lines at a uniform depth, a great improvement on the old fashioned way of broadcasting seed by hand, since the ground between the crops could be hoed. Tull stressed the importance of clean farming by keeping the ground free of weeds. To help put his ideas into practice he designed a horse-drawn seed drill and a horse hoe. Like his contemporary and supporter, Townshend, Tull was thought a crank, and his importance can be exaggerated. His originality was in basing his methods on observation, and as a pioneer of agricultural machinery.

The most famous of the progressive landowners was Thomas Coke of Holkham, in Norfolk (1754–1842). He improved his sandy estates by marling, and succeeded in growing heavy crops of wheat. He practised the most up-to-date farming methods such as crop rotation, and was the first Englishman to grow swedes on a large scale. Coke was very interested in improving the quality of his livestock. He introduced stall feeding of cattle, and cultivated artificial grasses for winter fodder. He encouraged his tenants to adopt the new farming practices, and granted them long leases of twenty-one years so that they were given time to make improvements, and to receive a fair return for their outlay. He broad-

cast the new methods by his practice of holding annual meetings of farmers, the 'Holkham Gatherings' or 'Sheep Shearings'. These meetings began in 1778 when Coke invited some of the local farmers to advise him on farm management. As Coke developed a model estate they became famous, and landowners from all over the country came to seek advice and new ideas. In some years as many as 7,000 people attended, even though travel was slow and difficult. The 'Gatherings' lasted for four days and were noted for the hospitality which Coke lavished on his guests. Each day began with a tour of part of the estate, which was followed by a discussion lasting several hours, when the humblest farmer could speak on equal terms with the greatest landowners. The 'Gatherings', which came to an end in 1821, helped spread knowledge of sound farming techniques, and played their part in raising the standard of English farming.

5   The sixth Duke of Bedford (shown on horseback) followed Coke's example, and held sheep-shearing festivals on his estate at Woburn

A contemporary of Coke, Robert Bakewell (1725–95), of Dishley, near Loughborough in Leicestershire, pioneered selective stock breeding. Hitherto, according to one writer on farming matters, breeders

were so attentive to objects of the smallest importance that those of the greatest consequence seemed to be utterly neglected; the disposition to fatten, early maturity, and a form indicating strength of constitution attracted less attention than the colour of a leg or the position of a horn.

Bakewell cross-bred different types of sheep which he imported from various parts of the country. The animals he used for breeding were carefully selected from the viewpoint of their meat and wool-producing qualities. Bakewell wished to perfect a type of sheep which was small-boned and short-limbed, with a barrel-shaped body carrying plenty of fat, for he realized that increased meat supplies would be needed to feed a rapidly growing population. Bakewell kept careful records of his experiments and he regulated the feed of his livestock. He grew turnips, cabbages and carrots as fodder, and irrigated his meadows, even digging a canal 2 km (more than a mile) long in order to water 80 hectares (200 acres) of land. He eventually succeeded in developing his famous New Leicester sheep which were said to be the hardiest when alive and the heaviest when dead. Bakewell's experiments in breeding cattle and horses were less successful, but the methods of artificial selection which he used have remained the basis of scientific stock-breeding ever since. The Colling brothers from Darlington did succeed in breeding a new type of cattle, the Durham shorthorn, with improved beef and dairy qualities. By the end of the century it seems likely that the average weight of cattle and sheep had been more than doubled. In 1710 the weight of oxen, calves and sheep sold at Smithfield market had averaged 170, 25, and 17 kilos (370, 50 and 38 lb); in 1795 the weights recorded were 365, 70 and 35 kilos (800, 150, and 80 lb) respectively.

One of the greatest names in eighteenth-century English agriculture was Arthur Young (1741–1820). A failure as a practical farmer, Young was unrivalled as an agricultural journalist, since he had the ability to express his ideas and observations in a way which the ordinary farmer could understand. He supported large-scale farming for profit, enclosures, and improved methods. In his writings Young attacked the open-field system as wasteful and out-of-date. In 1768 on his famous *Six Weeks Tour in the Southern Counties* he studied Norfolk farming and published the results. In 1770 he toured the North of England and noted the contrast between the low standard of farming there compared with the rest of the country.

Now it is highly worthy of remark that the husbandry of these farmers is universally bad; their fields are in a slovenly condition, and many tracts of land that yielded good crops of corn, within 30 years, are now overrun with whins, brakes and other trumpery. The farmers are a poor wretched set of people. If it be demanded, how such ill courses are to be stopped: I answer, Raise their rents. First with moderation; and if that does not bring forth industry, double them. But if you are to have a vigorous agriculture go forward, throw 15 or 20 of these farms into one, as fast as the present occupiers drop off. This is the only means in such cases to improve husbandry, and consequently to promote population.[1]

Later, Young toured Ireland twice (the second time because his servant had stolen his notes), Italy, and in the period 1787–9 visited France on three occasions. After each tour he published his observations. In 1784 he began writing the *Annals of Agriculture* in order to circulate information among farmers. He created agricultural clubs and societies, and in 1793, together with Sir John Sinclair, founded the Board of Agriculture, of which Young was the first Secretary. The Board did much to sponsor improved methods at a time when they were most needed.

Agriculture even received royal encourage-

6   George III rewards an industrious haymaker near Weymouth

ment. George III, 'Farmer George', took a keen interest in farming matters, and made part of his Windsor estate into a model farm. These men, the titled farmers, and others like them, improved the standard of English agriculture so that it acquired a European reputation. In the reign of Louis XVI Frenchmen were sent to study English farming methods.

The enclosure movement

The country dweller in the second half of the eighteenth century could hardly fail to notice the changes taking place around him. In his lifetime he saw the gradual increase of traffic on rivers and roads, the building of turnpike roads and canals, the growth of industry, and the beginnings of industrial towns and villages. But the change which altered the appearance of the countryside most was enclosures.

When a village was enclosed, every individual's scattered strips of arable land were consolidated into a compact unit, surrounded by a fence, hedge or wall, equivalent to the amount of land held formerly, together with a proportionate share of the common land. Except where voluntary agreement could be reached among all landowners in a village, each enclosure had to be authorized by a private act of Parliament. In order to obtain permission to enclose, a petition representing the holders of four-fifths of the land affected had to be drawn up. In this way the signature of a single important landowner could overcome the wishes of the majority, since the proportion was reckoned in land, not landowners. Indeed, until 1774 the villagers' first knowledge of an enclosure was often the arrival of commissioners to survey and allocate the land. In that year however, Parliament declared that notice of enclosure had to be posted on the church door of each parish affected for three consecutive Sundays in August or September.

The petition was duly considered by Parliament which was largely composed of country squires and great landowners. Counter petitions from the villagers were rare, since they were unable to afford the expenses of bringing witnesses before the Parliamentary Committee set up to inquire into the matter, and of hiring solicitors and counsel to present their case. Once the bill had passed through Parliament commissioners, usually three in number, were sent to the parish with complete authority to enclose it. They were appointed by Parliament, but they were in practice nominated by the petitioners, and they might even include the lord of the manor himself or his agent. Even though occasions on which the commissioners deliberately misused their power seem to have been rare, the system clearly favoured the great landowners. Not until 1801 was this abuse stopped by Parliament. It was forbidden to appoint as a commissioner any person who had an interest in the land which was to be enclosed.

The whole parish was surveyed by the commissioners, whose task was to discover the extent, condition, and value of every property, and to adjudicate conflicting claims. The commissioners then made their award, i.e. they redistributed the land. Much of the waste and common land disappeared, and provision was made for new roads where necessary. When the work had been done the village was transformed. The open fields had gone for ever, and in their place were compact farms separated from each other by hedges and walls.

The poor often suffered great hardship as a result of enclosure. Many of the poorer land-owners had no clear title to their land, and even where documentary evidence was held, it often rested on obsolete maps, or manorial court rolls. Land ownership which depended upon hearsay evidence and custom does not seem to have been considered sympathetically by the commissioners. Some people had no legal rights to their land at all. The squatter, who had cleared a patch of land on the waste, was evicted unless he could prove that he had cultivated his holding for twenty years.

Once the village had been enclosed, the poor lost their rights to the common and waste, which had enabled them to keep geese and poultry, a few cows and pigs, and to collect wood for fuel and building purposes. The portion of land which the smallholder received in compensation did not offer him the same variety of benefits. The real value of the common land rights is debatable, since the grazing on common land was often worth very little. Yet the open field system gave most villagers a share in the land, together with the feeling of independence which went along with it. Arthur Young, an enthusiastic sup-porter of enclosures, recognized that their social results were often unfortunate. In 1801 he wrote: 'In nineteen out of twenty enclosure acts the poor are injured, in some cases, grossly injured.'[2] Even a commissioner declared:

I lament that I have been accessory to injuring 2,000 people at the rate of 20 families per parish. Numbers, in the practice of feeding on the commons, cannot prove their rights; and many, indeed most who have allotments, have not more than an acre, which being insufficient for the man's cow, *both cow and land are usually sold to the opulent farmers.*[3]

Many smallholders, bewildered by the rapid changes around them, or unable to bear the legal expenses of enclosure and the costs of compulsory fencing, sold their land. An un-known number migrated to towns seeking work. Those who remained in the village became landless labourers, dependent upon the wages of a wealthy farmer. Without the use of the commons the labourer had to buy all his food, and when prices rose steeply, as they did after 1793, he went hungry. If the wages of agricultural labourers doubled in the forty years after 1770 prices of foodstuffs trebled, so that his real earnings declined. Particularly in the rural South of England where the in-crease in population coincided with the decline of domestic industry, the plight of the agri-cultural labourer was pitiful.

It was for this reason that in 1795 a group of magistrates in the Berkshire village of Speen tried to relieve the poverty of the agricultural labourer by supplementing his wage to a level which just enabled him to keep himself and his family alive. The Speenhamland System had unfortunate effects however, since it en-couraged farmers to pay low wages. The burden of poor relief, which fell upon those who owned land, rose steadily each year, and discouraged farmers from paying adequate wages, since they already contributed to the maintenance of the parish poor. Free farm labourers could not hope to compete with subsidized labour, and many were pauperized. It seemed that thrift and efficiency were un-rewarded virtues, and that all alike had the right to be kept by the parish. The demoraliza-tion of the poor was highlighted by Arthur Young when he quoted a labourer as saying: 'If I am diligent shall I have leave to build a cottage? If I am sober shall I have land for a cow? You offer no motives; you have nothing but a parish officer and a workhouse.'[4]

Yet from a national viewpoint enclosures were certainly desirable. The driving force

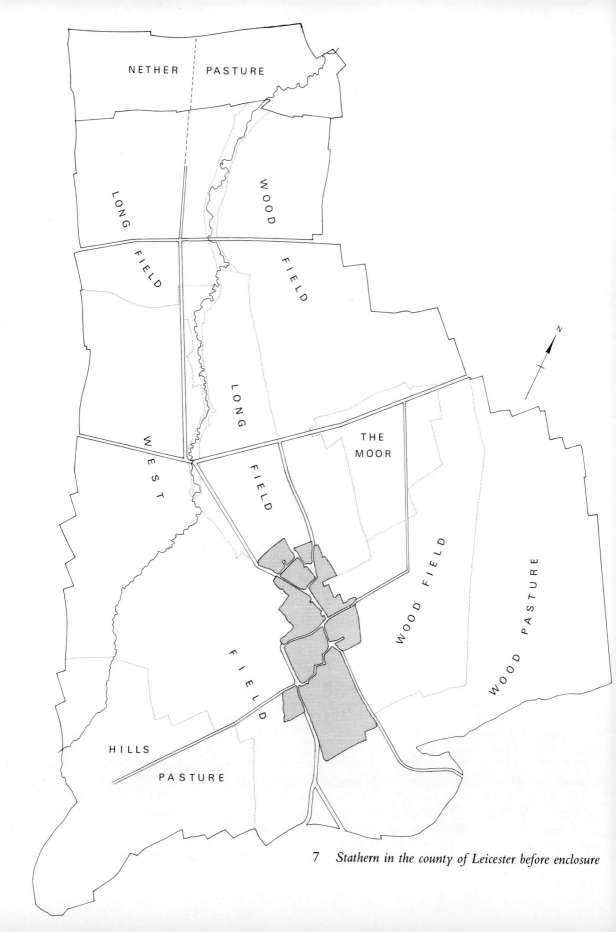

NETHER   PASTURE

LONG   FIELD

WOOD   FIELD

LONG   FIELD

WEST

THE MOOR

FIELD

WOOD   FIELD

WOOD   PASTURE

HILLS

PASTURE

7   *Stathern in the county of Leicester before enclosure*

Richard Earl Howe

Leonard
Bullivant

John Henley

Richard
Guy

Church-
warden's

Antony Good

In exchange

Churchwarden's

Richard
Watchorne

Martin Newbury

John Henry
Duke of Rutland

Feoffes of
Loughborough Bridges

Thomas
Roberts

Thomas Blankley
E   S

Henry Parnham

John Bugg

Barns

William Shipman

James Kemp

Thomas
Blankley
S

T. Blankley
S

Henry Parnham

John Barke

T. Roberts

Thomas Barke

Francis Sumner

Leonard
Bullivant

Robert Yalding

James Bampton

John Henley

James Bampton

Isabella Whittle

John Henry
Duke of Rutland

Francis
Sumner

A. Good

Rebecca Keal

Rev. Thomas Parke
Tithe

E. Bryans

John Henry Duke of Rutland

H. Parnham

J. Bampton

Philip Burton's trustees

Rev. Thomas Parke   Glebe

Robert Yalding

I. Cobley

Thomas Caunt

John Bockin

Ann Jarvis

T. Parke

Caunt C.

L. Wilford

W. Shipman

Thomas
Wilford

William Shipman

Rebecca
Keal

John Henry Duke of Rutland

Rev. Thomas Parke

Thomas Roberts

Duke of Rutland

8   *Stathern in the county of Leicester after enclosure, 1792*

behind the enclosure movement was a growing population, which meant that more food had to be grown if the country was to remain self-sufficient. This in turn brought about a continuous, if uneven, rise in food prices over most of the second half of the century, so that farming became more profitable, and investment in agriculture was encouraged. The statistics of enclosures show how agricultural change was influenced by rising prices. In the period 1730–44, when food prices were low, there were fewer than 100 enclosure acts. During the Revolutionary and Napoleonic Wars with France (1793–1815), when food prices were generally high, 1,934 enclosure acts were passed. The enclosure movement aimed at increasing yields per acre, and extending the area of land which was efficiently farmed. The abolition of the open fields and the introduction of improved farming methods were, as we have seen, closely related; the new methods required enclosed fields. Whereas the enclosure movement of the sixteenth century, which had been largely for sheep farming, had been checked by the Tudor governments' fear of food shortages, those of the eighteenth century were inspired by it.

Enclosures undoubtedly made for better farming. During the century the production of corn, wool and mutton showed considerable increases; the English wool clip doubled, while the acreage of cereals and the yields per acre were increased. Two million acres of waste were put under the plough, chiefly for growing corn. More food made possible the expansion of industrial towns, and probably saved England from defeat in the war with France. Meat supplies improved, even though it is unlikely that they kept pace with the growth in population, especially since much pasture was converted into arable for growing corn during the Napoleonic Wars. Economically then, enclosures can be easily justified; enclosures and agricultural progress went hand in hand, and by 1800 English farming had become the most efficient in Europe.

The net result of enclosures was to make farming a source of wealth for the whole nation instead of a means of subsistence for individual families. The land supplied not only foodstuffs for a growing population, but a wide range of raw materials for industry. When sheep and cattle were plentiful and cheap, leather workers, saddlers, shoemakers, cutlers, candle-makers, glue manufacturers, and many others were better off. Flax and wool for clothing, tallow and leather, malt for brewing, horses for transport, and wood for furniture, machinery, wagons and coaches, house-building, fuel, and other uses too numerous to mention, were all products of the land. Everyone benefited from a flourishing agriculture. A bad harvest forced food prices up and reduced the purchasing power of the population. Dear food meant social unrest and a demand for higher wages, cheap food meant that people had more money to spare for buying manufactured goods. A thriving countryside stimulated the economy in other ways too. On the one hand it was the source of labour for growing industries. On the other the great landowners not only provided the governing class at national and local level, they also initiated much industrial activity. They promoted transport improvements such as turnpikes and canals, exploited the mineral resources of their land, and opened iron, copper and lead works. In all these ways the development of English agriculture in the eighteenth century was an integral part of the Industrial Revolution.

REFERENCES

1   Arthur Young, op. cit., Vol. II, pp. 94–5.
2   Arthur Young, *Inquiry into the Propriety of applying Wastes to the better Maintenance and Support of the Poor* (1801), p. 42.
3   Arthur Young, *Annals of Agriculture*, XXXVI, p. 516.
4   Arthur Young, *Annals of Agriculture*, XXXVI, p. 508.

CHAPTER 3
Finance and Banking

Two important reasons why Britain became the birthplace of the Industrial Revolution were plentiful supplies of capital and the development of a banking system, without which the growth of trade, industry and communications would have been stifled. In very primitive societies where everyday needs are simple, the small number of goods produced can be distributed by a process of barter. As the number of goods and services multiply however, so money becomes indispensable as a means of exchange, and the more complex the society the greater its need for a monetary system whereby money can circulate freely and rapidly. Thus manufacturers who wished to build new premises, install fresh machinery, or borrow money to tide them over a temporary difficulty, landowners who wished to improve their estates, canal and turnpike trusts, and many others, all needed easy access to capital in order to carry on their activities.

At the beginning of the eighteenth century England had a mixed currency, for gold and silver coins, and banknotes, existed side by side. It was also a sound currency. Governments since the reign of Elizabeth I had come to realize the truth of the saying that 'bad money drives out good'. If a government debased its coinage by adding a percentage of base metal the value of the coins went down, and good coins rapidly disappeared from circulation. In 1696–9 the Government had carried through, at its own expense, a great recoinage, when all worn or clipped coins were replaced with new ones, with milled edges as a precaution against clipping.

As trade and industry grew a serious shortage of gold and silver coins developed. Since the stock of precious metals could not be increased fast enough to meet the needs of industrialists, merchants and shopkeepers, various ways of overcoming the difficulty were found. Some ironmasters, like John Wilkinson of Shropshire, who had large wages bills, printed their own tokens which were used by the local people in place of coins of the realm. Some industrialists paid their workers in 'truck', or kind. The worker might be given a proportion of his wage in the goods he produced, such as coal or clothes, or he received coupons which could only be exchanged at the employer's store or ale-house. Inevitably the system was open to abuse. High prices were charged in these 'truck shops' because there was no competition for custom. The value of a man's wages was correspondingly reduced and he was restricted in what he could buy. Workers who were allowed credit fell into the power of their employer, and were unable to change their job easily. Thus the workers came to detest the system, and the rise of cooperative stores in the North of England in the early nineteenth century was due partly to their determination to rid themselves of 'truck'. The 'tommy shop' finally became a thing of the past in the 1870s, after a series of Truck Acts, beginning in 1701, had been passed in an effort to remove the abuse. The real answer to the shortage of coins was the extended use of banknotes. Paper money developed out of a system of buying on credit, which had been in existence since the Middle Ages. Merchants or manufacturers gave their creditors promises to pay, or 'bills of exchange', which became substitutes for cash. Their value, however, depended upon the honesty and permanence of the firms which issued them, and since in time there were so many, there grew up a need for firms which would guarantee payment—i.e. banks.

In the Middle Ages the need for credit was supplied by the Jews, since Christians were forbidden by their religion to lend money for interest. Thus the idea of banking has a long history, but the ancestors of modern banks were the London goldsmiths of the Civil War period in the middle of the seventeenth century. They were entrusted by merchants with large sums of money, called 'running cashes', or as we know them today, current accounts, which they kept in their strongrooms. Since they would only be asked at any one time for the return of a small part of the money deposited with them, the goldsmiths loaned money to customers in need of credit. The lender was given a receipt for the amount he had deposited, and received interest on it, while the borrower paid a higher rate of interest, which would vary according to circumstances. The difference between the two rates of interest gave the goldsmith his profit. In this way the goldsmith performed a very valuable service. He enabled capital to circulate from those who had surplus funds they did not wish to leave standing idle to those who needed cash. Goldsmiths also issued promises to pay stated amounts, in other words, banknotes, which were accepted as money since the holders had confidence that they could be taken to the goldsmith who had issued them and exchanged for cash. Their customers often arranged for the transfer of money from their accounts by means of written instructions, instead of making payment in coin or banknotes, thus originating the modern cheque.

Goldsmiths and other wealthy men also lent money to the Government which needed large sums, especially in wartime. This was a risky business, however, for kings did not always repay their debts, but when, in 1689, as a condition of being offered the crown, William III agreed that Parliament should control the nation's finances, people were more prepared to lend money to the Government. It was the desperate need of William III's Government for huge sums of money to

continue the first of two great wars against the France of Louis XIV, the War of the League of Augsburg (1689–97), and the War of Spanish Succession (1701–13), which led to the twin institutions of the Bank of England and the National Debt. In 1694, as a convenient way of raising money, the Government granted a charter of privileges to a small group of businessmen, and allowed them to form a joint stock banking company. They were authorized to raise a joint stock of £1,200,000 which they loaned to the Government at 8 per cent interest. In 1708 Parliament consolidated the privileges of the Bank of England by passing an act declaring that no other joint stock bank with more than six partners could be formed in England, so that for over a century the Bank of England was the only joint stock bank which could issue notes.

Since the Bank of England was the Government's banker it enjoyed the reputation of being extra safe. Thus from the initial £1,200,000 there grew up a permanent debt, as successive governments raised greater and greater sums of money from their subjects. One of the most obvious results of the eighteenth-century wars was the enormous increase in the size of the National Debt, which has come to assume astronomical proportions. Its growth can be appreciated from the following set of random figures. In 1713 the Debt stood at £56 million; by 1763 it had reached £132 million, by 1783 £241 million, and by 1815 £834 million; in 1918 it stood at the immense figure of £8,000 million. Efforts to reduce it had shortlived success, for it grew much faster in wartime than it could be reduced in peacetime. Both Sir Robert Walpole in 1717, and William Pitt the Younger in 1786, established Sinking Funds into which £1 million raised from taxation was to be paid each year. The interest which accrued on the Fund would repay part of the capital sum. Wars ruined their attempts, though even in peacetime Walpole raided his Fund for other purposes, so that he only succeeded in getting the Debt down to £46 million. By the middle of the eighteenth century it had become clear that the Debt would never be repaid, but this knowledge ceased to cause anxiety. The National Debt did not lessen the wealth of the community, since it represented the transfer of cash from individuals to the Government, which paid interest on the money it borrowed. The loans would be repaid out of future borrowing by the Government.

The Bank of England's monopoly of joint stock banking meant that it was not possible for strong banks with country branches to develop, and the Bank of England was unwilling to establish them. The provinces therefore lacked banks until the growth of industry created sufficient demand for them. Country bank means private bank. The first country bank, called the 'Old Gloucester Bank', was formed by a Bristol merchant, James Wood. After 1760 many private banks were set up, generally by local shopkeepers. London paid for its foodstuffs from the countryside with bills of exchange. As trading increased some provincial shopkeepers began to deal in bills, giving their clients cash in exchange for them, and charging a percentage, called a discount, for running the risk that the bill might prove worthless, and for the inconvenience of having to wait for their money. Many banks were started by corn merchants and wool merchants with spare capital. Several Welsh country banks arose from the cattle trade with England. Money was a scarce commodity in Wales, and cattle drovers returning home with cash sometimes set up banks and issued banknotes. One such bank helped its illiterate customers by using the picture of a black sheep to denote one pound, and a lamb ten shillings. Some manufacturers created banks in order to help their own businesses. Ironmasters especially needed much capital to pay the wages of the large numbers of men they employed, and both Lloyd's and Barclay's Banks had their beginnings in the iron industry.

Banks usually loaned money for short terms only. Long-term investment was supplied by people who were prepared to accept the considerable risks involved, for in the absence of limited liability an investor was liable to the entire extent of his savings for the debts of a company in which he had bought shares. From the last quarter of the seventeenth century a specialized market in stocks and shares grew up, since one disadvantage with this type of lending was that an investor had to sell his shares if he wanted his money back. Dealers in stocks and shares were called stockbrokers. They bought and sold shares, charging a commission on each transaction. Until 1773 they conducted their business in London coffee houses, but by then they had become sufficiently important to set up their own headquarters in a special building called the London Stock Exchange.

The banking system which had developed by the beginning of the nineteenth century had several weaknesses. Within the memory of people living in 1815 there had been no country banks, except in a few of the larger towns, but by the start of the Napoleonic Wars there existed over three hundred country banks, and by its end nearly nine hundred. Since joint stock banks were illegal in England and Wales most of these banks were small, with few reserves to meet an emergency. In 1797 fears of an invasion caused a run on the banks as people changed their paper money into gold, thereby protecting their savings, and many banks had to close their doors. To save the situation Pitt's government ordered the Bank of England to suspend payments of its notes in cash, and gold coins almost disappeared from circulation. One consequence was that the measures taken before the war to restrain the rash issue of paper currency by certain country banks were dropped. In 1775 notes under £1, and in 1777 notes under £5, had been made illegal; the great increase in paper money which resulted from the lifting of this ban did much to encourage wartime inflation. One landowner, Lord King, became so concerned over the difference in value between notes and their equivalent in gold that he demanded payment of his rents in gold coin, 'the good and lawful money of Great Britain'. This forced the government to pass an act in 1811 making Bank of England notes compulsory tender, so that for the first time the country had a forced currency. Meanwhile, a Bullion Committee appointed in 1810 to investigate the depreciation of the nation's currency fixed the blame squarely on the over-issue of notes. It recommended an early return to the system of cash payments by the Bank of England, but wartime conditions made this impracticable, so that cash payments were not resumed until 1821.

The slumps of 1814–16 and 1825, when scores of banks tumbled down, led to a complete overhaul of the banking system. A government memorandum of 1826 stated that

much of the prosperity of the country for the last century is to be ascribed to the general wisdom, justice and fairness of the dealings of the Bank. . . . But the progress of the country during the last 30 or 40 years in every branch of industry and trade has been so rapid that the Bank of England, which was fully adequate to former transactions, is no longer sufficient, without new aids, to meet the demands of the present times.

A Bank Act of that year, following Huskisson's belief that 'paper and coin could not circulate together; the paper would drive out the coin', forbade the issue of notes smaller in denomination than £5, though it did not compel country banks to keep adequate gold reserves. In the same year a Newcastle merchant, Thomas Joplin, who had been impressed by the achievements of Scotland's joint stock banks in financing new industries within her borders, succeeded in his campaign to end the joint stock monopoly of the Bank of England. Joint stock banks were permitted outside a sixty-five mile radius of London, and later, in 1833, they could be formed inside this circle, though they were not allowed to issue their own notes.

In 1844 the most important banking legislation of the century was passed. Under the terms of the Bank Charter Act no new note-issuing bank could be established. Existing banks with note-issuing rights retained the privilege, but were not allowed to increase their issue. Joint stock banks which opened a London branch, amalgamated with a London bank, or went bankrupt, forfeited their note-issuing powers. The government's intention was to give the Bank of England a monopoly of issuing notes in England and Wales, but this was not achieved until 1921, when the last surviving private note-issuing bank amalgamated with Lloyd's. Finally, the Bank Charter Act separated the note-issuing department of the Bank of England from its ordinary banking department. The Bank was authorized to issue £14 million of notes backed by securities instead of bullion, a figure which rose to £19 million as various country banks surrendered their note-issuing powers to the Bank of England. Above that amount all notes had to be backed by gold in the Bank's vaults. In 1928 an Act of Parliament raised the limit to £260 million.

The country banks gradually disappeared after 1826, as they were replaced by the more substantial, reliable joint stock banks. Experience had shown that small banks had difficulty in surviving the crises which swept the country at regular intervals. The growth of large-scale industries also meant that private banks lacked sufficient funds to finance their business deals. Moreover, the extensive use of cheques, which was a more convenient method of payment than the transfer of notes and coin, accelerated the formation of joint stock banks. In 1854 the joint stock banks joined the London Clearing House where settlement was made on all the cheques drawn on the member banks. The banks kept their reserves in the Bank of England, which acted as the 'banker's bank', and from 1854 the banks settled their debts to each other by cheques drawn on the Bank of England. In 1864, to simplify matters, the Bank itself joined the Clearing House. Finally, the Limited Liability Acts of 1858, 1862, and 1879 stimulated the development of joint stock banking. The act of 1879 followed the collapse of the City of Glasgow Bank in 1878, when holders of the bank's shares were called upon to pay £2,750 for every £100 share they owned. Thereafter the liability of shareholders in joint stock banks was limited to three or four times the amount of capital they had invested. Joint stock banks now entered a period of territorial expansion, opening branch offices in various parts of the country, and amalgamating with private banks. As their businesses expanded they moved their headquarters to London in order to be near the money market of which they formed a part. Securing a foothold in London by uniting with a London private bank had the added attraction of membership of the London Clearing House. A typical example of amalgamation was the formation of the modern Barclay's Bank in 1896 by its union with nineteen private banks.

After 1914 the amalgamation process continued, but with the difference that now very large and powerful banks with many branches united. Eventually banking in England and Wales was dominated by the Big Four, the Westminster, Lloyd's, Midland, and Barclay's Banks. It was only in Lancashire and Yorkshire where specialized knowledge of the textile industries was essential, that smaller banks resisted the centralizing tendency. Instead of being absorbed they were affiliated to the major banks. In 1946 the Bank of England was nationalized, so that it ceased to be, if only by name, a private company. The fact that the Bank of England acts as the agent of the Government in carrying out its monetary policy reminds us of the important part played by the banks in the accumulation of capital and the rise of modern industry. They enabled capital to be stored safely, so that people were encouraged to make profits and to save, knowing that they were protected from ordinary risks of loss. By enlarging the currency, and by lending money to businessmen they promoted the development of every kind of industrial enterprise, on which the nation's wealth and prosperity depended.

CHAPTER 4
Overseas Trade in the Eighteenth Century

Before industrial change can take place capital must be accumulated, so that people can afford to buy more goods, and businessmen have the necessary cash to begin producing more to meet the increased demand, and so add to their profits. This is what we mean when we say that 'money breeds money'. The accumulation of capital in the seventeenth and eighteenth centuries was therefore an essential preparation for the Industrial Revolution. One of the most important sources of capital was the profits from trade, which had been growing in volume since the Middle Ages. The expansion of trade was bound to precede the expansion of industry, for as long as production was chiefly limited to meeting the needs of the population, industrial growth was slow. Thus the remarkable increase in trade during the eighteenth century, which stimulated existing industries, created new ones, and made England a wealthy nation, was both a cause and a result of the Industrial Revolution. In the words of Voltaire, one of the greatest French thinkers of the century,

It is only because the English have taken to trade that London has outgrown Paris, both as to its size and the numbers of its inhabitants, and that England can have two hundred men-of-war, and subsidize allied kings. All this fills the English merchant with justifiable pride, and enables him to compare himself, not unreasonably, with a Roman citizen.[1]

Yet for much of the century trade was a form of economic warfare as well as a means of exchanging one country's products for those of another. According to the mercantilist principles which regulated trade and industry (as far as the government could in those days), the chief purpose of trade was to bring into the country bullion, i.e. gold and silver, in the

belief that the country with the greatest stocks of precious metals would become the most powerful. The underlying aim of each nation was a favourable balance of trade, and as long as exports exceeded imports all was thought to be well. Thus trade was welcomed, when manufactured goods were exported (except machinery, whose export was forbidden), or raw materials, which could be turned into finished articles, were imported. Home industries were helped by bounties, and protected from foreign competition by duties on imports, while agriculture was encouraged, not only to provide food for a growing population, but because the countryside was a reservoir of labour for industry, and recruits for the army and navy. The basis of mercantilism was laid down in the Navigation Acts of 1651 and 1660, and the Staple Act of 1663, which stated that goods from foreign countries had to be carried either in British or colonial ships, or in those of their own countries. Goods imported in foreign ships were subjected to a special tax. The chief purpose of the acts had been to wrest control of Europe's carrying trade from Holland, and by 1700 this had almost been achieved.

Britain's trade grew as a result of war and diplomacy, though during the course of war itself trade was disrupted. In 1700, apart from Jamaica in the West Indies, and four trading stations in India, England owned only the thirteen colonies in America. During the War of Spanish Succession (1701–13) valuable gains were made, and British trade increased at the expense of the French and the Dutch. The Methuen Treaty of 1703 with Portugal lowered duties on British exports of textiles and hardware to that country, in return for similar concessions on imported wines. This arrangement did much to encourage a preference for port wine instead of French claret. By the Treaty of Utrecht (1713–14) Britain retained the valuable naval bases of Minorca and Gibraltar, Newfoundland with its valuable cod fisheries, and Hudson Bay and Nova Scotia, giving her a foothold in Canada. In addition, permission for a limited trade with the Spanish Indies was obtained. By the right of *Asiento*, Britain was allowed to supply Spanish planters with 4,000 slaves annually, and to send one ship each year to the fair at Porto Bello.

In 1720 these privileges were given to the South Seas Company, formed in 1711 to exploit the trading possibilities with the Spanish colonies. In return for a monopoly of trade with the Spanish Indies the company took over responsibility for the National Debt. The company's prospects seemed so attractive that in a frenzied burst of speculation the company's shares rose tenfold, and many people made fortunes overnight. Confidence in the company, however, was suddenly undermined when it prosecuted one of many rival schemes which tried to take advantage of the mania for investment. The famous 'Bubble' burst, the price of the company's shares tumbled, and thousands were ruined.

The South Sea Bubble helped bring to power Sir Robert Walpole, who had managed to make a fortune out of the affair, while condemning the foolishness of the scheme. From 1721 to his fall from power in 1742 Walpole's position amounted almost to that of prime minister. During his period of office Walpole did much to encourage trade. Abroad, he followed a peaceful policy, believing that war was harmful to commerce. At home he simplified the customs duties on imports and exports, reducing them wherever possible, and gave bounties on the export of corn, silk, and gunpowder.

In 1739, however, England drifted into war with Spain. Relations between the two countries had been difficult for a long time. The Spanish resented the loss of Gibraltar, and the *Asiento*. English merchants were annoyed at being unable to trade freely with the Americas, where the Spanish authorities employed *guarda costas*, privateers armed with a special licence, to check smuggling. There were frequent quarrels between the two countries and, when a rather disreputable sea captain called Jenkins related to the House of Commons how, several years earlier, a Spanish *guarda costas* had searched his ship, bound him to a mast, and sliced off one of his ears with a sword, the Commons, in which merchants were a powerful pressure group, clamoured for war. The conflict widened when the War of Jenkins's Ear merged with the greater War of Austrian Succession (1740–8), in which Britain found herself fighting both France and Spain.

The results of the war were inconclusive. In North America the British had captured Fort Louisburg, and in India the French Fort Madras; by the Peace of Aix-la-Chapelle these conquests were exchanged. The truce in the Anglo-French colonial struggle was broken by the Seven Years' War (1756–63), a worldwide conflict, in the course of which France lost Canada and all her Indian possessions to Britain, whose trade benefited enormously from their acquisition. Though the American colonies were lost in the War of American Independence (1776–83), England remained their most valuable market, and trade between the new nation and the former Mother Country expanded rapidly as the Industrial Revolution in England got under way.

The pattern of British trade altered greatly during the century. In 1700 Europe was the source of fifty per cent of England's imports. From Scandinavia and Russia came iron, copper, and vital naval stores such as masts, sailcloth, rope and pitch; from the Mediterranean countries came wines, silks, dyestuffs and citrus fruits; from Ireland, which had mainly a pastoral economy, dairy produce, hides, meat, and tallow. Trade with France was slight, for she was regarded as England's traditional enemy, but small quantities of luxury items such as brandy, silk, velvet, tapestries, lace and brocade found their way into England. Imports from the Far East included silk, rice, spices, indigo, saltpetre, and tea, which was rapidly becoming the Englishman's ordinary drink. By the end of the century vast quantities of tea were imported. Until 1721 printed cotton fabrics figured largely in imports from India, but by an act of that year their use was forbidden in England, in order to protect the interests of the English woollen industry.

The chief export was woollen goods, which amounted to half the total value of goods sent abroad, but cutlery, wheat, salt, and re-exports of colonial products were also important. In addition, according to Daniel Defoe's *Plan of English Commerce* 'We send daily great quantities of wrought iron and brass into Holland, France, Italy, Venice, and to all parts of Germany, Poland, and Muscovy'. By the end of the century, however, cotton goods were about to overtake woollens as the major export, and exports of iron, coal, and pottery had grown considerably. On the other hand England ceased to be a corn-exporting country. Trade with the colonies and, after 1783, with the United States had grown to such an extent that the proportion of imports from Europe had declined to one-third, though the actual volume of trade with the continent had increased.

Trade with North America involved diverse types of economies. The plantation economies of the Southern States supplied tropical and subtropical products such as sugar, tobacco, rice, and cotton, which were in great demand in England and in Europe. The extent of the trade with this group of colonies may be shown by the volume of goods imported via Liverpool. During the period 1700 to 1796 imports of tobacco increased threefold, sugar fivefold, and cotton fifty-fold. On the other hand, the New England colonies to the north had little to offer Britain that she could not produce herself. Thus only the southern colonies fitted well into the Old Colonial System, which regulated trade between the American colonies and Britain down to the War of American Independence.

Under this system the function of the colonies was to supply Britain with valuable raw materials and foodstuffs which were unobtainable in Europe, and to take in exchange British manufactures. Thus the Government in London looked upon the colonies as a kind of vast, private estate existing for the benefit of Britain. The New England colonies had an adverse balance of trade since they were unable to pay for British manufactures with exports of raw materials and foodstuffs. Yet under the Old Colonial System they were not allowed to compete with Britain by setting up manufacturing industries of their own. Thus by an act of 1732 the Americans were forbidden to export felt hats which were very popular at the time, and an act of 1750 allowed the colonists to produce bar and pig iron, but not to establish rolling and slitting mills. Nor were the colonists supposed to trade with foreign merchants, although since this was difficult to enforce over three thousand miles of ocean, the Government usually turned a blind eye to it. Although it is true that colonial shipping and commerce were encouraged, and all *enumerated products* (a long list of goods which could only be exported to England) had a guaranteed market, by the 1760s the colonists had become angry at the restrictions on their development. The attempt to enforce the Old Colonial System more thoroughly after the end of the Seven Years' War was an important cause of the revolt of the American Colonies.

The Atlantic trade of the eighteenth century may be divided into four categories, viz with West Africa, America, Spanish America, and the West Indies, with Liverpool and Bristol as their focal points. Dominating this triangular network was the slave trade which occupied a very important place in the structure of English commerce. Mercantilist writers defended it on the grounds that it was 'very advantageous to Great Britain and necessary to

9   *Prince's Dock, opened in 1821*
The great expansion of Liverpool's trade in the late eighteenth and early
nineteenth centuries was reflected in the construction of new docks,
which transformed the Mersey waterfront

the plantations'. Slaves were in great demand by the planters of the West Indies and the Southern States of America as the colonies developed, and the number of slaves landed annually reached 70,000 by the 1780s, half of them carried in British ships.

The slaves were collected at central points on the African coast, where they were bartered for knives, trinkets, and bric à brac of all kinds. Their sufferings on the voyage across the Atlantic, the so-called 'middle passage', were terrible. William Wilberforce, addressing the House of Commons in 1789, described it as

the most wretched part of the whole subject. So much misery condensed in so little room, is more than the human imagination had ever before con-

ceived. . . . Let any one imagine to himself 6 or 700 of these wretches chained two and two, surrounded with every object that is nauseous and disgusting, diseased, and struggling under every kind of wretchedness! How can we bear to think of such a scene as this? . . . Death at least is sure ground of evidence. . . . It will be found upon an average that . . . not less than $12\frac{1}{2}$ per cent perish in the passage.[2]

On reaching their destination the slaves were auctioned, or exchanged for West Indian rum, sugar, and tobacco.

Until the middle of the century the slave trade was a thoroughly respectable, if a risky, one. Its profits fluctuated greatly, for an outbreak of disease on board ship, enemy action, or shipwreck could bring heavy losses, and Wilberforce argued that the slave trade, instead of being a benefit to English sailors, was their grave – 'More sailors die in one year in the slave trade than die in two years in all the other trades put together.'[3] Public opinion was also becoming concerned over its obvious inhumanity, and in 1772 Chief Justice Mansfield in the *Somerset Case* pronounced slavery illegal in England, thus emancipating about 10,000 slaves. Quakers and Methodists condemned the traffic, and a movement to abolish the slave trade grew up under the leadership of Thomas Clarkson and Granville Sharp. In William Wilberforce (1759–1833) they found the powerful spokesman in Parliament needed to put across their cause. The abolitionists attacked the slave trade on the grounds of its cruelty, which was undeniable. Pitt the Younger was reluctant to commit his government to this course, since after 1793 England was at war with France, and it seemed unwise to suppress what appeared to be a flourishing trade. Wilberforce persevered, however, and in 1807 slave trading in British ships was made illegal.

In the eighteenth century it was hard to distinguish between legitimate trade, and smuggling, privateering, and piracy. Smuggling, encouraged by high duties, was widespread, and approved of by public opinion. A wine merchant in Cornwall, writing to Lord Dartmouth, President of the Board of Trade, gave his opinion that, although nine out of ten people drank tea twice a day, only one person in a hundred bought duty-paid tea. Considerable quantities of wool, whose export was forbidden, were shipped abroad where higher prices were obtained. Unknown quantities of tobacco, wine, brandy and silk were smuggled into the country, and the inland revenue officers had little chance of checking smuggling so long as its rewards were so great. The real cure was to remove the incentive for smuggling. In 1784 Pitt reduced the duty on tea from the very high figure of 119 per cent to $12\frac{1}{2}$ per cent, and in 1786 he negotiated the

Eden Treaty with France, whereby Britain and France lowered their duties on each other's goods. These first steps towards freer trade were abruptly halted, however, by the outbreak of the Revolutionary War with France in 1793.

Although the long war with France, when much of Europe was cut off from British exports, almost certainly slowed down the growth of trade, Britain's trade throughout the eighteenth century grew much faster than her population. The demand for more goods hastened the introduction of large-scale processes and labour-saving devices in industry. Goods became cheaper, since the cost of an article which is mass produced is lower than that of which only a few are made. Cheaper goods meant larger markets. After 1785, when steam-powered machinery began to make its presence felt, trade expanded enormously. The demand for raw materials for industry, and foodstuffs to feed a growing population created wealth in those countries which produced them, so that they were able to buy manufactures. British merchants and industrialists were well placed to take advantage of this situation, for Britain was the birthplace of the Industrial Revolution. Secondly, those industries which were first transformed – textiles and iron – were those whose products were in everyday use, so that the markets to be exploited were vast. The growth of trade was therefore one of the vital factors in the Industrial Revolution. Without a great expansion of trade, which created new wealth, markets, and sources of supply of food and raw materials, the Industrial Revolution could not have taken place.

REFERENCES

1   Voltaire, *Lettres Philosophiques*, X, 'Sur le Commerce', ed. Morland, XXII, pp. 110–11.
2   *The Parliamentary History of England*, XXVIII.
3   *The Parliamentary History of England*, XXVIII.

CHAPTER 5
Water Transport

Internal trade and transport, like overseas trade, was stimulated by the growth of population and industry during the eighteenth century. The growing manufacturing areas and seaports, with their concentrations of population, demanded supplies of food and raw materials. Daniel Defoe tells us how in particular the City of London exerted a strong pull on the produce of all parts of the country. Cheese and dairy produce came from Gloucestershire, Cheshire, Warwickshire, and other counties, cattle from Wales and Scotland, and cider from Devon, after it had been shipped around Land's End and along the south coast. Every August many thousands of turkeys and geese were driven to the capital from Norfolk and Suffolk. Manufacturing areas like the West Riding obtained their food supplies from the surrounding counties, and even farther afield. Agricultural products such as grain, cattle, dairy produce, lime, manure and marl; raw materials, especially coal, wool, wood, iron and building materials; and manufactures of all kinds were transported about the countryside. The volume of traffic and the amount of goods carried increased steadily every decade.

In 1700 goods were transported chiefly by water – along the coast and navigable rivers. Most important towns were situated at convenient points on rivers or coastal inlets, and the English coastline was dotted with ports and harbours. Land carriage was only used for short distances, or where water transport was not available.

Coastal shipping had obvious advantages over the carriage of goods by road. Heavy, bulky materials could be taken more quickly and cheaply by sea. London and the south coast was supplied with 'sea coal' from the Northumberland and Durham coalmines. Nearly four thousand ships were employed in the coal trade alone. Scottish cattle were shipped to the pastures of East Anglia, where they were fattened for the London market. The Cornish tin miners were supplied with coal brought by sea from South Wales.

Yet sea transport faced hazards from sudden storms and rocky coastlines poorly equipped with lighthouses. The Norfolk coast, according to Defoe, was 'particularly famous for being one of the most dangerous and most fatal to the sailors in all England; and the more so because of the great number of ships which are continually going and coming in their passage between London and all the northern coasts of Great Britain'.[1] He relates how one night in 1692 the greater part of two fleets was driven ashore in Cromer Bay, and two hundred ships and over a thousand sailors perished. During the frequent wars of the century, coastal traffic was disrupted by French privateers, and English press gangs who seized merchant seamen as recruits for the navy. The mariner also faced the practice of wrecking, which was either deliberately luring a ship on to the rocks, or enjoying the proceeds of a wreck sent by fortune.

Rivers were valuable for trade and transport not because they were excellent for these purposes, but because roads were so bad. English rivers are generally short and winding, and except for those in the eastern counties, have a rapid fall. The areas they served were limited, and many mineral-producing parts of the country were far from navigable water. Summer droughts, and periodic flooding and freezing in winter, made them unfit for use at certain times of the year. There were also artificial obstructions like fords, low bridges, and weirs for driving waterwheels, the chief source of industrial power for much of the century. Before rivers were improved by the addition of towpaths the barges were usually pulled upstream by gangs of men who scrambled along the banks. When the barge was stranded in shallow water the barge-master had to send upstream to request the millowner to open his sluice gates and allow a 'flash' of water to flow downstream to refloat the barge. The millowner's reluctance to lower the level of his water supply often gave rise to bitter disputes. After 1650 many rivers were improved; meanders were eliminated by short 'cuts'; fords were replaced with bridges, and shallows were overcome by the construction of small 'pound' locks, while towpaths provided for horse-drawn barge traffic.

Thus by 1700 the five main rivers of England and Wales were navigable along considerable stretches of their length. The Thames was a chief factor in the growth of London. The Severn, and its tributaries the Stour and Avon, served Shrewsbury, and parts of Wales, the West Midlands, and Somerset. Cheshire and South Lancashire were served by a third group of rivers. The Mersey and the Irwell were trade routes for Liverpool and Manchester. On the east coast the Humber and Trent, together with their tributaries, linked Nottingham, Burton and Derby, with the sea, and opened York and the West Riding to maritime trade. Finally an important group of rivers flowed into the Wash. The Ouse served places like Ely, Cambridge and Bedford, the Nene Peterborough, the Welland Stamford, and the Witham Lincoln. Other rivers had local importance, such as the Tyne and Wear for the north-eastern coalmines, and the Exe and Parret, which served Exeter and Taunton.

The economic importance of navigable rivers was great. A river which had been made navigable became the chief method of transport for the surrounding countryside, and those parts of the country which had to rely on roads found that prosperity reached them later. The secondary rivers also played an im-

portant role in stimulating industry. Thus the Aire and Calder served the West Riding woollen industry. Between 1726 and 1733 the river Don was made navigable to within three miles of Sheffield. At about the same time the owners of the saltfields near Nantwich in Cheshire obtained parliamentary permission to deepen the river Weaver, which enabled them to obtain more coal cheaply from the mines of South Lancashire. In the early nineteenth century it could be said of the river Ure, a tributary of the Yorkshire Ouse, that 'The traffic on the river for coals, timber, flax, and other articles, was extensive; for Knaresborough was then one of the greatest linen manufacturing towns in England and Boroughbridge was its port'. Rivers, therefore, were busy trade routes, and some are still used today by ocean-going ships.

Canals

By 1750 the mileage of navigable rivers in Britain had been doubled, but there were still many areas without adequate means of water transport. The improvement of rivers foreshadowed the creation of a system of artificial waterways, since it was a logical, if bold, step, to advance from making a 'cut' to shorten a river navigation, to constructing a proper canal. Canals had many advantages over rivers; they could be built to serve the needs of industry; they were ideal for the transport of heavy goods like stone, coal and timber, and safe for fragile articles like pottery, while their slowness was not at the time a disadvantage. Canals were of vital importance in the industrial development of the latter part of the century, since many industries came to depend upon coal. The link between canals and the coal industry cannot be exaggerated.

The first canal in Britain was the Exeter Canal, built in 1566, but it was not until 1755 that the Canal Age began. In that year a group of businessmen in Liverpool and St Helens decided to cut a canal in preference to widening the Sankey Brook. The Sankey Navigation, as it was called, was completed in 1757, and connected the expanding coalmines at St Helens with the river Mersey, enabling Lancashire coal to be transported cheaply to the Cheshire salt industry. It was the problem of transporting coal which prompted a great nobleman, the third Duke of Bridgewater, to build a canal from his mines at Worsley to Manchester. The Duke of Bridgewater owned extensive deposits of coal, but was unable to exploit them because of the high costs of carrying coal by packhorse into Manchester (9/- a ton for a distance of 11 kilometres—7 miles). In 1759 he engaged to survey and build his canal a Derbyshire millwright, James Brindley (1716–72), who became the greatest of canal engineers.

The chief difficulty was the crossing of the river Irwell, which Brindley proposed to overcome by an aqueduct. Contemporaries thought the idea of one ship sailing over the top of another foolish and reckless, but Brindley had the Duke's confidence and went ahead. The aqueduct at Barton, 180 metres (200 yards) long, and 11 metres (12 yards) wide, carried the Bridgewater Canal over the Irwell at a height of 12 metres (39 feet). People from miles around came to see the 'greatest artificial curiosity in the world', described as

... a navigable canal in the air; for it is as high as the tops of the trees. Whilst I was surveying it with a mixture of wonder and delight, four barges passed me in the space of about three minutes, two of them being chained together, and dragged by two horses, which walked upon the battlements of this extraordinary bridge.[2]

The canal, opened in 1761, was an important reason for the development of Manchester, where the price of coal was reduced from 7d to 4d a hundredweight. Coal was becoming increasingly important for domestic use, and in industry, especially after the coming of steam power in 1785. The success of the canal encouraged the duke to link his collieries at Worsley with the port of Liverpool, by

extending his original canal to Runcorn, 56 kilometres (35 miles) away. The Bridgewater Canal (1767) halved the cost of coal in Liverpool, from 12/- to 6/- a ton.

Industrialists soon realized that canals would open up much wider markets for their goods. Josiah Wedgwood, a Staffordshire pottery manufacturer, was especially interested in a safe method of transporting his fragile wares, and he became chairman of the Grand Trunk Canal Company in 1766. At the same time a second group of businessmen promoted the Staffordshire and Worcestershire Canal to connect the Grand Trunk Canal, or the Trent and Mersey Canal as it came to be called, with the river Severn. Both groups of promoters employed Brindley as engineer. The Staffordshire and Worcestershire Canal was finished in 1772, the year of Brindley's death, and the Trent and Mersey in 1777. The latter was 150 kilometres (93 miles) long, and linked the Midlands with Liverpool and Manchester. Within a generation the country was covered with a network of canals, linking all the major industrial areas with navigable waterways. Birmingham became the hub of a complicated web of canals. In 1768 the Birmingham Canal was authorized, linking the town with the Staffordshire and Worcestershire Canal, and thus with the port of Bristol. By 1790 Birmingham had water communication with London via the Coventry and Oxford Canals. London and the Bristol Channel were linked by three more canals. The first was the Thames and Severn Canal (1783–89). The Kennet and Avon Canal (1794–1810) was a broad canal, 92 kilometres (57 miles) long, with a staircase of 29 locks at Devizes. It was engineered by John Rennie (1761–1821), and cost £90,000. Its rival, the Wiltshire and Berkshire Canal (1795–1809) was a narrow canal, serving an agricultural area, but it made a modest annual profit until the middle of the nineteenth century. London was also linked with Northampton by the Grand Junction Canal (1793–1805).

In northern England another network of canals was constructed, particularly in South

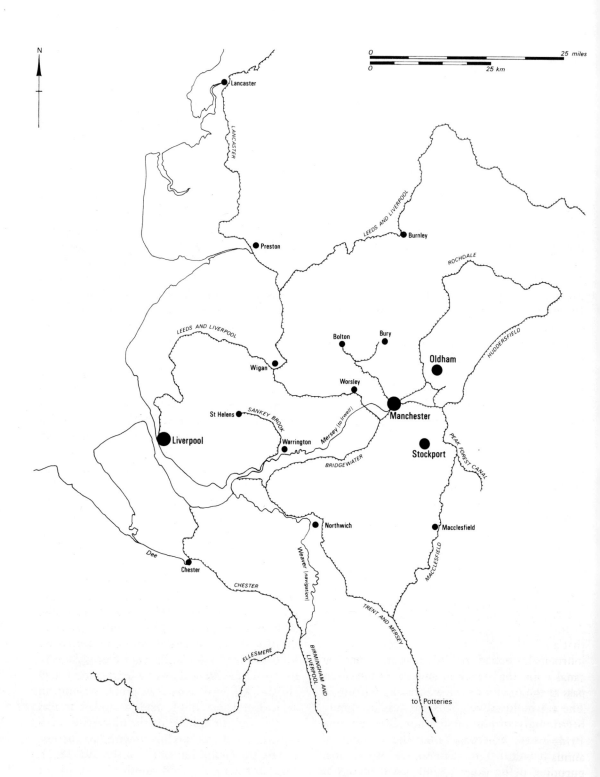

N

Lancaster

LANCASTER

LEEDS AND LIVERPOOL

Preston

Burnley

ROCHDALE

LEEDS AND LIVERPOOL

Bolton   Bury

Oldham

HUDDERSFIELD

Wigan

Worsley

St Helens   *SANKEY BROOK*

Mersey (to Irwell)

Manchester

Warrington

Liverpool

BRIDGEWATER

Stockport

PEAK FOREST CANAL

Northwich

Macclesfield

Dee

Weaver (navigation)

MACCLESFIELD

Chester

CHESTER

ELLESMERE

BIRMINGHAM AND LIVERPOOL

TRENT AND MERSEY

to Potteries

0 ────────────── 25 miles
0 ────────────── 25 km

10   Canals and navigable rivers in Lancashire and Cheshire in 1830

Lancashire and the West Riding, which provided a cross-country link between the ports of Liverpool and Hull. After the Leeds and Liverpool Canal had been authorized in 1770, three tributary canals were built. The Chesterfield Canal connected an important mining area with the river Trent. The Chester Canal ran from the river Dee to Nantwich, and the little Bradford Canal connected Bradford with the Leeds and Liverpool Canal, which was finished in 1816. In Scotland there were two important canals; the Forth–Clyde (1768–90), and the Caledonian Canal in the Highlands, begun in 1803 and completed in 1822.

Canals gave the country the most efficient system of transport it had known. Some 3,700 kilometres (2,300 miles) of canals were built, and along them merchandise of all kinds was carried. Telford declared that

Canals are chiefly used for the following purposes: 1st for conveying the produce of mines to the sea shore. 2nd conveying fuel and raw materials to some manufacturing towns and districts, and exporting the manufactured goods. 3rd conveying groceries and merchant goods for the consumption of the district through which the canal passes.

All parts of England gained in some way from the easier interchange of the products of different areas, but two regions in particular benefited. One was the Black Country to the north of Birmingham, the other was the North Staffordshire potteries around Stoke.

Nevertheless, canals had certain disadvantages. They were the result of individual enterprise and were built with no unified plan in mind. They varied in depth and width, so that a manufacturer sending a barge on a long journey, as well as paying dues to several canal companies, had to ensure that it could pass through the smallest lock on the route. The early canals were very successful—at the beginning of the nineteenth century the Bridgewater Canal was earning £100,000 annually—but many were built for speculative purposes, or after an insufficient appraisal of their prospects. During the 'Canal Mania'

11 *Inland navigation*
'Few improvements of modern times have contributed so much to increase the commerce and wealth of this country, as canal navigation' (quoted in W. H. Pyne, Lancashire Illustrated *[1827], from which the engraving is taken)*

(1791–4), when enthusiasm for canals reached its height, many unsound schemes were financed. This was especially so in the rural South of England, where the volume of traffic was often so low that the canals did not even pay their way. Canals were also limited by the facts of geography. Those passing through hilly areas had numerous locks. There were 92 locks in the 56 kilometres (33 miles) of the Rochdale Canal. Locks made the journey slow and tedious, and restricted the amount of traffic which could use the canal, because they were usually built no larger than was thought necessary at the time. By 1840 canals were losing business to the railways, which ran to a timetable, and offered safe, rapid carriage of raw materials and perishable foodstuffs. Many canals were taken over by railway companies, and either closed or run by them. Others went bankrupt, deserted almost as quickly as once they had been welcomed, and few survived as paying propositions.

REFERENCES

1   Daniel Defoe, *A Tour Through the Whole Island of Great Britain* (Everyman).
2   J. Newbery, *Lady's Pocketbook.*

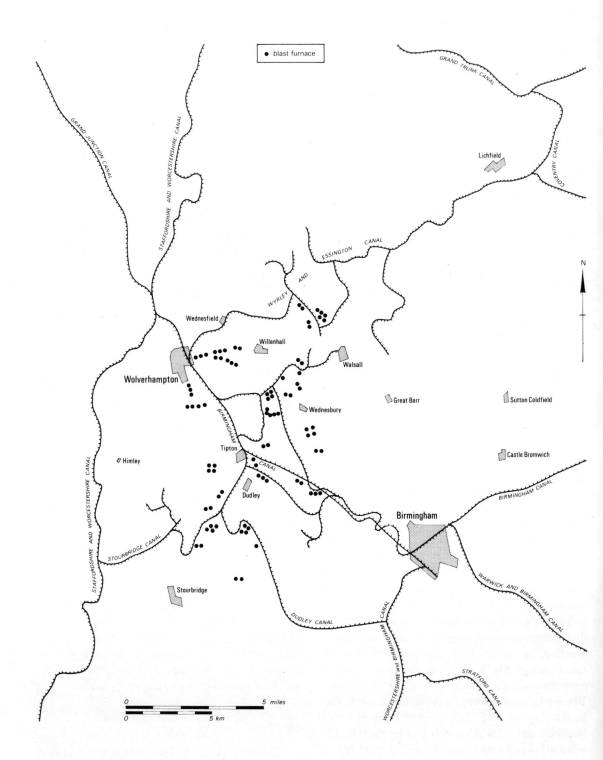

● blast furnace

GRAND TRUNK CANAL

GRAND JUNCTION CANAL

STAFFORDSHIRE AND WORCESTERSHIRE CANAL

COVENTRY CANAL

Lichfield

ESSINGTON CANAL

WYRLEY AND

Wednesfield

Willenhall

Walsall

Wolverhampton

Great Barr

Sutton Coldfield

BIRMINGHAM

Wednesbury

Himley

Tipton

CANAL

Castle Bromwich

Dudley

BIRMINGHAM CANAL

Birmingham

STOURBRIDGE CANAL

STAFFORDSHIRE AND WORCESTERSHIRE CANAL

WARWICK AND BIRMINGHAM CANAL

Stourbridge

DUDLEY CANAL

WORCESTERSHIRE and BIRMINGHAM CANAL

STRATFORD CANAL

0   5 miles

0   5 km

12   The West Midlands canal system in 1826

Most Englishmen in the eighteenth century complained about the weather, and the state of the roads, just as they do today, but with more reason. A road map of England in 1700 would have shown an intricate network of roads linking villages and towns, but this appearance would have been completely misleading. The typical road was a dirt track, dusty in summer, soft and muddy in winter, and full of ruts and potholes which made travel dangerous. Many roads were so narrow that they were barely wide enough for one cart, let alone for another to pass in the opposite direction. Where conditions were very bad travellers often left the road, and went over the fields, but where the surface of the road had sunk beneath that of the adjoining fields, or where enclosure had taken place, no detour was possible. Breakdowns, which happened frequently, caused great inconvenience and annoyance. Many roads were impassable to heavy traffic in winter. Villages and towns expected to be isolated during winter months, and laid in provisions to withstand this natural siege. Industrialists stockpiled essential raw materials during the summer to last them until spring. Few people undertook a journey in winter if they could possibly avoid it.

The amount of traffic on the roads in the eighteenth century was tiny compared with today. Goods were only taken by road where no other form of transport was available. Middle-aged men in 1800 could remember the time when people in outlying districts ran to see the curiosity of a cart. The usual method of carrying heavy goods by road was by covered wagon, pulled by a team of horses. Barring accidents, the wagon could average between 3 and 5 kilometres (2 or 3 miles) per hour. Where the countryside was too hilly for heavy stage wagons, as in northern England, it was usual to take goods by packhorse, in spite of the limited quantity which could be carried by each animal. The humble pedlar, often a rogue or a vagabond, was a familiar figure on the landscape, supplying villages and remote areas with their miscellaneous wants. The ordinary traveller made his way most comfortably by post-chaise, stage coach, and on horseback, if he could afford to, and on foot if he could not.

Road travel was not only slow and uncomfortable, it could also be dangerous. Until the roads became busier, highwaymen had matters much their own way, for there was no police force in the countryside to catch them. The exploits of highwaymen have made them appear romantic figures, gentlemen of the road, but they were not averse to waylaying the poor, and there was little difference between them and common footpads who robbed with violence in dark town streets. Little wonder that passengers,

13   A stage wagon

faced with these possibilities of an interrupted journey, often referred to stage coaches as 'God permits', because they arrived God willing.

Roads in northern England were especially bad, and it is not surprising that canals were first built there. Arthur Young wrote of the road from Chorley to Wigan in Lancashire

I know not, in the whole range of language, terms sufficiently impressive to describe this infernal road. To look at a map, and perceive that it is a principal one, not only to some towns, but even to whole counties, one would naturally conclude it to be at least decent; but let me most seriously caution all travellers, who may accidentally purpose to travel this terrible county, to avoid it as they would the devil; for a thousand to one they break their necks or their limbs by overthrows or breakings down. They will here meet with ruts which I actually measured four feet down, and floating with mud only from a wet summer; what therefore must it be after a winter? The only mending it receives in places is the tumbling in some loose stones, which serve no other purpose than jolting a carriage in the most intolerable manner.[1]

With few exceptions, roads in southern England were also atrocious. Young's description of the road from Billericay to Tilbury, in Essex, which was a main one, illustrates this point well.

It is for near twelve miles so narrow that a mouse cannot pass by any carriage; I saw a fellow creep under his waggon to assist me to lift, if possible, my chaise over a hedge. The ruts are of an incredible depth—and a pavement of diamonds might as well be fought for as a quarter. The trees everywhere over-grow the road, so that it is totally impervious to the sun, except at a few places. And to add to all the infamous circumstances which concur to plague a traveller, I must not forget the eternally meeting with chalk-waggons; themselves frequently stuck fast, till a collection of them are in the same situation, and twenty or thirty horses may be tacked to each, to draw them out one by one.[2]

Except for some turnpikes, proper road maintenance was almost unknown, so that with the gradual increase of traffic, road surfaces steadily deteriorated. Under the Highways Act of 1552 the parish was responsible for the upkeep of its roads. A local surveyor was elected by the parish each year to supervise the job of repairing the roads. He was often appointed against his will, usually had little knowledge of how to provide a proper road surface, and was unpaid. Statute labour was provided for six days of the year, when the local farmers had to allow their carts to be used for hauling stones from the quarry, and the rest of the men turned out as labourers. The worst potholes and ruts were roughly filled with boulders as quickly as possible, and the rest of the time taken as a holiday.

Thus even the busy main roads lacked a decent surface, and during the century various suggestions for improving them were made. One idea was to have two tracks instead of one. Efforts were made to limit the weight of wagons, and in 1753 a Broad Wheels Act was passed by Parliament, compelling wagons to have wheels nine inches wide, in the belief that broad wheels caused less damage to the road surface. This proved to be false, as the road surface was ground to powder, which was blown away by the wind, and washed away by rain. The real answer lay in the turnpike system.

14 Road mending in Yorkshire
The men are breaking the stones and spreading them

As early as 1663, in the reign of Charles II, justices of the peace in certain areas had been allowed to levy tolls for repairing their roads, but the first turnpike trust was not established until 1706. A turnpike trust was a group of men permitted by Parliament to put gates across certain roads, or parts of roads, and to charge a small sum, called a toll, for the right to pass through them. Typical charges were: wagons with four horses 1/6, coaches 1/-, cattle $\frac{1}{2}$d and sheep $\frac{1}{4}$d. In return the trust had to keep their roads in good repair. The gates were called turnpikes because they turned on hinges, and had sharp points like pikes on them to prevent horsemen from jumping over them. During the century over 2,000 turnpike acts were passed, and by 1830 there were 35,000 kilometres (22,000 miles) of turnpike road administered by 1,100 separate trusts.

Daniel Defoe was an enthusiastic supporter of turnpikes, but his opinion was not shared by those who had to pay tolls where formerly they had travelled freely, and tolls were sometimes referred to as highway robbery authorized by Parliament. Serious turnpike riots occurred near Bristol in the summer of 1749, when the posts at various toll-gates were blown up, and a body of commissioners took it in turns to stand guard and insist that the tolls were paid. During similar riots in Leeds in 1753 several people were shot dead in the streets. Some trusts were inefficient or corrupt, farming out the tolls to contractors who paid a lump sum in return for the right to make a profit from collecting the tolls. Sometimes there was not enough traffic on the turnpike to provide for the costs of maintenance. This may account for Arthur Young's description of the turnpike between Sudbury and Bury St Edmunds as 'Ponds of liquid dirt and a scattering of loose flints just sufficient to lame every horse that moves near them'.[3] Another disadvantage was that each trust was responsible for short stretches of road only, so that on a long journey tolls might have to be paid several times. Nevertheless, turnpikes were usually an improvement on the roads they replaced, and when foreign travellers in England compared English roads very favourably with those in their own country there is no doubt that they were referring to turnpikes.

Yet turnpikes accounted for a mere sixth of the total road mileage. More than 160,000 kilometres (100,000 miles) of road remained under the control of the parish, repaired by the old-fashioned statute labour, or by paupers who were paid out of the proceeds of a local highways rate. If many turnpike surveyors had no real knowledge of road engineering, building materials, and convexity, it is hardly surprising that the unpaid parish surveyor failed to provide a proper surface. In the second half of the century, however, there appeared a number of famous road builders, employed chiefly by the turnpike trusts, to build and maintain roads according to scientific principles, instead of the traditional makeshift methods.

The first important road builder of the century was a soldier, General Wade (1668–1748), who built over 300 kilometres (200 miles) of roads in the Scottish Highlands after the 1715 Jacobite rebellion. Previously, highland roads had been barely distinguishable from the natural surface of the surrounding countryside. Wade's roads made the highlands accessible, and reduced the independence of the Scottish chieftains. They were designed for military needs, however, and were of little value to farmers and traders.

John Metcalf (1717–1810), or 'Blind Jack of Knaresborough', was blind from the age of six years as a result of smallpox. Yet in spite of his blindness he surveyed the route himself, inspecting the surface with his stick, and then gave instructions to his workmen. He was said to have refused a lift once on the grounds that he was in a hurry. Metcalf built 290 kilometres (180 miles) of road in Yorkshire, Lancashire, Cheshire and Derbyshire. He tackled roads over the difficult terrain of the Pennines, and excelled in constructing roads over boggy ground. He solved the latter problem by laying bundles of heather as a foundation, which was pressed down, and covered with gravel. He paid great attention to drainage, providing his roads with ditches and convex surfaces so that they would drain easily. Metcalf's roads included part of the turnpike from Harrogate to Boroughbridge, the hilly road from Whaley Bridge to Buxton, and the road from Wakefield to Huddersfield over Crosland Moor, which Metcalf himself said needed no repairs for twelve years after it had been built.

Thomas Telford (1757–1834), a Scot, was one of the great British civil engineers. A man of many talents, he built docks, ports, roads, bridges, and canals. The Caledonian Canal in Scotland, the Ellesmere Canal in Shropshire, and the Gotha Canal in Sweden are among his achievements. He also engineered the Menai Suspension Bridge linking Anglesey with the mainland. In 1802 Telford went to Scotland, which was worse off for roads than England, and constructed over 1,400 kilometres (900 miles) of roads, including the Glasgow to Carlisle road. Telford built bridges where necessary on the grounds that they were less expensive than detours, and he planned the route so that no main road had a gradient of more than one in forty. He made his roads with strong foundations, gave them a camber of one in twenty, and dug drainage ditches along their sides. His best known work was the London to Holyhead road, begun in 1815, which was the finest road in England in the coaching era.

John Loudon Macadam (1756–1836), was born near Ayr, where his father had founded the local bank. When Macadam was fourteen years old his father died, and he was sent to New York for training in commerce by an uncle. On his return to Scotland in 1783 he settled first in Ayrshire, where he became Deputy Lieutenant of the county and improved the local roads, and then in Falmouth, Cornwall, where he continued his road-making experiments. In 1816 he was elected surveyor for the Bristol turnpike roads, which he soon improved, earning himself a national reputation at the same time. Macadam paid little attention to the foundation of his roads, believing that the surface was the most important. His method was to put down two or three layers of small, broken stone which traffic consolidated into a hard-packed, water-tight surface, thus preventing water from soaking into the soil underneath. The merits of the roads built by Telford and Macadam were hotly debated, but those of Macadam were cheaper, and his method was eventually adopted. Macadam's influence was chiefly in the repair of existing roads, and it is from his name that we get the term 'tarmac', or 'macadamized', used by the road builders of today.

The improvement in roads brought a great increase in traffic. Coaching services became more speedy, frequent and reliable. The monthly coach between London and Edinburgh took 12–14 days over the journey in 1763; in 1830 it took 48 hours. London to Dover took 10 hours, and London to Brighton $5\frac{1}{2}$ hours. Travellers from London to Ireland were able to reach the port of Holyhead in 27 hours, instead of the 3 days usual in 1785, thanks to Telford's road. Fast, armed mail coaches first operated by John Palmer of Bath in 1785, carried the mails as well as passengers between London and the principal towns. In their heyday, 1815 to 1835, stage coach firms employed 3,000 coaches, and provided the fastest regular services in Europe. Each run was divided into stages of about 19 kilometres (12 miles), when the horses were changed. Coach operators made contracts, usually with innkeepers, for the supply and stabling of horses. With these arrangements coaches could average 16 kilometres (10 miles) per hour; faster speeds killed too many horses, and by law the horses were not allowed to gallop, though this rule was often ignored by coachmen making up for lost time, or racing a rival. Each coach carried its firm's colours, and the driver, if a good one, had his admiring fans, much as a first-class racing driver today.

Another means of road transport being developed at the time was the steam carriage. In the 1820s several people were building them, and by 1833 steam coaches operated between Cheltenham and Gloucester, and London and Brighton. Steam traction companies faced fierce opposition from coach firms and railways however, and they had to pay on turnpikes tolls twenty times those of horse-drawn coaches. By 1864 their speed had reached 30 m.p.h. (48 k.p.h.), but the passing of the 'Man and Flag' Act, which laid down that self-propelled vehicles be restricted to 4 m.p.h. (6 k.p.h.), and were to be preceded on the road by a man with a red flag, led to their virtual disappearance. This act, which was not repealed until 1896, delayed the development of the motor car industry in this country. In the meantime, the stage coach had met a form of opposition it could not hope to overcome — mechanical fire-horses. The coming of railways killed the stage coach industry, as well as causing the decline of canal companies. Nevertheless, the transport improvements outlined above made possible the rapid industrial development which was so marked a feature of late eighteenth-century England.

REFERENCES

1   Arthur Young, *Six Months' Tour of the North of England*, Vol. I, p. 430.
2   Arthur Young, *Six Weeks' Tour Through the Southern Counties of England and Wales* (1772), p. 88.
3   Arthur Young, *Six Weeks' Tour Through the Southern Counties of England and Wales* (1772), p. 319.

15 The new steam carriage

CHAPTER 7
Science, Technology and Industry in the Eighteenth Century

By the end of the eighteenth century a series of inventions had transformed the manufacture of cotton in England, and had created a new method of production—the factory system. The iron, engineering, and chemical industries also experienced important changes, although their transformation was completed somewhat later. The most important technological changes involved the harnessing of the expansive force of steam, improvements in blast furnace techniques, such as the use of coke, and then coal, in smelting iron ore, the greater use of coal in producing heat and energy, the introduction of improved machinery, and large-scale manufacture of acids, alkalis and dyes for industrial use. All these changes are described below in separate chapters. The purpose of this chapter is to examine why these changes came about when they did.

The Industrial Revolution was not something which happened overnight. With the possible exception of France, England in 1700 was already the most heavily industrialized country in Europe. Daniel Defoe described early eighteenth-century England as a country of flourishing trade and manufacture, and of rapid economic development.

New discoveries in metals, mines, minerals; new undertakings in trade, inventions, engines, manufactures. These things open new scenes every day, and make England especially shew a new and differing face in many places, on every occasion of surveying it.[1]

Many areas were already specializing in the manufacture of goods for which they became famous. Newcastle had its shipyards and ironworks, Sheffield was noted for its cutlery, Birmingham for its metal goods ('Brumm-

16 *Wensleydale knitters*
Men, women and children all knitted in their spare time

agem ware'), South-west Lancashire for its glass and 'cottons', North Staffordshire for its pottery. The major coalfields were already being worked, while tin and copper were mined in Cornwall, and lead in Cumberland, West Durham, and Derbyshire. Clay, slate and stone were quarried extensively. Many lesser industries such as the manufacture of silk, lace, paper and leather goods, were securely established. The greatest industry of them all, the woollen industry, was found in most parts of the country, but with the South-western Counties, East Anglia, and the West Riding of Yorkshire the chief areas of manufacture.

We should gain a wrong impression if we imagined that England was a land of large-scale industry. Most people still earned at least part of their living from the land. Many industries were essentially domestic, that is, all or most of the manufacturing processes were done in the workers' homes, or in small workshops attached to them, and not in factories and mills. The only factory in the modern sense was John and Thomas Lombe's silk mill near Derby, which employed three hundred workers when it was built in 1717. But domestic industry did not mean primitive industry, and capitalists played an important role. The merchant clothier who employed hundreds of outworkers in rural areas was just as much a capitalist as the nineteenth-century millowner. Part of his capital (wealth) was tied up in the purchase of raw materials, and he had to wait for his profit until he had sold the finished products. Coalmines and blast furnaces also constitute capital, and the men who owned them were capitalists. Thus capitalism, large-scale production, and competition, certainly existed in some industries long before 1700, preparing the way for the more remarkable changes which justify the term 'Industrial Revolution'.

England's economic development had reached the stage where great industrial changes were both needed and wanted. Clearly one reason was the growth in population which was no longer limited by the demand for labour and the supply of food. The expansion of England's population can be traced back to the early decades of the eighteenth century which were blessed with good harvests, so that food was plentiful and cheap. The growth in numbers meant a demand for goods of all kinds, which tended to push prices up, thereby encouraging people to find new and better ways of making them. It meant more people to make goods as well as more people to buy them. Yet the startling rise in numbers appeared late in the century, and the example of Ireland, where the population also grew rapidly, shows that by itself an increase in population does not necessarily bring industrial change.

England had great natural resources of coal and iron, often found close together, and water, which was vitally important in many industries, either as a source of power, or in the manufacturing processes themselves. An abundant rainfall meant that in hilly areas like the slopes of the Pennines there were many fast-flowing streams which provided water power. No part of the country was far distant from the coast or navigable rivers, so that transport problems were eased before the days of canals and railways.

England also enjoyed internal peace and stability. Apart from the Jacobite rebellions of 1715 and 1745 there was no serious internal strife, and the long period of peaceful rule under Robert Walpole who was, from 1721 to 1742, the equivalent of our modern prime minister, enabled the Hanoverian dynasty to establish itself securely. England's immunity from invasion was a priceless gift bestowed upon her by nature. It allowed her industry and commerce to develop freely without the damage of war experienced by many continental countries, so that although Britain was at war for much of the century the effects of war were less harmful than they might have been. Some industries were stimulated by war and Britain certainly gained important colonies and trading advantages from her victories. The Act of Union (1707) between Scotland and England created a free trade area in Britain, in contrast to Germany, where there were over three hundred states, and France, where innumerable tolls and tariffs held back industrial growth.

Widespread industrial progress would have been impossible without an expansion of foreign trade. By the early part of the eighteenth century England had captured from Holland much of the carrying trade of Europe, and had laid the foundations of a worldwide empire by winning the first round of the colonial struggle with France. After the Seven Years' War (1756–63) the latter's possessions in India and North America were taken by England. Spain could not prevent English merchants from exploiting the opportunities for trade with her empire in Central and South America, and the growing American colonies demanded British manufactures. Tropical and subtropical products such as

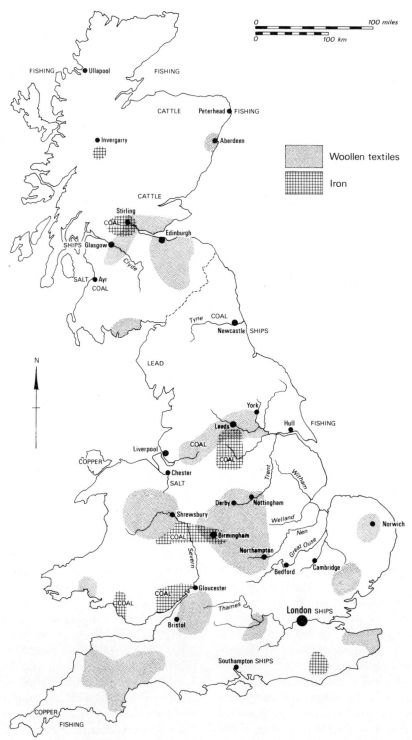

Britain in the early eighteenth century. Chief industries and navigable rivers

FISHING • Ullapool
FISHING

CATTLE
Peterhead • FISHING

• Invergarry
• Aberdeen

CATTLE

Stirling
COAL
Edinburgh
SHIPS Glasgow
Clyde
SALT • Ayr
COAL

Tyne COAL
Newcastle SHIPS

LEAD

N

York
Leeds
Hull FISHING

COAL
Liverpool
COAL

COPPER
• Chester
SALT

Trent
Witham

Derby • Nottingham

Welland
Nen

Shrewsbury

COAL
Birmingham
Northampton
Great Ouse

Norwich

Severn
Bedford
Cambridge

COAL Gloucester
COAL
Thames

London SHIPS

Bristol

Southampton SHIPS

COPPER
FISHING

Woollen textiles
Iron

0 ———— 100 miles
0 ———— 100 km

sugar from the West Indies, spices from India and the Far East, rice and tobacco from the southern colonies of America, found ready markets in Britain and European countries, to which they were re-exported. As trade expanded, so supplies of capital were accumulated, without which the mines, factories, ironworks and canals could not have been built.

There was also a great increase in scientific knowledge and its application to industry. During the seventeenth century mechanics became the most important branch of the natural sciences, so that science was closely associated with contemporary developments in mathematics. Scientific advancement owed much to Sir Isaac Newton (1642–1727), one of the world's greatest scientists. By the time he was twenty-four years old Newton had worked out a system of differential calculus, whereby the areas under curves and the volumes of solid figures could be calculated. He investigated the composition of light and the nature of colours by passing beams of white light, e.g. sunlight, through prisms, and he discovered the laws of gravity. His treatise on mathematics, the *Principia* (1687), in which he explained how the behaviour of the planets, the tides, and the motion of objects on earth were governed by a single mathematical law, revolutionized scientific thought.

Numerous societies were formed to encourage the spread of scientific knowledge. Two of the most famous were the Royal Society and the Lunar Society. The Royal Society, founded in 1662 under the patronage of Charles II, sponsored scientific accounts of technical processes. Among them were included:

The Histories of making Bread; of Malt; of brewing Beer and Ale in several places: of Whale-fishing: of the Weather for several years: of Windmills and other Mills in Holland: of Masonry: of Pitch and Tar: of Maiz: of Vintners: of Shot: of making Gunpowder: and of making some that is twenty times as strong as the common Pistol powder.[2]

Inventions attributed to the influence of the Society include thermometers, gravity scales, telescopes, barometers, and surveying and geological instruments.

The Lunar Society was formed in Birmingham in 1776. Its membership included many famous men of industry and science such as Matthew Boulton, James Watt and Joseph Priestley. The members met in each other's houses on the night of the full moon, so that they could travel home in the moonlight. Any member could take a technical or business problem along to the meeting for the advice of the others, so that all could benefit from the ideas and specialized knowledge of each individual. The Lunar Society and many similar societies in provincial towns gave money for scientific experiments, and offered prizes for the solution of practical problems. So fashionable was the interest in science and new industrial techniques that the *Gentleman's Magazine* in 1779 declared that it would publish the 'discoveries of every new invention, and the improvements in every useful art'.

The investigations of scientists into problems of measurement and weighing, theories of heat and energy, and strengths of materials such as timber, stone and metals created knowledge which was of great value in the development of the steam engine and other technical inventions. When the spread of technical knowledge was combined with a long tradition of fine craftsmanship, the skilled mechanics who could develop new machinery and instruments became available. The increasing number of patents registered every decade in the eighteenth century showed that growing numbers of people had acquired useful technical knowledge, and it was from this background that inventors like James Watt emerged.

Although some inventors, such as Edmund Cartwright, the inventor of the power loom, were gifted amateurs, most were men with technical knowledge. Such were the iron-masters Dud Dudley and Abraham Darby, who discovered how to use coal in smelting iron ore. Others were humble craftsmen or farmers in search of better ways of doing things. An example of the latter was John Arbuthnot, who farmed land at Mitcham in Surrey. Arthur Young described him as

a good chemist and well informed in mathematical mechanics [and added:] *The executions of this real genius in Husbandry embraced a great variety of objects, and I scarcely recollect one, in which he was not successful; he cultivated lucerne upon a large scale; he tried many breeds of sheep, and fixed upon South Downs as the most profitable, long before they were heard of in the farming world; his inventions in the mechanics of agriculture, in drills, horsehoes, rollers, drain ploughs, hoppers for the delivery of manure, and a variety of other articles were of decided merit; in a word, he brought to every part of agriculture a mind richly stored with a variety of knowledge.*[3]

Though the names of men like Townshend, Tull and Bakewell spring first to mind when considering technical improvements in farming, up and down the country there were many farmers who in their own localities contributed to the development of farming. Agricultural change, though slow in becoming general, was important because its results affected most people, either because they earned whole or part of their living from farming, or because lower food prices made the wages of industrial workers go farther. The English labourer spent a smaller fraction of his income on food than his European counterpart, and his higher purchasing power and standard of living created a demand for more manufactured goods.

It was the increased demand—for goods of all kinds, and for cheap, reliable, *mechanical* power—that really lay behind the Industrial Revolution. This can be most clearly shown in the cotton and iron industries. In the cotton industry there was a serious bottleneck in the production of yarn by the middle of the century. In Lancashire weavers walked several miles each day collecting the yarn needed to keep their looms busy. John Kay's flying shuttle, which speeded up the work of the weaver, and the spread of weaving to the countryside, only made the shortage of yarn worse. Nowhere else in Europe was the countryside so full of industry. Yet once all suitable new sources of labour for spinning had been absorbed, an expansion in the putting out system was impossible, for there was a limit to the amount of extra work an employer could obtain from his workers. Thus the mechanical spinning inventions, such as the spinning jenny, the water frame (1768) and the mule (1779) were substitutes for human skill. Steam-powered spinning, introduced in 1785, revolutionized cotton production within a generation.

In the iron industry the shortage holding back production was fuel and power. Wood was used in the eighteenth century for a host of purposes ranging from ships, machinery, building, furniture and drainpipes, to fuel and the production of alkali and tar, but its scarcity was an acute problem which led to the search for an alternative fuel. By 1784 technological advance culminating in Henry Cort's puddling and rolling processes had freed the iron industry from its dependence on diminishing timber supplies, and enabled it to use coal, which was plentiful and cheap, in the production of iron. Cheap iron meant that iron was used instead of wood wherever possible. After 1775 tireless steam engines began to replace water-wheels which were too dependent upon the weather. The conquest of the fuel and power problems was the most vital technological achievement of the century.

By the end of the eighteenth century new processes, new machines, and steam power were displacing human labour and water power in the cotton, iron, coal and engineering industries. The effects were so remarkable that the term 'Industrial Revolution' was coined to describe them. Yet if historians are in general agreement as to the causes of this revolution, its origins and extent are still disputed. Some historians trace the origins of the Industrial Revolution from the seventeenth century, others as late as 1780, after which industrial growth was rapid. Some historians see it ending in 1830, or 1850, or even as a continuous process which has not yet come to an end. Certainly, the truth of the prophecy made in 1787, that the steam engine would change the appearance of much of the civilized world, such was the incredible variety of uses to which it could be put, was apparent within half a century. It is less easy to be precise about the effects of the industrial changes upon the lives of ordinary people. In part at least this book is a commentary on those changes.

REFERENCES

1   Daniel Defoe, *A Tour Through the Whole Island of Great Britain* (Everyman), Preface to Vol. II, p. 133.
2   Thomas Sprat, *History of the Royal Society of London* (1667), p. 258.
3   Arthur Young, *Six Weeks' Tour Through the Southern Counties of England and Wales* (1772).

Many accounts of the Industrial Revolution start with the mechanical inventions in the cotton industry and the rise of the factory system. But changes in the coal and iron industries, and the development of steam engines for pumping water from mines, crushing ores, blowing the blast, and driving the rolling mills in the iron industry should provide the real starting point, since it was coal as fuel, iron as the structural material, and steam power provided by James Watt's steam engine which made mechanization in many industries possible.

Coal had been mined in Britain since Roman times, when its tendency to become 'round stone masses' made it a curiosity worth mentioning by contemporary historians. At the beginning of the eighteenth century nearly all the present day coalfields of England were worked, though the mining methods were very primitive, and the pits were small. The miner's equipment consisted simply of a pointed shovel, a pick, a 'tomahawk', which was a sort of wedge for loosening heavy blocks of coal, and corves, or baskets, for getting the coal to the surface. Much coal lay just below the surface and, although a few pits reached a depth of 60 metres (200 feet), vertical shafts rarely exceeded 15 metres (50 feet). The coal was hauled to the surface either by a hand windlass, or by some form of animal or water power, or carried up in baskets on the backs of the miners. Water from these workings could still be easily drained by means of an 'adit', or drainage channel.

Originally coal had been dug out of the ground where it outcropped on the surface of the earth, and these mines looked like small quarries. The coal was extracted by digging an 'adit' into the side of the hill, which be-

sides acting as a drainage system also gave easy access to the workings. By 1700, however, shallow mines were becoming exhausted, and small 'bell' or 'beehive' pits had to be dug in order to reach the coal seam. Pits like these near Chesterfield in 1697 were described by Celia Fiennes, a contemporary traveller and diarist.

They make their mines at the entrance like a well and so till they come to the coal, they dig all the ground about where there is coal, and set pillars to support it, and so bring it to the well, where by a basket like a hand barrow by cords they pull it up.[1]

The pillars meant that much coal was lost, so the next development was the bord-and-pillar type of working. The mine was divided into separate, self-contained compartments by leaving solid ribs of coal. Within each area 'bords' (the Saxon word for roads), were cut through the seam at right angles to each other, leaving pillars of coal up to 55 metres (60 yards) square. These were removed soon after they were formed by cutting slices about 5 metres (6 yards) wide from one side of the pillar. As each slice was cut, the roof was supported by timber props. Then the props were removed, and the roof was allowed to collapse, when another slice was cut. The process was repeated until as much as possible of the pillar had been removed. From the bord-and-pillar system there developed longwall mining. By this method a wall of coal about 90 metres (100 yards) long was excavated. Then as successive bands of coal were mined the roof was supported by rows of dry stone walls built at right-angles to the coal face.

In 1700 most of the coal produced was used locally, since coal was heavy and bulky and,

18 Bradley Mine, near Bilston in Staffordshire

until the development of canals, England's transport system was quite inadequate for its wide distribution. The chief exception was the Northumberland and Durham coalfield, described in 1784 by Faujas de Saint-Fond, a French traveller.

The coal mines in the neighbourhood of Newcastle are so numerous that they may be regarded as not only one of the immense magazines of England, but also as a source of a profitable foreign commerce. Vessels loaded with coal for London and different parts of Europe set forth daily from this port. Besides this commerce, the navigation which results from working these mines gives an incalculable advantage to the navy, by forming a great nursery of seamen. In time of war more than a thousand vessels can be armed, and do considerable damage to the enemy's commerce.[2]

The coal from the north-eastern collieries was carried along wooden wagon-ways to loading quays or 'staithes', which were jetties built out on piles over the banks of the rivers Tyne and Wear. The coal was tipped into the barges, or 'keels', by means of inclined planes, or 'spouts', and floated down to Newcastle or Sunderland. Then it was transferred to colliers which took the coal by sea to London—'sea coals from Newcastle'.

Although most of the coal mined during the early part of the eighteenth century was burned in the domestic hearth, coal was becoming an important raw material. Coal was used by blacksmiths in their forges, in the manufacture of salt, in burning lime for agricultural purposes, and in producing heat in a variety of processes, such as dyeing cloth. Soap-boilers, brewers, potters and brickmakers also used coal. During the course of the century coal was substituted for wood in the iron industry. The technique of smelting iron-ore with coked coal, instead of charcoal, introduced by the Darbys of Coalbrookdale in the period 1700–50 and, later in the century, Henry Cort's puddling and rolling processes which enabled raw coal to be used in the manufacture of bar iron in quantity, greatly increased the demand for coal. The development of the steam engine by James Watt created a vast new market for coal, which was needed not only in the production of iron for making the engines, but in providing steam to work them. Finally, railways and steam shipping, which were developed in the nineteenth century, consumed enormous quantities of coal, so that the output of coal, which was $2\frac{1}{2}$ million tons in 1700 had quadrupled by 1800, and in 1913 it reached the record figure of 287 million tons.

The growing demand for coal was met by developing larger and deeper mines. By 1700 the shallow coalmines were becoming exhausted, but mining at great depths meant difficult problems of drainage, since any type of mine soon accumulated water, and unless it could be removed, work was paralysed. One method of keeping mines clear of water was the rag and chain pump, described by an eighteenth-century writer as

an iron chain with knobs of cloth stiffened and fenced with iron, seldom more than nine feet asunder. The chain is turned round by a wheel 2 to 3 feet in diameter furnished with iron spikes to enclose and keep steady the chain so that it may rise through a wooden pump 3, 4, or 5 inches bore and from 12 to 22 feet long, and by means of the knobs bring up with it a stream of water.

19 Drops at Wallsend
The loaded wagons were lowered into the ship's hold. The bottom was then unlocked, and the coal was allowed to fall into the hold. (Notice the 'spout' for loading barges)

This method of pumping survived for many years in some mines, in spite of the heavy labour involved, but elsewhere mechanical pumps were installed. Thomas Savery at the end of the seventeenth century invented a 'fire engine', or steam engine, for pumping water from Cornish tin mines, and about 1708 this was improved by Thomas Newcomen. Newcomen's engine was invaluable in making deep mines possible and, although it consumed great quantities of coal, this was of secondary importance where coal was plentiful. Consequently, his engine was widely used in collieries long after Watt's engine became available.

Another difficulty was providing a continuous flow of fresh air through the workings, in order to prevent the concentration of poisonous or inflammable gases in the mine. Carbon monoxide, or 'chokedamp', is a colourless, odourless gas which overcame the miner with hardly any warning; birds, or small animals, were taken down the mine, and their collapse gave the miner a chance to make his escape. Methane, or 'firedamp', is an inflammable gas which caused great loss of life through explosions. In the early days of coalmining it was the job of a fireman clad in leather soaked with water to go down the mine and, with a lighted candle at the end of a long pole, explode small pockets of 'firedamp', after which the mine was thought safe to work in. This was a hazardous task, and sometimes the miner was fatally injured. Small mines could be ventilated by the primitive method of lowering a bundle of gorse down the shaft, and shaking it up and down vigorously, thus removing the stale air and allowing fresh air to take its place. In larger mines it became common practice to have two shafts, known as 'downcast' and 'upcast' shafts. The 'downcast' shaft was used by the miners to get to and from the coal face. At the bottom of the 'upcast' shaft a fire was kept burning continuously, producing an upward draught which carried away the foul air. It was not until 1807 that the first practical mechanical ventilator, John Buddle's air pump, was introduced. By 1830 more efficient exhaust fans had been developed. Stale air was drawn into a rotating drum equipped with fan blades, and then expelled from its circumference to escape up a widening chimney into the atmosphere above. Where underground workings became very extensive, proper ventilation depended upon regulating the flow of air through the tunnels. Trapdoors were spaced at regular intervals, and children, called 'trappers', opened and shut these doors so as to cause a steady movement of air through the mine.

Until the introduction of the safety lamp in 1815 no satisfactory method of lighting coal mines was found. Candles were understandably not very popular with miners. About 1740 Charles Spedding of Whitehaven in Cumberland invented the flint and steel mill. A boy stood by the hewer and caused a small toothed wheel to revolve against a flint, producing a shower of sparks. An even safer light could be obtained from piles of putrid fish, whose phosphorescent glow just enabled the miner to see what he was doing, but its use in a confined space was unpleasant. The use of lamps with unprotected flames caused such frequent explosions in the Northumberland coal mines, however, that in 1813 the Sunderland Society for the Prevention of Accidents in Coalmines was formed by the Reverend John Hodgson of Jarrow, who had lost most of his parishioners in the Felling Colliery disaster. He persuaded the scientist Sir Humphry Davy to design a safety lamp. The flame inside Davy's lamp was surrounded by a wire gauze, which, being a good conductor, dispersed the heat of the flame. It could not easily pass through the gauze and ignite any inflammable gases present in the atmosphere. George Stephenson also invented, independently of Davy, a safety lamp which worked on similar principles. Though the use of safety lamps did not eliminate the risk of explosions, their number was greatly reduced.

The coal trade was greatly affected by the

technological changes which occurred in many industries during the Industrial Revolution, but coalmining itself did not undergo a revolution. Transport was improved by the network of canals and inland waterways which had been completed by the early nineteenth century, enabling coal to be distributed cheaply and efficiently over a wide area. In the north-eastern collieries ponies were employed for hauling sledges along the underground galleries, and after 1767 iron rails began to replace the wooden tramways which were used to take the coal to the nearest navigable water. Increased production of coal was achieved, however, largely by human labour, and at the cost of much suffering. Until 1842 women and children were employed underground in many mines for heavy haulage jobs. They pushed or pulled corves and wagons loaded with coal up inclined planes, sometimes in narrow seams where it was impossible to stand upright. Long hours were worked in conditions of great discomfort and considerable danger. Before Watt's steam engine drove winding gear coal was raised to the surface by horse-drawn winches. Miners often went up and down the shaft by the same means, and accidents were common. In spite of the tremendous extension of markets for coal in the nineteenth century, it was only late in the century that mine owners seriously considered mechanization. Until then the industry continued to use much the same methods it had adopted when increased demand made deep mining a necessity.

REFERENCES

1   *The Journeys of Celia Fiennes* (Cresset Press, 1949), p. 96.
2   Faujas de Saint-Fond, *A Journey through England and Scotland to the Hebrides in 1784*, ed. Sir Archibald Geikie (1907), Vol. I, p. 135.

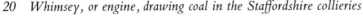

20   Whimsey, or engine, drawing coal in the Staffordshire collieries

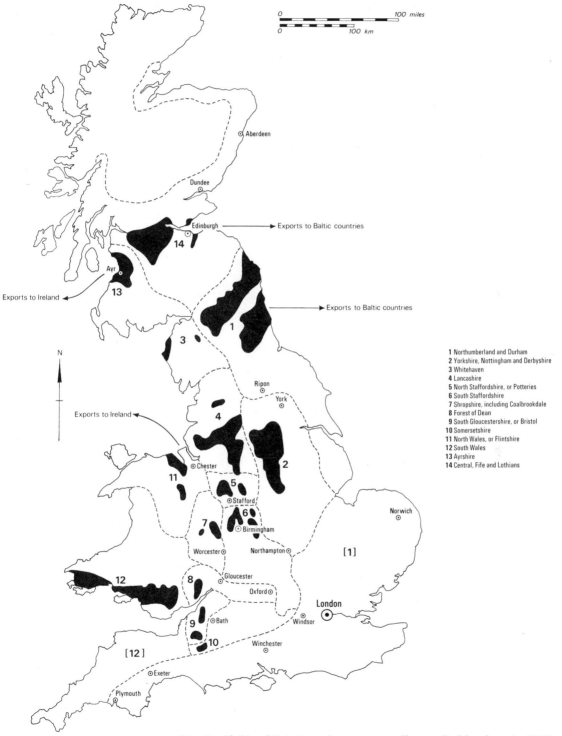

21 *Coalfields of Britain and areas normally supplied by them in 1830*

CHAPTER 9
The Iron Industry in the Eighteenth Century

Iron implements had been made in this country for many hundreds of years. Most villages and towns had their local blacksmiths who supplied the needs of the surrounding district. Scythes and sickles for the reaper, pots, pans, and kettles for the housewife, gates and ornamental railings for the rich man in his hall, horseshoes for the rider—the list is endless. The demand for the blacksmith's work was universal. Yet the iron industry in 1700 was not flourishing. Although England had abundant deposits of iron-ore, almost half the needs of the country had to be imported from Sweden.

At the beginning of the eighteenth century iron was made using charcoal as fuel. Iron-ore, mixed with limestone and charcoal, was smelted in a blast furnace, which was usually sited in the countryside near iron-ore deposits and woodlands. Mining and smelting were invariably parts of the same undertaking. Thus many landowners developed their estates by becoming ironmasters, like Lord Ashburnham in Sussex, and the Dudleys in the Midlands. The blast furnace was about 9 metres (30 feet) high, built of brick or stone, and capable of resisting great heat. An opening at the top was provided for filling the furnace, which once lighted was kept burning continuously, since restarting was a long and expensive business. The furnace was replenished either by tipping barrow loads down the opening, or by running trucks with false bottoms over the top of the furnace, and allowing the contents to drop into it.

When iron-ore, limestone and charcoal were heated together, the molten iron separated itself, and ran into a hearth beneath the furnace. The iron was then allowed to flow down into a sand mould. There was a central

22 *Blast furnaces at Hanley in Staffordshire*

channel called the 'sow', and many branches off it called 'pigs'. The resulting iron was called pig iron. When the molten iron was ladled into clay moulds of the required shape it was called cast iron. Pig iron and cast iron were very brittle due to carbon impurities, and their uses were limited. The impurities were removed by the blacksmith working in his forge, or finery. The iron was repeatedly heated and hammered, and the result was bar iron, or wrought iron, which was tough and pliable. The quality depended upon the skill of the blacksmith and the number of times the iron had been wrought by the hammer to make its texture more uniform. The bar iron could then be made into articles, or rolled into thin plates, and slit into rods at the rolling and slitting mills.

The chief centre of the old iron industry had been the Weald of Sussex and Kent, which in Elizabethan times, Camden tells us, resounded day and night with the beating of hammers upon iron. It was in the Weald that the first blast furnace was introduced into England from the continent in 1490. By 1700, however, the Weald as an iron-producing region was fast declining, and the number of blast furnaces had been reduced to about a dozen. The Weald was once heavily forested, but its trees had been cut down for making charcoal. As well as a shortage of timber the Weald suffered from other serious disadvantages. The local ores were of poor quality, and since the area has a relatively low annual rainfall, the water supplies often proved inadequate during the summer months. The industry, therefore, migrated to other parts of the country, especially Shropshire, South Wales, and Northern England, where both water supplies and woodlands were comparatively plentiful, so that even before 1700 it was beginning to grow up on the coalfields.

The iron industry was composed of three main branches; mining, smelting, and the conversion of the iron into finished articles. The first two were hardly flourishing. The iron industry was confined to areas which had both iron-ore deposits and woodlands. These were seldom near large rivers, and the small streams which drove the water-wheels were often inadequate. A poor transport system set limits to the growth of the industry; if timber had to be carried more than 15 kilometres (10 miles), fuel costs made English iron uncompetitive with iron imported from the Baltic countries. Finally, charcoal was very expensive and becoming hard to get in sufficient quantities. In the metal-working sections activity was brisk, but as long as the industry depended upon charcoal for fuel its growth was stunted, and its very survival uncertain.

Thus there was every incentive to discover a means whereby coal could be used instead of charcoal in the smelting process. Coal had long been used by the blacksmith in his forge, and attempts to smelt iron-ore with coal had been made in Derbyshire since Elizabethan times, but without success. It now seems very likely that Dud Dudley of Worcestershire succeeded during the first half of the seventeenth century in making pig iron using charked coal as fuel. The main product of the blast furnace in his time was pig iron suitable for conversion into malleable iron. To make his main product, bar iron, Dudley still had to refine in a charcoal finery.

The doubts expressed over Dudley's claims have rested largely on the sulphur and phosphorus content of coal, impurities which embrittled the iron produced using coal as fuel, and coke's lower reactivity with oxygen, compared with charcoal, which made it very difficult to produce the very high temperatures needed in the blast furnace. Dud Dudley, however, was both aware of the varying sulphur content in coal and of its effect upon iron, and he was also highly knowledgeable in iron metallurgy, being able to recognize the properties of different types of cast iron. Dudley was fortunate in that the local coal lost most of its sulphur content when it was coked in large lumps. In *Metallum Martis* Dudley relates how at Himley, in Staffordshire, he built a larger furnace, 8 metres (27 feet) square, after several trial *blows*, and provided for his blast furnace bellows 'larger than ordinary bellows are'. This would seem to indicate that he was aware of the need for greater blast pressures and volumes. His modest claim that he had not yet 'fully perfected or raised his invention to the quantity of Charcole Iron Furnaces, the Author's quantity being but seven Tuns per week' cannot easily be dismissed. His secret, however, died with him, and the credit for reprieving the iron industry from dying a natural death went to the Darbys of Coalbrookdale, in Shropshire.

About 1709 Abraham Darby was producing cast iron smelted with coal. He overcame the problem of the embrittling agents in coal by coking the 'clod' coal of Shropshire, which was especially suitable for use in the blast furnace, and by keeping the limestone in contact with the fuel longer than was usual with charcoal. Thirdly, he increased the furnace temperature with a more efficient blast. The iron produced, however, was unsuitable for making bar iron. The second Abraham Darby improved his father's process. He dammed the stream, making a pool above the water-wheel, so that the greater velocity of the water from the pool to the wheel increased the blast, and in 1742 he replaced the leather bellows with wooden ones which were more efficient. By 1749 he was producing small quantities of bar iron from coke-smelted pig iron. Mrs Abiah Darby, wife of Abraham Darby II, later recounted that

Had not these discoveries been made, the iron trade of our own produce would have dwindled away, for woods for charcoal became very scarce and landed gentlemen rose the price of cord wood exceedingly high—indeed, it would not have been to be got. But from pit coal being introduced in its stead the demand for wood charcoal is much lessened, and in a few years time I apprehend will set the use of that article aside.[1]

Thus the Darbys' inventions were very important in the development of the English iron industry. They began the alliance of coal and iron on which so much of the progress of the Industrial Revolution was based. After 1760 the industry grew steadily. The new blast furnaces with few exceptions used coke for fuel, and the industry expanded where coal was readily available.

The Darbys' success in making pig iron cheaply with coal as fuel emphasized the shortage of bar iron. The forging of bar iron from pig iron was a slow business, creating a bottleneck in its manufacture, so that further progress in the iron industry depended upon the discovery of a means of speeding up its production. The solution was found separately at about the same time by Peter Onions, a foreman at an ironworks in Merthyr Tydvil, and Henry Cort of Portsmouth. Cort is generally given the credit for the puddling and rolling processes which he patented in 1783 and 1784, and Peter Onions remained relatively unknown.

In Cort's method iron-ore was smelted with coal as fuel in a reverberatory furnace, that is a furnace where the coal was kept separate from the ore, which was smelted by the flames bouncing down, or reverberating, from the roof of the furnace. This prevented impurities in the coal getting into the iron. The molten iron was 'puddled', or stirred, with iron rods until all the carbon, which burned with a blue flame, had been removed. The iron then thickened into pasty lumps called *blooms* which were taken out by tongs. The *blooms* were hammered into bars and rolled into plates by water-driven machinery.

Cort's processes were revolutionary. Bar iron of good quality could now be produced without using charcoal, and quickly, for 15 tons could be rolled in the time taken previously to produce 1 ton. The iron industry was able to expand rapidly to meet the growing demand for a wide range of iron goods without having to rely on imports. Cort, who was honest and good natured, had little business sense, and he did not benefit much from his discovery which made fortunes for men more astute than himself. He never received the royalties of ten shillings a ton to which he was entitled, and in 1789 he fell into debt. He lost his patent rights, and it was only due to Pitt's influence that he obtained a pension, on which he lived until 1800.

The iron industry, freed from its dependence upon charcoal, now advanced rapidly, and the output of iron increased three-fold in the next twenty years. The industry also became increasingly concentrated on the coalfields, notably in South Wales, the Black Country, South Yorkshire, and the Lowlands of Scotland. Large-scale production was developed in order to take full advantage of the new processes and machinery available. Previously, ironworks had been limited in size by the supply of nearby timber. Typical of the new capitalist ironmasters was John Wilkinson, 'Iron-mad Wilkinson', who gave instructions that he was to be buried in an iron coffin. He owned coalmines, and extensive ironworks at Bersham in Denbigh, Bradley in Staffordshire, and Broseley in Shropshire, which he connected with the Birmingham Canal. He founded an ironworks in France, and held shares in Cornish tin mines. He built up what almost amounted to a local kingdom, and between 1787 and 1808 even issued his own coins, which were widely used in the West Midlands. The Darbys were also enterprising. The first iron rails in this country were laid at Coalbrookdale in 1767, and the first iron bridge was constructed near by over the river Severn in 1779. It was 7 metres (8 yards) wide, 30 metres (100 feet) long, and consisted of a single impressive arch. Other great ironmasters were the Crawshays of South Wales and the Walkers of Rotherham.

While the iron industry came to the fore-front, steel remained of minor importance in the eighteenth century. Tiny amounts were made for cutting tools, and other items such as watch-springs and swords, where great strength and hardness were required. Steel was made by heating purest bar iron between layers of charcoal in a special furnace, but it was expensive. Benjamin Huntsman, a Sheffield clock-maker, was dissatisfied with the steel he obtained, and was anxious to find a way of making flawless steel for his watch and clock springs. In the middle of the century he developed his famous crucible process for making steel. Huntsman took small quantities of pure bar iron and smelted them in sealed fireclay crucibles, clay pots nearly a foot high, at a very high temperature. The result was cast steel of the finest quality. At first the Sheffield cutlers did not welcome his invention, but decided to adopt it after Huntsman had been invited to live and work in Birmingham. Huntsman, who did not patent his invention, tried to keep his process a secret, but he was unable to do so for long. There is a story that a local ironmaster, Samuel Walker of Rotherham, disguised himself as a beggar and was permitted to warm himself by Huntsman's furnaces, thereby discovering the secret. The price of steel remained high, however, and the output of steel was unimportant until the middle of the nineteenth century.

Great industrial and social changes came with the sudden expansion of the iron industry. Richard Crawshay's Cyfarthfa ironworks rapidly transformed the tiny village of Merthyr Tydvil into an industrial centre. By the beginning of the nineteenth century the Taff valley had thirteen blast furnaces, and a huge water-wheel 16 metres (52 feet) in diameter. Most of the inhabitants depended upon the industry for their livelihood. Contemporaries laughed at Wilkinson's idea that ships could be made of iron—yet he launched the first one on the river Severn in 1787. The uses to which iron could be put were almost unlimited. Wilkinson made iron chairs, vats for breweries, and 65 kilometres (40 miles) of cast iron pipes for Paris, as well as innumerable other articles. Mills were built with iron floors, which could be cleaned more easily than wooden floors, and the risk of fire was reduced. Iron machinery of all kinds was developed, for it was subject to less wear, and soon wooden machines were being replaced with ones made of iron. It was the alliance of iron machinery and steam power which made Great Britain in the nineteenth century the greatest industrial nation the world had ever known.

REFERENCE

1   Quoted in T. S. Ashton, *Iron and Steel in the Industrial Revolution* (Manchester University Press, 1963).

Steam as a source of power had been known for centuries, but an effective steam engine, or *fire engine*, as it was sometimes called, was only developed towards the end of the seventeenth century. About 1660 the Marquis of Worcester invented a device whereby steam power was used to work a fountain. Denis Papin, a refugee French scientist, made experiments with steam in England and Germany, and in 1680 produced his *digesteur*, or steam engine. Papin also invented a safety valve. The first practicable engine, however, was Thomas Savery's, patented in 1698, and designed for pumping water from Cornish tin mines. It made use of atmospheric pressure to raise water from the mine workings into a tank, and steam pressure to force the water from the tank in order to drain away. Savery claimed that his invention, which he called the *Miner's Friend*, would be useful for land drainage, town water supplies, as well as for fire-fighting and driving mill machinery, but it had a number of disadvantages. It could only raise water slowly about 6 metres (20 feet) at a time to a maximum of 30 metres (100 feet). The engine also consumed great quantities of coal and, lacking a safety device, it was liable to explode without warning.

In 1709 Thomas Newcomen (1663–1729) invented a pumping engine which, although clumsy and inefficient, quickly replaced Savery's. His engine consisted of a boiler, cylinder, piston, and a huge wooden 'balance beam', pivoted at its centre. One end of the beam was attached to the piston, which fitted into the cylinder; the other end was connected to a pump rod. Steam was passed from the boiler into the cylinder, forcing the piston upwards. The balance beam 'see-sawed', and the pump rod descended. On the downward

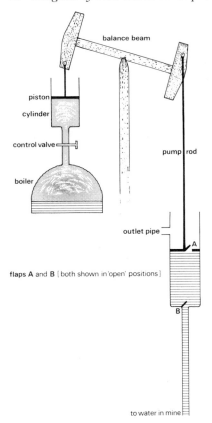

23 Diagram of Newcomen steam pump

stroke of the pump rod, the pressure of water closed flap **B**, while water forced its way past flap **A**. Cold water was now sprayed into the cylinder, condensing the steam, and creating a partial vacuum. The pressure of the atmosphere then forced the piston down, and the balance beam 'see-sawed' again. The pump rod was lifted (the weight of water closing flap **A**), and water was raised to the surface.

Samuel Smiles wrote a picturesque description of a Newcomen engine in operation.

It was an apparently very painful process, accompanied by an extraordinary amount of wheezing, sighing, creaking, and bumping. When the pump descended there was heard a plunge, a heavy sigh, and a loud bump; then, as it rose, and the sucker began to act, there was heard a creak, a wheeze, another bump, and then a rush of water as it lifted and poured out.[1]

Newcomen's engine was capable of raising water from great depths, but since the water could only be lifted about 15 metres (50 feet) on each stroke, in deep mines it was raised in stages from one level to the next above it, and several pumps would be at work at the same time.

The value of Newcomen's engine should not be overshadowed by Watt's rotary engine. After several improvements had been added, such as a safety valve by Henry Beighton in 1717, it remained almost unaltered for fifty years, and was used in some collieries until the beginning of the nineteenth century. Well over one hundred engines were built for the north-eastern coalfield. Over forty were erected for Cornish tin mines in the period 1745–75, and we know of about thirty for Derbyshire. The Newcomen engine was also installed in Lancashire coalmines—there were seven on the St Helens coalfield alone—and we have not taken into account all the mining areas of England and Scotland. The widescale use of the Newcomen engine, bearing in mind that it was costly to build and install, proves that its industrial importance was great. But both Savery's and Newcomen's engines were pumps. It was James Watt who developed the steam engine into the greatest source of industrial power the world had known.

James Watt was born in 1736 in the little town of Greenock in Renfrewshire. He was the sixth child born to the wife of Thomas Watt, but the first to survive infancy, so it is not surprising he was sickly as a youth. He went to the local grammar school, where he showed ability in mathematics and a passion for mechanical things. On leaving school he was employed in his father's workshop until his mother's death in 1753, and his father's business difficulties forced him to decide upon a career. He went to stay with relatives in Glasgow, where he hoped to learn the trade of mathematical instrument maker. There was little opportunity in Glasgow, however, and Watt journeyed to London, where he became an apprentice instrument maker. In 1756 Watt returned to Scotland with £20 worth of instruments. One of his relatives, George Muirhead, was a professor at Glasgow University, and it was through him that Watt was offered employment by the university, and allowed to open a shop in the college itself. This was fortunate for Watt, since he was not a burgess of the city, and thus did not have the right to set himself up as a craftsman there. His business flourished, and within two years he was allowed to open a shop in Glasgow itself, where he employed several journeymen.

The turning point in Watt's career came in 1764, when he was asked to repair a model of a Newcomen engine belonging to the University. He knew a little about steam because he had recently experimented with a Papin *digesteur*. Watt soon realized that the repeated heating and cooling of the cylinder wasted much fuel and energy, and he turned his attention towards making the engine more efficient. Watt himself described how the answer to his problem came to him.

One Sunday afternoon I had gone to take a walk in the Green of Glasgow, and when about half way between the Herd's House and Arn's Well, my thoughts having been naturally turned to the experiments I had been engaged in for saving heat in the cylinder, at that part of the road the idea occurred to me, that, as steam was an elastic vapour, it would expand, and rush into a previously exhausted space; and that, if I were to produce a vacuum in a separate vessel, and open a communication between the steam in the cylinder and the exhausted vessel, such would be the consequence.[2]

By condensing the steam in a separate chamber or condenser, a change in the temperature of the cylinder itself was avoided, and the coal consumption of Newcomen's engine was reduced by more than half. Watt also modified the engine so that the piston was driven by steam pressure instead of atmospheric pressure.

A model of the engine was made within a few weeks, but it was another matter to construct an engine for use in industry. James Watt was not a rich man, and he was lucky to be introduced to someone who could help him develop his engine. John Roebuck was a founder of the Carron Ironworks and, at the time he met Watt, he was developing a coal-field leased from the Duke of Hamilton. Roebuck was worried by the problem of draining his coalmine, and realized that Watt might be able to provide him with the solution. He urged Watt to continue work on the steam engine. A full-size engine was built, but it would not function, chiefly because inferior workmanship, on which Watt was forced to rely, and poor materials, meant that the parts were inaccurate. Watt persevered, however, and made sufficient progress in a year for Roebuck to decide to form a partnership with him. In 1769 he built his first steam engine, called *Beelzebub*, which he set up near Edinburgh, but it soon ceased working. In the same year Watt went to London to take out a patent for his engine. On his way back to Scotland he broke his journey at Birmingham in order to visit Matthew Boulton, a friend of Roebuck. This was the origin of a friendship between them, and an important event in Watt's life, for without Boulton's financial backing, Watt's steam engine might never have become a commercial proposition in his own lifetime.

Matthew Boulton was already, at the age of thirty-nine, a famous Midlands business-man. His father had died in 1759, leaving him his business premises at Snow Hill, in Birmingham. A year later Boulton married a wealthy heiress, and with the fortune he had suddenly acquired he built, at a cost of £9,000, a large factory at Soho, 3 kilometres (2 miles) north of Birmingham. Here Boulton, a 'toy manufacturer', made a great quantity of metal goods ranging from fancy buttons, watch chains, and sword hilts, to clocks, chandeliers, snuff boxes, statuettes, and fashionable steel buckles. Boulton employed over 600 skilled craftsmen, and his workshops were the most up-to-date in the world, attracting many sightseers. He could provide Watt with the accurate workmanship which was vital for the development of the steam engine. Watt himself was keen for Boulton to share in his partnership with Roebuck, but the latter, who had a two-thirds share in the rights of the invention, was unwilling to offer Boulton anything more than a licence to make the engine for three midland counties. In a letter to Watt, Boulton rejected these terms, saying: 'It would not be worth my while to make for three counties only, but I find it very worth my while to make for all the world'.[3]

In 1773 Roebuck went bankrupt, and this led to the famous partnership of Boulton and Watt. In exchange for cancelling a debt of £1,200 which Roebuck owed him, Boulton took over his share of the rights to Watt's invention. Boulton was interested in the steam engine, firstly because he could see the immense possibilities of the engine if it could be developed, and secondly because his Soho Works depended for its water power on Hockley Brook, which often dried up in summer. The Edinburgh engine was dismantled, and rebuilt at the Soho Works by Boulton's skilled workers. John Wilkinson, the Shropshire ironmaster, supplied the cast iron cylinders, accurately bored by his cannon lathe at Broseley. Boulton managed to persuade Parliament to renew the patent for a further twenty-five years, and a year later, in 1776, the first engines were sold. The success of the venture seemed assured.

Nevertheless, the cost of developing the steam engine exceeded all forecasts, and for several years the firm went through a difficult time. The project had to be heavily subsidized from the profits of Boulton's toy factory. Initially, most of the orders came from Cornish tin miners, many of whom refused to pay the royalties. Purchasers of the engine had to pay for the cost of building and installing the engine, together with a third of the annual saving in fuel costs for twenty-five years. It was only in 1799, after endless lawsuits, that Boulton and Watt recovered £30,000 due to them. There was also trouble with competitors who infringed their patent. A notable example was Jonathan Hornblower, who built an engine with two cylinders. He was sued, and ruined when he lost the case. The firm survived these critical years, and their fire-engine soon proved its complete superiority over Newcomen's. In 1781 Boulton was able to write to his partner: 'The people in London, Manchester and Birmingham are steam-mill mad.'

In 1781 Watt took out a second patent, for rotary motion, which enabled the steam engine to drive all types of machinery in industry. The device which Watt used, known as the *sun and planet* motion, was suggested to him by William Murdock, the trusted foreman of Boulton and Watt, and an inventor in his own right. Hitherto, the steam engine had been a reciprocating engine, suitable only for pumping. The device for rotary motion gave the engine power to revolutionize industry. Watt improved his engine in other ways too. In 1782 he made a double-acting expansive engine; in 1784 he added the device of parallel motion, and finally, in 1788, the governor, which enabled the speed of the engine to be regulated, and thus a smooth movement obtained. Any of Watt's inventions would have made him famous; taken together they put him into that class of men who have changed the course of history.

The steam engine was of vital importance to the Industrial Revolution. It did not create the factory system, but gave it an irresistible force of expansion. Without steam power, production could only have been increased within narrow limits; with it, mass production

and the large-scale development of industry became possible. For much of the eighteenth century industry was dependent upon water power—even the beginning of the factory system in the cotton industry was based upon the water frame. The water-wheel, which had been used for centuries, was the only important alternative to animal and man power. It was to be found in textile mills, flour mills, in ironworks, indeed in nearly all branches of industry. Water power, however, had several disadvantages. It restricted industries to places where there were good supplies of fast running water. Water supplies could be disrupted by flooding in winter, and drought in summer. Often the water supply was inadequate, and artificial waterfalls had to be created, or water stored in reservoirs by means of pumping engines. Once the Watt engine had proved itself, industry could develop near its sources of raw materials. Steam power transformed industry for it was not dependent upon geographical position, and industry, freed from its dependence upon water power, was able to exploit the advantage of Britain's abundant coal resources.

With the invention of rotary motion there was a keen demand for the steam engine. It was used in the Soho factory to work bellows, hammers, and rolling mills. Wilkinson and the Darbys of Coalbrookdale soon ordered engines. In 1786 the Albion flour mills in London caused a sensation when they were equipped with two steam engines which worked fifty pairs of millstones. The transformation of the cotton industry was regarded as little short of miraculous. The first steam-powered spinning mill was set up by Robinson in 1785 at Papplewick, in Nottinghamshire. Other manufacturers at once followed his example. Such was the demand for the engines by cotton manufacturers that Boulton pessimistically feared that the limits of expansion in that industry had been reached. From 1794 the steam engine was gradually introduced in Yorkshire woollen spinning mills. It was also used in a variety of other industries, including brewing, pottery, crushing sugar-cane, and minting coins. By 1800 the firm of Boulton and Watt had sold 500 engines; there were 32 in Manchester, 20 in Leeds, and 11 in Birmingham.

The steam engine reinforced the tendency of many industries to concentrate in towns and villages on the coalfields, near their markets and labour supplies. To a much greater extent than before, industry became interdependent. The expansion of the basic industries such as coalmining, iron and steel, textiles, and engineering, was both caused by, and was essential to, the progress of each of the others.

The age of steam power had begun. James Watt, however, who died in 1819, had only witnessed its first stirrings.

REFERENCES

1   Samuel Smiles, *The Lives of the Engineers* (1862), Vol. III, pp. 9–10.
2   Correspondence of James Watt, quoted by J. P. Muirhead, *The Life of James Watt.*
3   Letter of Matthew Boulton to James Watt, 21 June 1781, quoted in Samuel Smiles's *Lives of Boulton and Watt*, p. 293.

CHAPTER 11
The Revolution in the Textile Industries

The English woollen industry grew in earnest when Flemish weavers crossed to England shortly after the Norman Conquest, so much so that in the reign of Edward III its growing importance was one cause of the Hundred Years' War with France. The prosperity of medieval England was largely due to the wool trade. The Woolsack, the Lord Chancellor's seat in the House of Lords, is a reminder of the great wealth which England derived from the wool trade.

The woollen industry in 1700 was carried on in most parts of the country. Fine broadcloths were made in Kent and Surrey. Colchester in Essex, and Norwich in Norfolk were thriving centres. Nottingham and Leicester were noted for their woollen stockings. Further north came the West Riding of Yorkshire, with its cloth markets at Wakefield, Halifax, Leeds, Huddersfield and Bradford. Yorkshire was well known for its coarse cloth. In Lancashire, Manchester, Oldham and Bury manufactured woollen goods long before cotton made its appearance. The south-western counties were dotted with cloth-making towns. In Somerset they were closely packed, and Defoe reported the opinion that Frome was destined to become one of the greatest English towns. This area owed its importance primarily to the high quality wool of Cotswold sheep. The woollen industry was also found in Hampshire and Berkshire, in the Midlands, though not to any large extent, and in Wales. Thus the industry was certainly not localized. Nevertheless, it had three main areas: the West Riding, East Anglia, and the South-west.

The woollen industry was organized under the domestic system, though the meaning of this term varied from one part of the country

24 *Cottage spinning*
A large number of poor people were employed in cottage industry, even after the introduction of machinery had lowered their wages to one halfpenny per pound weight of thread

to another. Under this system the work was done in the home, and factories or large workshops were rare. Most cottagers could make or afford the simple tools needed for spinning and weaving. The weaver's cottage was a home and workshop, and all his family helped to make cloth from raw wool. His children washed the wool, removed bits and pieces clinging to the fleece, and sorted the wool into graded heaps. His wife and daughters spun the wool into yarn, either on a spinning wheel, or on the more primitive distaff and spindle. The weaver wove the yarn into cloth on a hand loom, sometimes working single-handed, sometimes employing several men under him. In this form of the domestic system, found in the West Riding, the weaver controlled production, owning both the tools and the raw materials, and marketing the finished cloth. In 1806 around Leeds there were more

25 Yorkshire cloth-makers taking their cloth to market

than 3,500 weavers, all approximately equal, for the man who owned several looms was exceptional. Thus the manufacturer was not a 'big businessman' but a craftsman, working with his hands on home-made implements. He also probably owned a few acres of land, and produced enough food to keep himself and his family. Since part of his living was obtained from the land, which could not be taken away from him, he tended to be independent, and proved less willing than his counterpart in Lancashire to enter a factory in the early days of the Industrial Revolution.

In the South-west and South-east of England the domestic system had developed differently. Here the woollen industry was largely in the hands of wealthy merchant clothiers. Once production had outstripped local demand the trader, or middleman, was needed to link producer and shopkeeper. At a fairly early date the capitalist merchants, with their reserves of cash and the ability to wait for a profit, controlled all the processes from start to finish. The merchant bought the raw wool, often in very large amounts, and arranged for it to be carded, spun, woven, and fulled. He employed agents for the distribution of the raw materials and finished cloth. The cottagers were no more than outworkers, dependent upon the wages of a capitalist. Since the cottager did not always own his loom, he had

only his labour to sell. The chief difference between him and the nineteenth-century factory worker was his escape from factory discipline.

The eighteenth century has sometimes been called the 'golden age of industry' by those who have assumed that the worker was happier before the coming of factories, when the craftsman worked in the familiar surroundings of his home. But his working conditions were cramped and unhealthy, and more often than not hardship forced him and his dependants to work very long hours in order to scrape a bare existence. Nor was the element of industrial strife absent, for there were frequent riots, as when the wool-combers of Tiverton, in Devon, objected to the attempts of merchant clothiers to import cheap combed wool from Ireland in 1720 and 1749. Law and order was only restored after a pitched battle. Riots were frequent when trade was bad, or when it was believed that traditional methods of work were threatened by new machines.

Just before the beginning of the eighteenth century the silk industry had been greatly stimulated. After the Edict of Nantes, which had given religious toleration to French Huguenots, had been withdrawn in 1685 by Louis XIV, many skilled craftsmen had fled from persecution, and a colony of silk weavers had settled in Spitalfields, whence their fame spread rapidly. Since silk could not be cultivated in England due to the unfavourable climate, silk thread was smuggled into the country from Italy. The supplies were so cheap that it was firmly believed the Italians had machines for throwing silk. The secret (for the machines did in fact exist) was closely kept. In 1716 John Lombe risked his life on a perilous mission to Leghorn to obtain drawings of the machine. On his return with the designs in 1717, he and his brother Thomas Lombe built the first factory in England on an island in the river Derwent, near Derby. The building astonished everyone by its size, for it was 150 metres (500 feet) long and six

26 The preemer boy
The two men in the background are 'rooing' the cloth with teasels. The preemer boy is using an iron comb, or preem, to detach the bits of wool clinging to the teasels just used

storeys high, and contained three hundred operatives. Their job was to mend the threads when they broke. This factory was the forerunner of the modern factory system, with its machines, mass production, and specialization. Lombe rapidly made a fortune of £120,000 and, when Parliament in 1732 refused to renew the patent for the silk-throwing machine, he was compensated with £14,000. Silk was manufactured in Derby, Stockport, London and Macclesfield, but the industry did not develop on a large scale. There were no changes comparable to those which took place in the Lancashire cotton industry. This was due partly to the high price of raw silk, which had to be imported, to the competition with

silk from the continent, and to the fact that no new techniques were introduced into the industry.

Until the seventeenth century the word cotton described certain coarse woollens made in Lancashire. In 1700 the cotton industry proper was in its infancy, and most of the cotton goods sold in this country came from India. The printed fabrics were very popular, and in that year the powerful woollen manufacturers, eager to protect themselves from foreign competition, persuaded Parliament to pass an act prohibiting the import of printed fabrics from India, Persia and China. When this act proved ineffective, another was passed in 1721 which laid down heavy fines on people found to have them in their possession. But Parliament could not alter fashion, and the demand for cotton goods grew. The two measures merely had the effect of protecting the germinating cotton industry in Lancashire just when it most needed help against foreign competition, and it was soon in a strong position. The port of Liverpool was near by for the raw cotton supplies from Brazil and the East. Lancashire also had a damp climate needed for cotton spinning, and Manchester quickly achieved a reputation for its cottons. Although no effort was spared by woollen manufacturers to destroy the cotton industry, it grew rapidly.

The cotton industry, like the woollen, was at first a cottage industry, but at an early date wealthy merchants began to take control of production and distribution. The cottagers received their raw materials from a class of men called fustian masters, who bought linen thread and raw cotton to be worked into its finished state. During the course of the century the industry was transformed by a series of inventions which based it upon the factory system, and enabled it to outstrip the woollen industry by 1801.

The first important invention was Kay's Flying Shuttle in 1733. John Kay (1704–64) was born near Bury, in Lancashire, but moved to Colchester where he worked as a weaver. Here Kay turned his attention to improving the handloom. Unless two workmen were used, the width of the cloth was limited, since the weaver had to throw the shuttle from hand to hand. Kay fitted the shuttle with four small wheels, and arranged for it to travel along a wooden groove. The 'fly shuttle' was knocked to and fro by hammers attached to strings which the weaver manipulated. Kay's invention allowed the weaver to make wider pieces of cloth, and to work more quickly. This had important consequences. Formerly it had taken four or five spinners to produce sufficient thread to keep one weaver fully employed. Kay's invention increased the demand for thread, which now became in short supply.

There was thus a need for a spinning invention to redress the balance.

The first people to invent a spinning machine were John Wyatt and Louis Paul. Paul had bought the rights to a machine for boring metals, which Wyatt had invented. This led to a partnership between the two men. Wyatt had already thought out a design for a spinning machine, and in 1733 a model actually worked, but it was not until 1738 that a patent was taken out. Wyatt's machine consisted of two pairs of rollers; the second pair of rollers, which rotated slightly faster than the first, stretched the yarn, which was wound on to revolving spindles, thus imparting a twist to the thread. Wyatt and Paul set up a workshop containing the machines but the venture was a failure. The rights to the invention were sold to Edward Cave, who established a small factory with five machines at Northampton. This little-known workshop was the first cotton spinning mill in England. Wyatt and Paul, however, were really before their time, and the invention was not a success. Meanwhile, there was increasing anxiety in the cotton industry over the gap between spinning and weaving. This gap was closed by three men whose inventions appeared within a few years of one another—James Hargreaves, Richard Arkwright, and Samuel Crompton.

James Hargreaves (1720–78) lived in Blackburn, where he was a weaver and carpenter. According to tradition, Hargreaves got the idea for his invention by watching his wife's spinning wheel continue to revolve after it had been knocked over. The jenny consisted of a wooden frame having spindles at one end, and a moveable carriage at the other. The spindles were rotated by bands attached to a roller which was turned by a large, hand-operated wheel. The threads from the rovings to the spindles passed between a pair of rails which could be clasped together, holding the threads fast. The spinner drew out the threads from the rovings by moving the bar backwards. After a certain distance the thread was clasped between the two bars, while the backwards movement of the carriage, and the turning of the spindles continued, so that a twist was imparted to the threads. The threads were then depressed by a wire so that they could be slowly wound on to the spindles by moving the bar forward. Hargreaves's spinning jenny spun several threads simultaneously, and within a few years spinning jennies with eighty threads had been made.

Hargreaves's machine was not at first well received by spinners. In 1767, when he sold his first jenny, his home was broken into by a mob, and his machines smashed, while he himself was forced to leave the town and settle in Nottingham, where there was less opposition to his ideas. There he took out a patent for his invention, but unscrupulous manufacturers refused to pay the royalties, and Hargreaves's appeal to the courts was turned down on the grounds that his jennies had been used in industry before the patent operated. James Hargreaves, therefore, like many inventors, did not reap the full benefit of his ideas, but nevertheless, when he died in 1778 he left a considerable estate of £4,000. The spinning jenny was widely used, especially in Lancashire, and within a few years of Hargreaves's death over 20,000 jennies existed. The jenny was simple to make, was cheap, and could be used in the domestic system, which it briefly revived. But the days of cottage industry were already numbered, for in towns like Nottingham and Cromford, spinning was being done in mills. This change, which was to revolutionize the cotton industry, was largely due to Richard Arkwright, whom Carlyle described as 'that bag-cheeked, pot-bellied, much enduring, much inventing barber'.

Arkwright was born in Preston in 1732, but when he was eighteen years old he settled in Bolton as a barber and wig-maker. Living in a cotton town he was soon aware that a fortune could be made by someone who could speed up the spinning process, but the origin of his invention is wrapped in mystery, and it does not seem likely that the idea of the water frame was his own. This machine, made in 1768, was similar to the spinning machine invented by Wyatt in 1733. It was made of wood, and had four pairs of rollers which were driven in the first instance by horse power, then by water power.

Arkwright was ambitious (he once boasted that it was his aim to make enough money to pay off the National Debt), and a good businessman, qualities rarely found in an inventor. He moved to Nottingham, where he managed to get financial backing from a country bank. In 1777 he built a spinning mill at Cromford, near Derby, not far from Lombe's silk mill. Within eight years the mill, or factory, with its several thousand spindles driven by water power, was producing great quantities of thread which was stronger and superior to that made by the most skilful spinner using a spinning wheel or jenny. This made it possible to weave pure cotton fabrics where formerly a mixture of linen and cotton had been necessary. Arkwright now expanded his business, building another spinning mill at Belper, also near Derby, and two mills in Lancashire, one near Chorley, and another in Manchester, which were the largest factories in England.

Meanwhile, rival manufacturers questioned his right to the patent. It seems possible that the water frame was really the invention of Thomas Highs of Leigh. Highs had been helped by John Kay of Warrington, who was afterwards employed by Arkwright for a while, until he was suddenly dismissed, accused of theft, a charge which Arkwright did not follow up in the courts. Arkwright was unable to explain his invention satisfactorily and in 1785 he was deprived of his patent. This setback did not materially affect his fortunes, for by now he had become one of the wealthiest men in the kingdom. In 1784, in partnership with David Dale, he had founded the New Lanark Mills on the banks of the Clyde. He improved his other factories, and at Nottingham made use of the steam engine. In 1787 he became Sheriff of Derby. When he died in 1792 he left an immense fortune of

£½ million. Arkwright's fame rests not on his inventive genius, which is doubtful, but on his success as a businessman, and the fact that he, more than anyone else, can be regarded as the real creator of the modern factory system.

Two more inventions, Crompton's mule and Cartwright's power loom, completed the transformation of the cotton industry. Samuel Crompton (1753–1827) was the son of a small landowner near Bolton. Hall i' th' Wood, where the Cromptons lived, was the birthplace of his invention, and is now maintained as a museum. Crompton's mule, finished in 1779, combined the principles of the spinning jenny and the water frame, and it was chiefly for this reason that Crompton did not try to patent his invention. The thread produced by the jenny was fine, but broke easily; that made by the water frame was strong but coarse. The mule combined the best features of both. Since he was unable to protect his rights in

the mule, Crompton was faced with the choice of making his idea public, or destroying the machine he had taken four years to build. He decided to rely on the generosity of manufacturers who promised him compensation for his idea, but the subscription raised a paltry sum. Crompton had little business sense, and did not set himself up as a manufacturer, and therefore gained little benefit from his invention.

The mule was at first made of wood, and was small enough for use in the cottage, but by 1783 large metal mules were in operation. In 1790 William Kelly designed an automatic mule with three hundred spindles driven by water power. From this time the mule rapidly replaced the jenny. By the early nineteenth century there were several hundred cotton spinning mills, housing millions of spindles, and cottage spinning in the cotton industry was almost extinct. As well as making spinning

27 Spinning by steam power

a factory operation, the mule also influenced weaving, for it produced thread fine enough for the manufacture of muslin. Bolton and Glasgow became the centres of this new industry. In 1812 Crompton was awarded £5,000 by Parliament, but his debts were pressing, and he did not live long to enjoy his pension. A statue erected to his memory in Bolton many years later by manufacturers whose fortunes he made possible, stands as silent evidence of the importance of his invention.

Spinning was now done by power-driven machinery housed in factories, but cotton weaving was still done on the handloom. The weaver was consequently in great demand, and his wages rose accordingly. Weavers became the highest paid workers in the land, and they aped the middle classes. Their prosperity, however, was soon cut short by Cartwright's power loom, invented in 1785.

There had been several earlier attempts to make a power loom, notably by two Frenchmen Vaucanson and Jacquard, but their results were impracticable. Edmund Cartwright (1743–1823) was a Fellow of Magdalen College, Oxford, before he became a clergyman. When he learned of the crisis in the cotton industry he became interested in developing a weaving machine. In 1785 he patented his invention, and in 1787 set up a small factory at Doncaster containing twenty looms, and two years later, a steam engine made by Boulton and Watt. Power looms were introduced gradually at first, for they were unpopular with weavers, but their progress was inevitable. In 1793 James Robertson built a workshop containing two looms. In 1800 a factory with two hundred looms was built in Manchester. In 1803 Horrocks of Stockport made an all metal loom, and the number of power looms multiplied rapidly. The power loom closed the gap between spinning and weaving, for two looms watched by a boy produced more than three times the quantity of cloth made by a weaver on his handloom. The effect of Cartwright's inven-

28 *Bell's cylinder printing machine*
One machine, attended by one man, could do the work of one hundred men using hand-blocks for printing

tion on the prosperity of the handloom weaver was disastrous. In 1800 when the first power loom was introduced in Manchester his wages had averaged 25/- per week; in 1820, when there were 2,000 looms in Manchester his wages had dropped to 14/-. The plight of the handloom weaver in the early nineteenth century was terrible.

The greatest textile changes took place in spinning and weaving, but there were important changes in other branches of the industry. In America Eli Whitney's 'saw gin', which separated the seed from the cotton fibre, enabled short staple cotton to be used to meet the growing demand from Lancashire for cotton. Machinery was used in printing. John Bell in 1783 used copper cylinders in a revolving press instead of plates which had to be applied to the cloth by hand. The bleaching properties of chlorine were publicized in Glasgow by James Watt, whence its use spread rapidly to England. Previously cloth had been bleached by exposing it to the sun, or by using dilute sulphuric acid. Henry and Taylor of Manchester developed brilliant dyes, notably scarlet, yellow, green, and 'Turkey Red'.

By 1830 the cotton industry was becoming firmly based on the factory system, and was concentrated in two major areas, South Lancashire and Clydeside, but progress in the woollen industry was much slower. The spinning jenny only came into general use in Yorkshire about 1785, the date when the jenny was being replaced in Lancashire by the water frame and the mule. The woollen industry was more widespread than cotton, so that new techniques were introduced more gradually. Weaving labour was plentiful in woollen areas, and there was not the same urgent demand for mechanical spinning and weaving. It was difficult to apply machinery to wool, the strands of which broke more easily than cotton. Nor would it have been easy to have persuaded the Yorkshire weaver to enter factories; he usually possessed land and the independent spirit which went along with it. It was impossible to remain a farmer and work the long hours demanded by the factory system, and the latter had to wait for its development until after 1840, when the improved power loom brought about the extinction of handloom weaving. The woollen industry was also fettered with restrictions of bygone years. The wool trade had been highly regulated since the Middle Ages, and the traditions handed down by the guilds were difficult to overcome. Another reason for the slow advance of machinery was the difficulty of increasing the supplies of raw wool, and it was not until wool was imported from Australia in large quantities that the factory system could make much progress. Finally, the demand for woollen goods was much narrower than for cottons, which had a world-wide market.

CHAPTER 12
The Chemical, Gas and Pottery Industries

Unlike most manufacturing industries, whose goods were used in everyday life, most of the products of the chemical industry were absorbed by other industries, so that their progress and that of the chemical industry were interdependent. This was clearly shown by the growth of the textile industries, and of cotton in particular. The increasing demand for soap for washing raw wool and cotton, and bleaching agents and dyestuffs for the finishing processes, was the foundation on which the chemical industry grew. Yet without the introduction of bleaching powder the stupendous growth of the cotton industry would have been checked. Both the traditional method of bleaching cloth by soaking it in sour milk and exposing it to the sun, and the later use of dilute sulphuric acid, were wholly inadequate once the annual output of Lancashire's cotton mills could be measured in millions of yards.

Not only textiles, however, but glass manufacture, soap, pottery, metallurgy, pharmaceuticals, and paper technology were closely associated with the chemical industry. Large quantities of alkali were needed by glass and soap makers. Lead oxides and other chemical substances were required by the glass industry for the production of different types of glass, and by the pottery industry for obtaining different glazes. In metallurgy the progress of analytical chemistry led to the discovery of new metals such as potassium and sodium, while the chemical industry made the acids for refining metals. In the early part of the nineteenth century several new compounds were discovered which proved to be of great value in the medical field. Sir Humphry Davy in 1799 seems to have been the first to suggest the use of nitrous oxide as an anaesthetic,

29 Bleachfields near Glasgow

whose general use dates from the 1840's. In paper technology the introduction of chlorine enabled paper-makers to bleach printed linen rags, which could then be used in the manufacture of white writing paper. Thus the chemical industry played a vital role in the Industrial Revolution, and by the end of the nineteenth century it had become an industrial giant.

The most important product of the chemical industry in 1750 was sulphuric acid. Its continuous manufacture in Britain began when Joshua Ward and John White built sulphuric acid works at Twickenham in 1736 and Richmond in 1740, where the acid was made in large glass retorts at a fraction of its former price. Soon afterwards, John Roebuck (1718–94) introduced the lead chamber process. Lead chambers, which were resistant to the acid, had two important advantages over glass containers. They were not fragile, and they could hold larger volumes of acid. In Roebuck's process sulphur and saltpetre were burned over water in lead chambers. In partnership with

Samuel Garbett, a metal refiner, Roebuck built a sulphuric acid works in Steelhouse Lane, Birmingham, where the acid was used by jewellers for engraving, by 'toy' manufacturers for such things as brass founding, gilding and button making, and by metal refiners. Roebuck was also aware of the bleaching properties of dilute sulphuric acid, and in 1749 he set up another sulphuric acid works at Prestonpans, near Edinburgh, to meet the needs of textile manufacturers in that area. The use of dilute sulphuric acid instead of sour milk cut the time of the bleaching process by ninety-five per cent. By 1820, shortly before the large-scale use of sulphuric acid in the manufacture of soda, some 3,000 tons were produced annually, at a cost of $2\frac{1}{2}$d per pound.

Until the Leblanc process of manufacturing synthetic soda, the alkalis needed by glass and soap makers were obtained from plant ashes and, after 1730, from burning kelp, a brown seaweed. Both Joseph Black (1728–99), a chemist, and John Roebuck, tried to make soda from common salt, but it was a French scientist, Nicolas Leblanc (1742–1806), who first met with success. He treated common salt, (sodium chloride), with sulphuric acid, thus producing sodium sulphate. This was mixed with limestone and coal, and heated. The black residue was dissolved in water, which was then evaporated to leave soda. The Leblanc process, discovered in 1791, did not come into general use for over thirty years, since the practical difficulties of manufacturing soda as opposed to making it under laboratory controlled conditions, took some time to solve. Lord Dundonald and William Losh built an alkali works near Newcastle-upon-Tyne in 1796, but the large-scale exploitation of the Leblanc process came in 1823, when James Muspratt took advantage of the repeal of the salt duty by establishing a soda works at St Helens, in Lancashire. Soon an extensive development of the chemical industry took place in the areas around Warrington, Widnes and Runcorn. This region, in association with the rock salt deposits of Cheshire, and with a well-developed transport system providing easy access to coal and limestone supplies, was an ideal location for the industry.

In the meantime, another French chemist, Claude Berthollet (1748–1822), discovered in 1785 that chlorine was a powerful bleach, thus removing a serious obstacle to the growth of the British textile industries. When James Watt learned the news he immediately sent word of it to the textile manufacturers in Glasgow. Thence the use of chlorine as a bleach spread rapidly to all the textile-producing areas. In 1789 Charles Tennant, a Renfrewshire bleacher, began the manufacture of liquid bleach from chlorine and slaked lime. Shortly afterwards he obtained a patent for the manufacture of bleaching powder, and in 1799 he opened the St Rollox works, near Glasgow, which was the largest in Europe. The development of bleaching powder was of the utmost importance in the course of the Industrial Revolution. Many years later a German chemist, Justus von Liebig, declared that

But for this new bleaching process it would scarcely have been possible for cotton manufacture in Great Britain to have attained the enormous extent which it did during the nineteenth century, nor could it have competed in price with France and Germany.

Chemical works soon became very large and diversified as manufacturers found ways of turning former waste materials into valuable byproducts. Thus at first the hydrogen chloride generated by the Leblanc process was allowed to escape into the atmosphere, causing widespread damage to crops and property near the works. Fortunately manufacturers found that it could be used to make hydrochloric acid and chlorine. As nitric acid was needed for making sulphuric acid, the alkali manufacturer was soon involved in making these acids, as well as the various salts of alum, iron, copper and sodium.

The chemical industry was also closely associated with the rise of the coal gas industry in England, which dates from about 1812. The fact that coal gave off an inflammable gas was reported as far back as 1667, and almost one hundred years later George Dixon, the owner of a coalmine near Newcastle-upon-Tyne, collected a large quantity of coal gas, but his experiment ended with an explosion. The Earl of Dundonald was one of the early pioneers of gas lighting, and in 1787 he lit the hall at Culross Abbey with coal gas. In 1792 William Murdock lit his house in Redruth, Cornwall, with gas and, after further experiments, illuminated part of the Soho factory of Boulton and Watt with gas to celebrate the Peace of Amiens in 1801. In 1805 he provided a Manchester mill with gas lighting, and another in Halifax was similarly equipped by Samuel Clegg, until 1805 Murdock's colleague and afterwards his successful rival. Thus factory work was no longer limited to the hours of daylight, or carried on by the light of dozens of candles, which were fire hazards as well as being costly.

Gas street lighting was promoted by a German emigrant to England, Frederick Winsor. Winsor, unlike Murdock and Clegg, realized that if gas lighting was to become general, mills, houses, and street lights would have to be supplied by mains radiating from central gas-generating stations. By 1807 he had obtained enough money from public subscriptions to light Pall Mall by gas. In 1810 Winsor secured an Act of Parliament giving him permission to form the London and Westminster Gas, Light and Coke Company. By 1816 the parish of Westminster had twenty-six miles of gas mains under its pavements. By 1825 many churches, banks and other public buildings were illuminated by gas, and three rival companies operated north of the river Thames.

A minor social revolution followed the substitution of gaslight for candles. In the absence of any effective competition until the invention of the filament lamp in the 1860s, the gas industry flourished, creating many new jobs and a valuable export trade in gas

30 The retort house at Westminster gas works

31   The lamplighter on his round

appliances. Gas cooking did not become common until after 1870, but in other ways the life of the people was improved. The streets became safer at night when they were well lit. Attendance at educational and political meetings was encouraged, so that more people took part in community life. Gaslight was clean, convenient and safe. When Winsor, or one of his associates, wrote:

Must Britons be condemned for ever to wallow
In filthy soot, noxious smoke, train oil and
*   tallow;*
And their fumes for ever to swallow.
For, with sparky soot, snuffs, and vapours, men
*   have constant strife;*
Those who are not burned to death are
*   smothered during life.*

he exaggerated to gain greater effect. Yet there is no doubt that the gas industry helped to make life in Victorian England more pleasant and comfortable.

Great changes in the scale and methods of production also marked the pottery industry, which was transformed during the period 1760–1820. This industry was stimulated by the growing wealth of the nation, and by changes in fashion which accompanied it. The popularity of tea, coffee, and chocolate as beverages created a strong demand for a wide range of attractive earthenware to replace pewter mugs and wooden platters. Transport improvements such as the development of turnpike roads and inland waterways enabled Staffordshire potters to obtain their raw materials from further afield, and to sell their wares not only in most parts of England, but in Europe and North America. Technological advances in the pottery industry included the discovery of new glazes, bodies, and decorative methods, greater division of labour, and the introduction of factory methods of production. Where the steam engine was used for preparing the raw materials the unit of production became a factory, not a tiny workshop. The factory system in the pottery industry, however, differed greatly from that which operated in the cotton industry, where the worker was a machine minder. It was not until well into the twentieth century that the individual skills of the potter and artist were replaced by machinery.

Long before the Industrial Revolution pottery was made not only in North Staffordshire, but in many other parts of the country where suitable clays were found. By 1700, however, the pottery industry was beginning to concentrate in the Five Towns which now constitute Stoke-on-Trent. According to Dr Plot, who wrote a *History of Staffordshire* (1686),

The greatest pottery they have in this country is carried on at Burslem, where for making their

several sorts of pots they have as many different sorts of clay, which they dig about the town, all within half a mile's distance, the best being found nearest the coal; and are distinguished by their colours and uses as followeth:

1 bottle clay of a bright whitish, streaked yellow colour

2 hard fire clay of a duller, whitish colour

3 red blending clay, which is a dirty red colour

4 white clay, though a blewish colour and used for making a yellow ware, because yellow is the lightest colour they make any ware of

The industry was small-scale, producing a very limited range of wares such as butter pots, jars, and jugs for the local market. The typical pottery was a cottage with a lean-to shed, and since the roads were little more than narrow tracks, the potters sold most of their wares in nearby fairs and marketplaces such as Uttoxeter.

In the manufacturing process the clay was first 'blunged', i.e. it was put in a tank of water where it was stirred with a large wooden paddle. The resulting muddy liquid was sieved into shallow containers, or 'sun-pans', where the water was either evaporated by the heat of the sun, or by the heat from coal, which the potters mined themselves. When the clay had become soft and pliable it was 'wedged' by throwing one lump of it on to another in order to remove air bubbles which caused unsightly defects in the finished product. The wares were either thrown on the potter's wheel, or made by putting the clay into specially prepared moulds. After a first firing in beehive-shaped ovens or kilns, the wares were given a slip-wash of a different coloured clay which gave them a pleasing appearance. In the second firing the wares were glazed to make them non-porous. Glaze, essentially a thin coating of clear glass, was obtained by throwing fine sand, or salt, through a hole in the top of the kiln towards the end of the firing process.

Salt glazing, and the potter's lathe, were introduced towards the end of the seventeenth century by two Dutchmen, David and Philip Elers. The potter's search for a white body, as a substitute for porcelain, ended when John Astbury succeeded in making a light coloured stoneware. In 1720 Astbury discovered that by mixing pulverized flint with Devon clay he was able to produce white earthenware which could be fired at a very high temperature, thus rendering it harder. The clay he used was carried by ship from Bideford to Chester, thence by barge along the Weaver Navigation to Winsford, and by packhorse from Winsford to the Potteries. The flint was crushed by heavy rollers operated by a water-wheel. This process introduced a new industrial hazard into pottery making, for the flint dust inhaled by the workers caused a lung disease, and labour became difficult to obtain. The problem was overcome in 1726 when Thomas Benson took out a patent for grinding flint under water.

But it was due chiefly to the work of Josiah Wedgwood that pottery was converted

32 The Potbanks
The pottery was baked in these large kilns

from a local craft into an industry supplying an international market. Wedgwood (1730–95) was the twelfth child of Thomas and Mary Wedgwood. At the age of nine Wedgwood began work in his father's pottery at Burslem. Twenty years later he set himself up as a master potter in the Churchyard Works, in Burslem, where he perfected a type of green glazed ware which became very popular. In 1764 Wedgwood moved into larger premises near by in order to increase production of a new type of cream-coloured ware he had developed. Queen Charlotte, the wife of George III, ordered a cream-ware dinner service, and was so impressed that she allowed Wedgwood to advertise it as 'Queen's Ware'. This sold so well that Wedgwood wrote in 1767: 'The demand for this said Cream Colour, alias Queen's Ware, still increases. It is really amazing how rapidly the use of it has spread.'[1] Several years later his diary records the interesting note: 'I had been seriously advised not to trust myself with the miners in Cornwall, the tin trade being very low, they being convinced that Queen's Ware was the cause.'

Wedgwood was the complete industrialist. Enterprising, ambitious, with a remarkable flair for business, he supervised the manufacture of his pottery down to the smallest detail. He constantly experimented with new designs and materials in his search for improvements. Different lustres were applied to wares giving them the appearance of being made of pearl or metal. Jasper ware, perfected in 1775, with its white figures set in high relief against a coloured background, and black basalt, were among Wedgwood's creations. A self-trained chemist, Wedgwood developed the use of 'pyrometric cones' which changed colour as the temperature in the oven rose or fell, so that the accurate control of temperature needed in the firing of delicate wares could be achieved. He kept a careful record of all his experiments. According to one historian of the pottery industry, John Thomas, Wedgwood raised pottery manufacture from 'a matter of

guesswork and procedure by rule of thumb, to a matter of scientific measurement and calculation'.[2]

Wedgwood was also greatly concerned in developing the market for Staffordshire wares, not only in this country but abroad. He was an enthusiastic supporter of turnpike roads and canals, and he became chairman of the Trent and Mersey Canal. Wedgwood realized that the canal would not only afford cheap transport facilities for bringing Cornish clay to the Potteries, but would open up Europe and North America for Staffordshire wares. On its banks he built his famous factory, opened in 1769, which he called Etruria, because of his admiration for classical Italian design. Through his marketing techniques and the quality of his wares, Wedgwood captured a large part of the English market. He was the first potter to open a showroom in London where wealthy people could view and order goods in comfort. Other famous potters such as Josiah Spode copied his example.

Not content with his sales in England, Wedgwood opened showrooms in Paris, Amsterdam and Dublin. West Indian planters were among his best customers, and Wedgwood ware was exported to countries as far away as Russia, Turkey, and China, the original home of porcelain. In 1779 Wedgwood sold a Queen's Ware dinner service of 952 pieces to Catherine the Great of Russia. Each piece was decorated with a view of a famous nobleman's estate, drawn by some of the best artists Wedgwood could find. The set is now one of the treasured exhibits in the Hermitage. In making wares to be sold abroad, Wedgwood was careful to observe national habits and customs. His success in penetrating European markets alarmed foreign manufacturers so greatly that Lord North informed Wedgwood in 1776 that 'Staffordshire earthenware had interfered so much with the German manufactures, and particularly with those of Saxony, that the German powers propose laying still higher duties upon them'.

Inevitably, Wedgwood became involved in

influencing the Government's commercial policy. In 1773 he urged the Government to arrange more extensive trade between Britain and France. He stressed the need for preventing skilled British craftsmen being lured abroad by promises of rich rewards for betraying secret manufacturing processes to foreign firms. Wedgwood wanted potters' wheels and lathes put on the list of goods whose export was banned. He opposed the extension of a monopoly of the use of Cornwall's china clay to Richard Champion. Until 1754, when William Cookworthy discovered deposits of china clay in Cornwall, the only source of kaolin was North America. Cookworthy took out a patent for the manufacture of porcelain at Plymouth, but his business collapsed, and he sold his patent rights to Champion in 1774. Wedgwood failed to prevent the renewal of the patent, but in 1781 Champion decided to sell his rights to a group of five Staffordshire potters. Shortly afterwards Wedgwood leased clay mines near St Austell in Cornwall, thus securing essential supplies of kaolin.

Wedgwood did not patent his discoveries, and he had many imitators, chief among whom were the Staffordshire potters John Turner, William Adams and Josiah Spode. Their efforts and those of many lesser known potters made North Staffordshire the chief pottery area in the world. By the end of the century over 20,000 workers were employed by 200 master potters. Nevertheless, Staffordshire was not the only area where pottery was made. Leeds creamware was as good as Wedgwood. High quality porcelain was made in Swansea, Derby, Worcester, Chelsea, and Coalport in Shropshire. By 1800 English ceramics enjoyed a European reputation, and pottery was high on the list of exports. Faujas de Saint-Fond wrote that

in travelling from Paris to St Petersburg, from Amsterdam to the farthest point of Sweden, from Dunkirk to the southern extremity of France, one is served at every inn from English earthenware. The same fine article adorns the tables of Spain, Portugal and Italy, and it provides the cargoes of ships to the East Indies, the West Indies, and America.[3]

REFERENCES

1   *The Story of Wedgwood*, compiled by Alison Kelly in association with Josiah Wedgwood and Sons Ltd.
2   John Thomas, *Staffordshire Industries Past and Present*.
3   Faujas de Saint-Fond, op. cit., Vol. I, p. 112.

The Revolutionary and Napoleonic Wars with France which lasted, apart from a short break, from 1793 to 1815, were the longest and most costly wars Britain had ever fought. The number of men in the armed forces reached nearly half a million in the latter stages of the war. Britain's continental allies, Austria, Prussia and Russia, could not survive without subsidies, which severely strained Britain's financial resources. Since the war also coincided with a period of rapid change in industry and agriculture, its effects were considerable.

The double burden of fighting on land and sea, and of subsidizing allies, was a heavy one. Taxation rose sharply, provoking the author of a pamphlet, *Hog's Wash, or Politics for the People*,[1] to complain

If we fight and tax on for a year or two more,
The French, I dare say, will ne'er land on
  our shore,
For fear of the charge of maintaining the poor.[1]

Customs and excise duties were raised, and in 1798 an income tax of two shillings in the pound was introduced on incomes over £200 per annum. Yet though the various forms of taxation took away an estimated one-sixth of everybody's incomes, taxation met only one-third of the cost of the war, and the Government was forced to borrow money on a large scale. The National Debt increased from £240 million at the start of the war to £900 million in 1816. Government borrowing and payments of gold to England's allies caused inflation. Our gold reserves fell steeply, but the banks, which for the sake of convenience were allowed to issue paper currency, were still bound by law to pay the bearers of their notes the stated sum in gold. In 1797 a naval

mutiny at Spithead, and the threat of invasion, brought about a run on the banks as people tried to exchange their banknotes for gold, which would retain its value in the event of a national disaster, whereas the former would not. To avoid financial chaos the Government suspended cash payments. Freed from the check of keeping adequate gold reserves the country banks increased their circulation of notes, thus adding to the inflationary spiral, since more and more money was made available for any given quantity of goods.

Prices rose, so that the value of money fell and, while wages rose too, in general they did not keep pace with the rise in the cost of living. Skilled craftsmen, especially those in industries which served the war effort, did well, but the wages of unskilled workers, and those who lived in the countryside, rose very little or not at all. This was due more to the general increase in population, which meant that there was a surplus of labour in rural areas, and to the introduction of power-driven machinery which was steadily destroying domestic industries, than to the war. But the war certainly brought about rises in the price of food, since imports of foodstuffs from the continent to feed a rapidly growing population were reduced. The average price of wheat doubled during the war, causing great distress among the poorer sections of the community. In years of shortages such as 1795 and 1800 the price of bread reached famine levels, and food riots broke out. William Hale described in 1800 the poverty he had seen:

As a silk manufacturer I am in some measure acquainted with the distressed circumstances of many who, although they are in full employ, the whole amount of their week's industry is not competent to purchase for themselves and their children a sufficiency of the simple article of bread. But in the discharge of my parochial office I am frequently called upon to witness scenes of the most awful distress; to visit families who, to satisfy the cravings of hunger, have long ago been forced to part with their clothes and linen, and, almost expiring amidst the horrors of starvation, have scarcely a rag to cover their nakedness.[2]

Such misery was usually temporary in industrial areas, but in the rural south the problem of the unemployed was acute. It was to deal with this situation that in 1795 a group of magistrates meeting in the Berkshire village of Speen decided to grant poor relief according to the price of bread and the size of the labourer's family (see p. 175). This practice was soon copied throughout the South of England, and by 1830 Northumberland was the only English county which had not followed suit. Supplementing wages out of the poor rates, however, had unfortunate results. It prevented wages from rising, since farmers knew that their labourers would in any case be maintained out of the poor rate, to which they themselves contributed, and it accustomed labourers to receiving automatic charity. Frederick Eden, in his survey of the poor law administration, *The State of the Poor* (1797), reporting on a Devon parish, declared

No labourer can at present maintain himself, wife and two children on his earnings; they all have relief from the parish. . . . A very few years ago, labourers thought themselves disgraced by receiving aid from the parish, but this sense of shame is now totally extinguished.[3]

Elsewhere the same demoralization of the poor was to be found. In Reading

Many of the labouring class of the community possess very little economy or foresight. . . . Weavers who can earn 18s. a week do not hesitate to solicit relief, if a temporary stagnation of business curtails their common receipts, and reduces them to those difficulties which a little parsimony would have obviated.[4]

Yet, however unfortunate some of its results were, poor relief was necessary to guarantee the poor at least an income on which they could just manage to survive, and it probably damped down the spread of revolutionary ideas.

The impact of war on industry was varied. The iron industry responded to the demand for munitions and the disruption of Swedish and Russian supplies, by speeding up the introduction of steam power and Cort's puddling and rolling processes. The British iron industry became the most efficient in Europe. The metal industries flourished, especially copper, which was used to sheathe the hulls of warships. Coal production soared to meet the demands of industries using steam engines, and the metal working trades. Shipbuilding boomed as wartime losses had to be replaced. The Yorkshire woollen industry, which provided coarse cloth for uniforms, did well, but the decline of the East Anglian and West Country woollen industries was hastened. The cotton industry's progress was interrupted briefly when Britain and America quarrelled over the former's blockade of Europe. The Americans retaliated against the restrictions on their trade by passing the Non-Intercourse Act (1811), and by declaring war on Britain in 1812. Until peace was restored in 1814 Lancashire was starved of its supplies of raw cotton. The chemical industry grew rapidly, but those industries, such as pottery, which relied heavily upon exports, suffered from the loss of their European markets. The war greatly stimulated agriculture, and farming became very profitable. All available land was cultivated, as marginal land (i.e. land which in normal times was uneconomic to plough) was farmed. The enclosure movement accelerated. The General Enclosure Act of 1801 made enclosure easier, and in the period 1795 to 1812 1,500 enclosure acts were passed. Thus landowners did well, but as we have already seen, this prosperity was not shared by those without land, or by those who lost it through enclosures.

The war harmed trade. By the Berlin and Milan Decrees of 1806 and 1807 Napoleon tried to prevent the entry of British manufactures into the continent, and neutral ships were forbidden to call at British ports. England's defeat was to be brought about by economic collapse, caused by a glut of goods she had manufactured but could not sell. Britain retaliated by passing Orders in Council, which required all neutral shipping bound for Europe to call at British ports. The worst effects of the blockade were evaded by smuggling goods into Europe from bases such as Malta and Heligoland, and by developing new markets in South America, but the normal growth of trade was certainly slowed down.

If the war speeded up industrial changes, it postponed reforms which could have reduced the distress caused by them. The Parliamentary Reform Societies which had flourished before the war were regarded as unpatriotic and potentially dangerous in view of the experience of France, where a movement for moderate reform had led to revolution and war. Their activities were spied upon by a Government which professed to see them as a threat to internal order which could not be tolerated in wartime. Most of them were disbanded. The right of public meetings was restricted. Trade Unions were outlawed in 1799 and 1800 by the Combination Acts (see pp. 143–4) which forbade both workers and employers to combine to discuss wages or conditions, though the laws could not be enforced against employers. When hard times produced violent protests such as Luddism, the Government merely enforced severer penalties instead of improving conditions. Luddism, or framebreaking, so called after the action of a Leicester stockinger's apprentice, Ned Ludlam, who is said to have smashed some stocking frames with a sledgehammer, was made a capital offence in 1812, and twelve Luddites were hanged at York. In fairness to the Government's stern measures it should be pointed out that there was no effective police force in those days. Disorder was always just beneath the surface when an angry meeting could easily degenerate into a dangerous riot. Few towns had sufficient constables; Leicester had only six at the time of the Luddite disturbances. Most were little better off than two hundred years before when Shakespeare's Dogberry was a fair caricature of a typical policeman.

The general discontent in England during the Great French War found little organized expression, partly because people confidently hoped that peace would bring prosperity. Yet the six years after Waterloo mark one of the grimmest periods in English history, for agriculture and nearly all branches of industry and trade were hit by a severe postwar slump.

The very high wartime price of corn had encouraged the use of marginal land. Much of this land was now abandoned. The harvest of 1813 was good, and since corn could be imported in 1814 corn prices fell abruptly. Many smallholders who had taken up loans or mortgages in order to improve their land were ruined. They either became landless labourers or migrated to the towns or industrial villages. Everywhere, farmers complained of falling prices and landowners of falling rents.

Parliament, which was dominated by landowners, tried to help farmers by passing the Corn Law of 1815, which prohibited the import of foreign corn until the price of home grown corn had reached 80/- per quarter (13 kilograms). In doing this the Government was following a well-established policy. A corn law of 1773 had protected English farmers from imported corn until the price of the home crop had risen above 48/- per quarter. This upper limit was successively raised by further corn laws to 54/- in 1791 and 66/- in 1804. The purpose of the corn laws was simple. Average crops of home-grown corn were about equal to home consumption. By giving farmers a monopoly of the home market until prices had risen above a stated figure, the Government tried to assure them of an income which would make it worthwhile to grow corn. Yet, though the 1815 Corn Law kept prices higher than they would have been without protection, it did not fix a high price. Corn prices still fluctuated according to the state of the harvest, and in the 1820s the average price was as low as 58/- per quarter.

In its effort to restore farming to its former prosperity Parliament repealed in 1816 Pitt's income tax, which had been promised as a temporary wartime measure. Compared with manufacturing industry agriculture had more than its fair share of taxation. In addition to the land tax and income tax, landowners paid tithes to the Church, county and highway rates, and the poor rate, which had quadrupled by 1816. The weight of taxation was one reason for the depressed state of agriculture in the postwar period. Yet, in spite of these relief measures, farming was slow to recover, and it was not until after Queen Victoria's accession in 1837 that agriculture became prosperous. By then the burden of the poor rate had been greatly reduced, while the progress of manufacturing industry and railway building, by providing employment, helped farming in the form of increased demand for foodstuffs.

Unemployment and low wages were not confined to agriculture. The boom in the iron industry ended abruptly when peace was signed, since the Government cancelled its orders for armaments. The demand for manufactured goods from an impoverished Europe was low, and trade took several years to recover its normal pattern. Manufactures lay unsold in warehouses, or were auctioned for less than their cost price. The distress in Birmingham, described by the *Gazette* was typical of many manufacturing towns.

In consequence of the depressed state of the manufacturing classes in this town, we learn that many families have been compelled to vacate the small tenements in which they have hitherto lived, and are now crowded together in small houses, many of which are deprived of a free circulation of air.

There was a good deal of unemployment in the cotton industry, where the introduction of machinery, and the employment of young children, who were a cheap form of labour, made many men redundant.

A very good handloom weaver will weave 2 pieces of cloth, each 24 yards long. A steam loom weaver, 15 years of age, will in the same time weave 7 similar pieces. . . . It may very safely be said that the work done in a steam factory containing 200 looms would, if done by handloom weavers, find employment and support for a population of more than 2,000 persons.[5]

The demobilization in 1815 of many thousands of soldiers and sailors added to the numbers seeking work.

Conditions in mines and many factories, where long hours were worked for low wages, were terrible. Women and children were employed underground in coalmines, chiefly for dragging heavy trucks and baskets full of coal to the surface. Factory machinery was usually uncaged and dangerous, and accidents were common. Discipline was harsh. Workers could be fined for a multitude of offences, including unpunctuality, whistling, and opening windows without permission. Even Jedediah Strutt, in many ways an enlightened cotton manufacturer, included in his mill at Millford, near Derby, a private prison where offending workers could be put in the stocks. The industrial towns, with their rows of back to back houses, and unpaved streets, were insanitary, depressing places to live in. As late as 1844 Preston was the only town in Lancashire with a park.

Parliament did little to relieve distress, partly because its resources for doing so were very limited, and partly because it feared that reform would encourage a demand for revolutionary changes. Parliament also had little sympathy with, and understanding of, the problems of the poor, since its members were drawn exclusively from the wealthy classes. The Government tried to keep law and order by following a repressive policy, that is to say they tried to stamp out evidence of discontent instead of trying to remedy its causes. The Combination Laws were maintained, though many unions survived under the guise of friendly societies, which were still legal, or became secret societies indulging in brief but vicious strikes. Some of Parliament's measures, such as the repeal of income tax and the 1815 Corn Law, appeared selfish acts passed by landowners in favour of their own class. The abolition of income tax was balanced by raising customs and excise duties, which fell more heavily on the poor than the rich. Much of the taxation went to pay the interest on the National Debt, which meant that it was pocketed by holders of government stocks and bonds, in other words, the wealthy classes who escaped so lightly from taxation. Parliament also tightened up the Game Laws, again benefiting landowners, who had extended their parks and game preserves as a result of enclosures. Poachers were dealt with severely. Even the intention to poach could be punished, for anyone found at night with a net in his possession could be transported for seven years.

The freedom of the individual was restricted. In 1817 the renewed suspension of Habeas Corpus allowed magistrates to imprison people on mere suspicion. The Six Acts, or 'Gagging Acts' of 1819 speeded up the administration of justice, laid down severe punishments for seditious libel, and placed a stamp duty on newspapers in an effort to put them beyond the reach of the working man. The other acts authorized magistrates to search houses where they suspected arms were concealed, made military drilling by civilians illegal, and declared that six days' notice of any meeting of more than fifty people had to be given to the magistrates. Thus the failure of the Government to alleviate distress merely added to the discontent.

With times so hard riots and disturbances were commonplace. In 1816 there took place the Spa Fields riot in London. A large crowd assembled to hear Cobbett and Hunt address a reform meeting. Hunt arrived late, and Thistlewood, a dangerous agitator, persuaded part of the crowd to follow him with the intention of capturing the Tower of London. The mob broke into a gunsmith's shop on the way, but was eventually dispersed by the Mayor, who met them with soldiers and barred the way.

There was more unrest in 1817, for the harvest of 1816 was bad, and bread was dear. The Prince Regent's coach was stoned, and in Manchester several hundred cotton workers planned to march to London in order to present to the Government a petition complaining of the suspension of Habeas Corpus, the Corn Law, and high taxation, and requesting the Regent to dismiss his ministers. The March of the Blanketeers, so called because each man carried a blanket to keep himself warm at night, was broken up by soldiers, who arrested the ringleaders, so that very few got as far as Stockport, and only one man reached London. In the same year there occurred the Derbyshire Insurrection, stirred up by Oliver, a government spy, or *agent provocateur*, as a result of which three poor men were hanged, and eleven others transported to Botany Bay.

Apart from a violent strike in the cotton industry the year 1818 was relatively quiet, but in 1819 the 'Peterloo Massacre' took place. A meeting on the subject of constitutional reform was held in St Peter's Fields, near Manchester. It was attended by an estimated crowd of 60,000, carrying banners with slogans like 'No Corn Laws', 'Liberty or Death', and 'Taxation without Representation is Tyranny', while their orderly movements suggested that they had been drilled. The magistrates foolishly sent in foot soldiers to arrest the speakers. They were immediately hemmed in by the mob, and the magistrates, now fearful for the soldiers' lives, lost their nerve, and ordered the cavalry in reserve to charge. What happened was described in an open letter to Lord Sidmouth, the Home Secretary.

33 *'Manchester Heroes'*, 1819

The Yeomanry Cavalry made their charge with a most infuriate frenzy; they cut down men, women and children indiscriminately, and appeared to have commenced a premeditated attack with the most insatiable thirst for blood and destruction. They merit a medallion on one side of which should be inscribed 'The Slaughtermen of Manchester'.[6]

11 people were killed, and over 400 injured. The bitterness and indignation of the working classes was increased by the Government's congratulations to the magistrates on the action they had taken. As a result of Peterloo the Six Acts were passed.

Finally, in 1820, Edwards, a police spy, betrayed the Cato Street Conspiracy, which he himself had largely arranged. Thistlewood, recently released from gaol for his part in the Spa Field's riot, and several accomplices, planned to assassinate the Cabinet at a dinner,

and in the ensuing confusion, start a general uprising in London which would overthrow the Government. Thistlewood and four others were hanged, and five conspirators were transported.

The disturbances of the postwar years reflect both the extent of distress and the need for reform. They also help to justify the stern measures which the Government took to keep order. Though the country was never on the verge of rebellion, as the Government believed, law and order was severely strained. Lacking a police force, and efficient means of communication, the Government had to rely on the initiative of the magistrates on the spot, on police spies, the yeomanry, and the army, which was recruited from among the worst elements of the population, and whose loyalty was suspect. Thus the Government dared not introduce reform in case it provoked more unrest; instead it relied upon a repressive policy. It was not until 1822, when prosperity was beginning to return, that a more enlightened Tory government began its policy of moderate reform.

REFERENCES

1   Daniel Eaton, *Hog's Wash, or Politics for the People* (1793).

2   William Hale to Patrick Colquhoun (21 October 1800) Public Record Office, Home Office, 42/52 (quoted from *English Historical Documents 1783–1832*, Vol. XI, Eyre & Spottiswoode, 1969).

3   Sir Frederick Eden, *The State of the Poor in 1797*, Vol. II, p. 137.

4   Sir Frederick Eden, op. cit., Vol. II, p. 14.

5   Richard Guest, *A Compendious History of the Cotton Manufacture.*

6   Richard Carlile's 'eyewitness account', quoted in Robert Walmsley, *Peterloo: the Case Re-opened* (Manchester University Press, 1969).

CHAPTER 14
Free Trade

By 1820 England was emerging from the trade recession which had followed the coming of peace in 1815, and merchants were eager to develop fresh markets. The Industrial Revolution was gathering momentum, and with the spreading use of steam-powered machinery Britain's manufacturing capacity soared. This was especially so in cotton textiles which in 1802 overtook woollens as the country's chief export. Imports of raw cotton were 1·4 million kilograms (3 million lb), 21 million kilograms (47 million lb) in 1770 and 1800 respectively, and 135 million kilograms (over 300 million lb) in 1830. But many other industries such as ironmongery, cutlery and pottery showed great increases in production. British merchants, therefore, had little to fear from competition, and much to gain from any trade expansion. A petition of London merchants to Parliament declared

that freedom from restraint is calculated to give the utmost extension to foreign trade, and the best direction to the capital and industry of the country; that the maxim of buying in the cheapest market and selling in the dearest, which regulates every merchant in his individual dealings, is strictly applicable, as the best rule for the trade of the whole nation.

The Free Trade movement was a reaction against the multitude of regulations and customs duties which hindered industry and trade in the early nineteenth century. A Report of a Select Committee on Foreign Trade observed in 1820 that there were nearly two thousand regulations on commerce, and pointed out that

it will not appear extraordinary that it should be a matter of complaint to the British merchant . . . that, so far from being able to avail himself of favourable

openings as they arise, he must ascertain what he may venture to do without infringing the law.

These restrictions had been intended to serve three main purposes. There were regulations which encouraged merchant shipping, customs duties for raising revenue, and customs duties to protect certain industries by levying charges upon foreign goods entering the country. The constant additions and alterations of the previous century made the system hopelessly complicated, and with the expansion of British industry protection was becoming less and less necessary, except for a few isolated examples such as shipping and certain luxury industries. Many tariffs served none of their intended purposes. Sometimes duties were so high that either foreign goods were virtually excluded and the revenue gained was trifling, or they were smuggled into the country, so that neither revenue nor protection was forthcoming.

The first influential attack upon this system was Adam Smith's book *The Wealth of Nations*, published in 1776. Adam Smith believed that the fewer the regulations on trade the greater its volume would be. He attacked the restrictions on colonial trade on two grounds. Firstly because

The exclusive trade of the Mother Country tends to diminish, or at least, to keep down below what they would otherwise rise to, both the enjoyments and industry of all nations in general, and of the American colonies in particular. By rendering the colony produce dearer in all other countries it lessens its consumption, and thereby cramps the industries of the colonies, and other nations, which both enjoy less when they pay more for what they enjoy, and produce less when they get less for what they produce.[1]

Secondly, manufacturers were easily tempted to concentrate their sales in the colonies where there was little foreign competition. In his view 'The causes of decay in other branches of foreign trade . . . may all be found in the overgrowth of the colony trade'.[2]

Adam Smith's first great disciple was William Pitt the Younger, who in the 1780s greatly reduced the heavy duties on tea in order to discourage smuggling, and simplified the collection of duties by introducing a single rate of duty for each article instead of several different calculations. He reduced many duties in order to encourage foreign trade, and arranged a commercial treaty with France in 1787, whereby Britain reduced her duties on imported French wines and spirits in return for comparable French concessions on British manufactures. The treaty was unpopular with French industrialists, who feared the effects of open competition with British manufacturers, and the outbreak of war between the two countries in 1793 brought it to an end. Pitt also tried to implement Adam Smith's view that 'As the wealth and industry of Lancashire does not obstruct but promote that of Yorkshire, so the wealth and industry of Ireland would not obstruct but promote that of England'. In 1785 he tried to arrange a trade treaty between England and Ireland, which as far as trade was concerned was treated as a foreign country. In this instance, however, he was opposed by English manufacturers who feared competition from Irish industry, particularly linen, and Pitt was compelled to abandon the scheme.

Pitt's achievement as a free trader was small, but his work was taken up by William Huskisson, President of the Board of Trade (1823–8), when the arguments in favour of freer trade had grown. Prohibitive duties such as those on whisky were reduced, when it was found that the revenue actually increased, since the incentive for smuggling had disappeared. Duties on many raw materials such as wool, cotton, silk, copper, tin, zinc and lead were lowered, and a maximum tariff of 30 per cent of the value of the articles was fixed for imported manufactures. The export of raw wool, hitherto banned, was allowed on payment of a duty of one penny per pound, and the statute forbidding the emigration of skilled artisans, which was very difficult to enforce, was repealed. Only opposition from some manufacturers prevented Huskisson from freeing the export of machinery in 1825; instead, only machinery whose value lay chiefly in the materials of which they were composed, rather than the invention they embodied, could be sent abroad.

Trade with the empire was encouraged by a system of preferential tariffs, whereby colonial products like Australian wool and West Indian rum were allowed into England at lower rates of duty than those from foreign countries. Colonial preference, however, was later abandoned in the movement towards complete free trade, when privileged treatment was impossible. A Reciprocity of Duties Act (1823) enabled ministers to make trade arrangements with foreign countries, and in the next few years several such treaties were made with European countries, and the new South American states, whose independence from Spain Canning, the Foreign Secretary, recognized in 1823.

Huskisson also eased the operation of the Navigation Acts, although he proceeded cautiously as shipowners were worried by the effects of American competition on world shipping routes, and even Adam Smith had defended them on the grounds that they were necessary for the nation's safety, which outweighed any economic disadvantages they might have. In 1825 the colonies were given freedom to trade with all other countries on the same terms as England herself. Restrictions on foreign shipping were modified, and port fees on ships of the United States and Prussia entering British harbours were reduced, in return for similar concessions to British ships entering their ports, but it was not until 1849 that the Navigation Code was finally abandoned.

Besides his measures for encouraging foreign trade, Huskisson as President of the Board of Trade was responsible for the repeal of the Combination Laws in 1824 (see p. 144). He also attempted to replace the 1815 Corn Law by a sliding scale of duties which varied according to the price of corn. In his opinion the Corn Law failed to help the farmers, while in times of shortage they merely caused hardship for the poor. But the bitter opposition of the landed interests brought about his resignation in 1828, although a modified version of his sliding scale was introduced shortly afterwards by the Duke of Wellington.

During the 1830s the Whig governments were preoccupied with the passage of the first Reform Act (1832), and with social and administrative reform. Free Trade only re-appeared as a major issue when trade slumped badly in the early 1840s, and an expansion of international trade became desirable. During Sir Robert Peel's Second Ministry (1841–6) great progress towards Free Trade was made by a systematic reduction of duties. In 1842 those on raw materials were fixed at a maximum of 5 per cent, on partly manufactured goods 12½ per cent, and fully manufactured goods 20 per cent. To balance the loss in revenue an income tax of 7d in the pound on incomes over £150 was re-introduced. In 1845 duties on over five hundred commodities were abolished, including meat, livestock and potatoes. Duties on sugar, cheese and butter were reduced. In 1846 duties on all raw materials except tallow and timber were abolished. The export of machinery was permitted after 1843.

A Select Committee on Import Duties had reported in 1840 that 'On articles of food alone the amount taken from the consumer exceeds the amount of all the other taxes which are levied by the Government'.[3] Peel had done much by his budgets to reduce the cost of food, but the most important food tax, that on imported corn, still remained. The attack on the Corn Laws was mounted by the Anti-Corn Law League, formed in Manchester in 1839. Largely a middle-class organization, the League was led by Richard Cobden, a Manchester cotton manufacturer, and John Bright, a Rochdale carpet manufacturer and Quaker, who saw in the spread of Free Trade the best means of keeping peace between nations. Until 1843 the efforts of the League were confined to the northern industrial areas, where manufacturing industry had fallen upon lean times, but in that year the campaign became national rather than regional. Public meetings, which were often very emotional affairs, where the sufferings of the poor were vividly described, were held up and down the country, and the League soon acquired considerable influence. It benefited enormously from the introduction of penny postage in 1840, which made it possible to circulate cheaply thousands of pamphlets to electors, and from the growth of railways, which enabled its speakers to address meetings in the major towns. Monetary contributions poured in from manufacturers, so that by 1844 the League was spending £1,000 per week.

The chief argument of the Free Traders centred on the unfairness of the Corn Laws, and their irrelevance. Thus Cobden declared in the House of Commons (August 1841):

The bread tax is primarily levied upon the poorer classes; it is a tax, at the lowest estimate, of 40 per cent above the price we should pay if there were a free trade in corn. The report upon the handloom weavers puts down 10/- as the estimated weekly earnings of a family, and states that in all parts of the United Kingdom that will be found to be not an unfair estimate of the earnings of every labourer's family. It moreover states that out of this 10/- each family spends 5/- on bread. The tax of 40 per cent is, therefore, a tax of 2/- upon every labouring man's family earning 10/- a week, or 20 per cent upon their earnings. How does it operate as we proceed upwards in society? The nobleman with an income of £500,000 a year, and whose family consumes no more bread than that of the agricultural labourer, pays less than one halfpenny in every £100. . . . I am sure there is not an honourable Member of the House who would dare to bring in a bill to levy an income tax on all grades of society upon a scale similar to this, and yet I maintain that the bread tax is such a tax, and is levied not for the purposes of the State, but for the benefit of the richest portion of the community.[4]

The Free Traders also forecast that repeal would bring a better deal for the farmers, though here they were on less sure ground, since they neglected to take into account that increased prosperity would bring increased rents, so that there would be little scope for raising the wages of agricultural labourers. Thus Cardwell announced in the House of Commons that the increased prosperity of the country resulting from the repeal of the Corn Laws would benefit the farming community.

A man with 30/- a week would consume more bread, butter, beef, mutton, and other agricultural produce, than a man with 8/- or even 16/- and, when the consumption of agricultural produce was thus increased, the profits of the farmer would be increased likewise, and the condition of the agricultural labourer would be proportionately bettered.[5]

Yet the clearest argument against the Corn Laws came from an agricultural labourer who said: 'I be protected and I be starving.' Protection did not encourage efficient farming, and it is doubtful even if it helped the ordinary farmer, since corn prices still fluctuated seasonally. By 1845 Peel himself had been convinced by the arguments of the Free Traders, so that the maintenance of the Corn Laws depended upon good harvests. If the price of corn was to rise sharply, the demand for the repeal of the Laws would be irresistible. Thus Peel found himself in the unfortunate position of being unable to justify to himself the continued existence of the Corn Laws, yet as leader of the Conservative party, in which the landowning element was very strong, bound by his election promises to uphold them. Although he had modified the Laws in 1842 by

introducing a sliding scale which reduced the level of duties, and encouraged imports of corn, any attempt to do away with them entirely would have split his party.

Peel's hand was forced by events in Ireland. The English harvest of 1845 was poor and, when a disastrous potato blight ruined Ireland's staple crop, there were no home supplies of corn available to send to Ireland. The failure of the potato crop meant an appalling famine in Ireland, as a result of which nearly half a million peasants died of starvation. Drastic measures were urgently needed. Peel tried to convert his cabinet to the idea of repealing the Corn Laws, but failed and resigned. Lord John Russell's attempt to form an alternative government was only half-hearted, for he did not think that a Whig government would be able to overcome the opposition of the House of Lords, and he soon gave up the task. Peel now returned to office, and in 1846 carried through the repeal with

34 *'Peel's Cheap Bread Shop' (Punch, 1846)*

the support of the Whig party and some Conservatives, called Peelites. On the same evening the Protectionists voted with the Whigs against Peel on another issue, forcing Peel to resign. Thus ended his political career; he died in 1850 without regaining office.

Peel justified breaking his party and his election pledges by stating he had put the interests of the community before those of his party. His critics argued that he could have found some means of avoiding complete repeal, but it is unlikely that the Corn Laws could have been resurrected once corn had been imported duty-free. The plain fact is that Peel had changed his mind over the value of the Corn Laws, and in his resignation speech to the House of Commons he said:

It may be that I shall leave a name sometimes remembered with expressions of goodwill in the abodes of those whose lot it is to labour and earn their daily bread by the sweat of their brow, when they shall recruit their strength with abundant and untaxed food.

In the next few years Britain became for all practical purposes a Free Trade country as Gladstone, Chancellor of the Exchequer (1852–5, 1859–66) completed the work of Peel. Gladstone's principles were to raise revenue by small taxes on a few articles in general use, such as tea, sugar, tobacco and spirits, but to abolish duties on all other commodities. In 1853 he removed the duties on soap and cotton yarn and lowered those on tea, cocoa, fruit, eggs and butter. In 1860 the duties on dairy products and fruit were removed. Apart from forty-eight duties kept for purely revenue purposes, the only duties were those on paper and timber; these disappeared in 1861 and 1866 respectively.

The completion of Free Trade marked the triumph of the manufacturer over the landowner, and for a generation, while England's economy was the fastest growing in the world, it remained unchallenged. Free Trade suited the country with a long industrial lead, and one rapidly becoming a nation of town

35 *'The British Lion in 1850; or, the Effects of Free Trade'* (Punch, 1846)

dwellers, who welcomed a policy of cheap food. Thus when the gloomy forecasts that agriculture would be ruined by the repeal of the Corn Laws finally came true after 1875, the interests of the countryside were sacrificed to those of the industrial towns. No serious attempt was made to restore Protection until the beginning of the twentieth century, when industry faced severe competition from foreign manufacturers.

REFERENCES

1   Adam Smith, *The Wealth of Nations*, Vol. II, p. 98.
2   Adam Smith, op. cit., Vol. II, p. 103.
3   John Morley, *The Life of Cobden*, Vol. I.
4   Richard Cobden, *Speeches*.
5   Edward Cardwell, speaking in the House of Commons (February 1846), quoted in Elie Halevy, *History of the English People in the Nineteenth Century*, Vol. 4 (Benn, 1961).

CHAPTER 15
Railways

English society before the coming of factories and railways was very different from our own. Life tended to centre on one's town or village, for few people travelled outside their immediate neighbourhood, and local rather than national issues aroused most interest. There were few large towns, and even the largest, London, could be crossed on foot in a couple of hours. The man on horseback was the fastest means of communication, a fact which had remained unaltered for centuries. The improvements in roads, and the introduction of canals in the eighteenth century, both aimed at increasing the efficiency of the horse, by enabling it to move heavier loads more quickly

and cheaply. Yet by the beginning of the nineteenth century the existing means of transport were inadequate to meet the needs of industry and a rapidly growing population, and some form of mechanical transport was required. The solution was the steam locomotive, which became the symbol of an age for, by revolutionizing communications, it not only enabled industry to develop at a faster rate, but brought about great changes in the structure of society itself.

The history of railways, as we know them today, begins with the opening of the Liverpool to Manchester railway in 1830, but the principle of a railway—of a track constructed

36 Ralph Allen's wagon way, near Bath

for wheeled traffic — was centuries old. Wooden rails, along which crude trucks were manhandled, were used in some German mines by the middle of the sixteenth century, and they were certainly in use in England in 1609, when a wooden wagon-way from Wollaton Colliery, near Nottingham, provided a means of taking coal from the pithead to navigable water. Wagon-ways, or tramways, developed most rapidly in the coal-mining areas of Northumberland and Durham, where they were known as 'Newcastle roads'. Wagonways outside mining areas were rare, and Ralph Allen's wagon-way in his stone quarries at Coombe Down, near Bath, built about 1730, was exceptional. Roger North, who visited coalmines in the Newcastle area in 1680, wrote of 'The laying of rails of timber exactly straight and parallel, whereby the carts fitting these rails are drawn so easily that one horse can draw four or five chaldrons of coal', or approximately five tons. Sometimes thin plates of wrought iron were nailed to the wooden rails to reduce wear. These were called 'plateways', but they caused much wear to the wooden wheels of the carts, and the next improvement was to make the wheels of cast iron. Cast iron rails were first used in 1767 at Coalbrookdale, where the shortage of timber was becoming acute. In 1789 William Jessop used cast-iron 'edge rails', and transferred the flange from the rail to the inner side of the wheel. By 1810 wrought-iron rails were used, and in 1820 the Bedlington type of rail, which became general, was introduced.

Tramways were usually constructed so that they followed the surface of the ground, winding around hills instead of cutting through them. As most of the heavy traffic from collieries went one way the road was made to slope downhill in that direction where possible. The majority of tramways were short and simply constructed, and the Causey Arch, built in 1726, and the Beckley Burn embankment on the Tanfield line, in County Durham, were isolated feats of engineering. Towards the end of the eighteenth century tramroads were built as 'feeders' to canals. Canal companies welcomed them as valuable links with mining areas which could not otherwise be reached, so that coal and iron-ore could be brought down from the high ground to the waterway. Thus the influence of the canal was extended some 15–30 kilometres (10–20 miles) on each side. Railways, however, were unlikely to challenge canals as the chief means of transporting goods until horse traction was replaced by something more efficient, since railways worked by horses had few advantages over canals. Although James Watt's improvement of the steam engine had turned people's attention towards developing steam locomotion, many technical problems had to be solved. The rails broke easily under the weight of the early locomotives, and a high-pressure boiler had to be developed so that the size of the engine could be reduced without any corresponding loss of power.

The first steam carriage was built in 1769 by a Frenchman, Nicolas Cugnot, but it was not very successful. William Murdock, the versatile engineer employed by the firm of Boulton and Watt, also built a steam carriage in 1786, but was discouraged by Watt from proceeding any further. The real originator of the railway locomotive was Richard Trevithick (1771–1833), a Cornishman, who became familiar with the operation of steam engines at an early age. He built two steam road carriages in 1801 and 1803, called dragons by the local folk, and in 1804 designed a locomotive for the Penydarren Ironworks, near Merthyr Tydvil. It hauled a load of fifteen tons at a speed of 8 k.p.h. (5 m.p.h.), but the railway only operated for five months due to frequent breakages of rails, and the engine was put to work driving a steam hammer in the ironworks itself. Trevithick then built another locomotive for Wylam Colliery, near Newcastle, and in 1808 the *Catch Me Who Can*, which ran on a circular track near the site of present-day Euston Station in London. It caused a sensation among the spectators who

37 Tramways in the Newcastle area in the early nineteenth century

paid a shilling to watch it. Trevithick, however, lacked the determination to get his achievement recognized. He went to South America to set up several of his engines in silver mines and, after many adventures, died in Costa Rica in 1833. Meanwhile, the interest of some mine owners had been aroused, and in 1812 John Blenkinsop was commissioned by the proprietor of Middleton Colliery, near Leeds, to design an engine. Blenkinsop refused to believe that smooth wheels could get sufficient grip on smooth rails, so he provided the driving wheel of his locomotive with teeth which fitted into cogs on the rails.

His cog engine could haul a load of 94 tons at an average speed of 5 k.p.h. (3 m.p.h.). Other early pioneer locomotive builders were William Hedley, who made the famous *Puffing Billy*, Timothy Hackworth, and George Stephenson.

Yet the steam locomotive still had to prove itself, and the early railways were made for horsedrawn traffic, though stationary engines were sometimes used as well on steep gradients. Between 1801 and 1825 Parliament sanctioned twenty-one railways. The first public railway, opened in 1804, was the Surrey Iron Railway between Croydon and the

38   *The Sankey Viaduct on the Liverpool to Manchester Railway*

Thames at Wandsworth. It provided a railroad for wagons and carts, which paid tolls as on a turnpike, had towing paths as on a canal, and was the first stage of an intended line between London and Portsmouth. Its 14 kilometres (9 miles) cost £60,000 to build. The first public railway to use steam locomotives was the Stockton to Darlington Railway, authorized by Parliament in 1821 and completed in 1825, though until 1833 horses were the chief method of traction. The adoption of steam power was only seriously considered when Edward Pease, the promoter of the railway, saw one of Stephenson's locomotives working at Killingworth Colliery, and was converted to the idea of the locomotive. A second act of Parliament was therefore obtained, which allowed the company to erect one stationary engine, and to use locomotives for the conveyance of passengers and goods. But the railway was to be available to all who wished to put their carts on it, provided they paid the statutory tolls, and the gauge of the railway,

1·4 metres (4 feet 8½ inches), was the average width of a hundred local farm carts which Stephenson measured.

The success of the Stockton to Darlington Railway encouraged a group of Lancashire businessmen to promote a railway between Liverpool and Manchester. George Stephenson (1781–1848), fresh from his triumphant completion of the Stockton to Darlington line, was made chief engineer at a salary of £1,000 a year. While the line was being made, the directors held a competition to decide whether locomotives were superior to stationary engines, and a prize of £500 was offered to the designer of a locomotive which could successfully complete an exacting series of trials to be held on a section of level track at Rainhill in 1829. Four locomotives were entered: Burstall's *Perseverance*, Hackworth's *Sans Pareil*, Braithwaite's *Novelty*, and Stephenson's *Rocket*. Brandreth's *Cyclopede*, a wagon worked by a horse on a treadmill, was only considered because he was a director of the company, and it was not a serious competitor. The *Rocket* won the prize easily, reaching a speed of 56 k.p.h. (35 m.p.h.). By the time the Duke of Wellington opened the railway in 1830 George Stephenson and his son Robert had built another seven locomotives.

The Liverpool to Manchester Railway marked the beginning of the Railway Age, for it was the first railway to rely on steam locomotives alone. It was immediately successful, though at first many people were fearful of the risks of travelling so fast, or sceptical of the new locomotives. Thomas Creevey, who had a ride on the railway shortly before its opening, wrote:

I had the satisfaction, for I cannot call it a pleasure, of taking a trip of five miles. . . . The quickest motion is to me frightful; it is really flying, and it is impossible to divest yourself of the notion of instant death to all upon the least accident happening.[1]

He was determined that his first ride was also his last. A writer in the *Quarterly Review* commented sourly: 'The gross exaggeration of the powers of the locomotive steam engine may delude for a time, but must end in the mortification of those concerned.'[2] Events soon proved otherwise, however, and Stephenson's confidence in the locomotive was justified.

In 1830 there were fewer than 150 kilometres (100 miles) of railway in England; by 1855 over 13,000 kilometres (8,000 miles) of track had been laid, and the main outlines of the present system had been completed, largely as a result of two boom periods in construction, 1835–6 and 1844–6. The Grand Junction Railway, linking Birmingham with the Manchester to Liverpool Railway, and the London to Birmingham Railway, which was engineered by George Stephenson, were opened in 1838, giving a continuous rail link between London and Liverpool, though since three separate companies were involved, there was no through traffic, and no through rate. The Manchester and Leeds, and the Leeds, Selby

and Hull Railways linked the industrial north from coast to coast. The London and Southampton Railway was opened 1838–40, and the Great Western Railway, built by Isambard Kingdom Brunel (1806–59), linked the capital with Bristol and Taunton. It was completed in 1841. Soon afterwards London was linked with Brighton and Dover, and by the Great Northern Railway with Doncaster. There were also two rail links by the east and west coasts between England and Scotland. The Eastern Counties Railway, however, from London to Ipswich, authorized by Parliament in 1836, had built only 82 kilometres (51 miles) of its track by 1843, and was not completed until 1862, while the slowness of its journeys was a standing joke in *Punch*.

Thus by 1855 nearly all the main lines from London had either been built or planned for much of their length, the only addition being the Great Central, terminating at Marylebone Station, which was opened in 1899. Though the mileage of railways grew steadily during the century, most of the increase was in suburban areas, and in the construction of branch lines. Apart from these, the major alterations to the system were the electrification of important suburban lines, and the development of the London Underground.

In 1883 Sir William Siemens used electric traction in Northern Ireland on a short stretch of railway between Portrush and the Giant's Causeway. By the early years of the twentieth century part of the Manchester railway network, as well as the line between Liverpool and Southport, were electrified. On all main lines, however, the steam locomotive reigned supreme, and the very fast average speeds achieved were not surpassed until the 1930s. The London Underground system began with the Metropolitan Line, opened in 1863, which used steam locomotives in spite of the discomfort for passengers. The first deep-level electric subway came in 1890—the 5 kilometre (3 mile) long City and South London Railway. It was followed by the Central London Railway, or 'Twopenny

Tube' (after its original fare of twopence), in 1900, and by the Bakerloo and Piccadilly Line in 1905. From these beginnings there developed an entire railway grid under London's streets.

At first there was much opposition to the railway. Many landowners, who thought more of the privacy of their estates than the public good, were convinced that railways crossing their land would ruin their estates, and large sums of money were often paid to landowners reluctant to sell. One landowner on the London to Birmingham route sold a small strip of his park for £30,000, which was the value of his entire estate. Soon afterwards he obtained a similar amount from a different company for another corner of his land. It has been estimated that land cost £630 per mile on the London to Birmingham line, and £3,000 on the London to Brighton line. Farmers near large towns feared that food would be brought in more cheaply from out-lying districts. The magazine *John Bull* attacked the railways on several grounds. They were dangerous, and they ruined the countryside; they frightened cattle and hens, killed birds with their smoke, and set cornfields and houses on fire with their sparks. Turnpike trusts and canal companies, and stagecoaching firms, were naturally opposed to a rival transport system which would capture their business. The tolls on the various turnpikes between London and Birmingham for the first year after the opening of the railway amounted to £16,000, compared with £28,000 for 1836, while railways often competed directly with canals, so that many were forced to slash their rates, sometimes by as much as half.

A number of towns refused the railway companies permission to pass through them. The Five Towns of the Potteries thought themselves already well served with com-munications; Northampton did not wish to be the site of Brunel's railway workshops, which were built instead at Wolverton. For many years Oxford University prevented the railway from coming any closer than Didcot, while Eton College forced Brunel to make a three-mile detour when he laid down the track of the Great Western Railway. The Duke of Wellington did not welcome railways since they would encourage the lower classes to move about. Sabbatarians objected to Sunday travel, others thought that people would be encouraged to ride around the countryside in-stead of working. Yet the advantages of rail-ways were so obvious that nothing could halt their growth, and by 1855 over £300 million had been invested in them.

Railways grew bit by bit, since at first Parliament considered each proposed line on its merits, with little thought for a planned national network of railways. Parliament's chief concern was to act as a watchdog to en-sure that other interests, such as landowners, canal companies, towns, and businesses, were not unfairly harmed, and to uphold the principle of competition, so that railway com-panies could not abuse their position. Parlia-ment therefore tried to make the railway available for use to anyone who paid the required toll, but it was soon clear that no railway company could operate efficiently if private individuals could put their own carriages on the line at will. Thus Parliament was forced to recognize that competition on the same line was impracticable, and that each company was bound to have a monopoly over its own route.

Once railway companies controlled their own track, fierce competition developed between them. Rates and fares were forced down, but soon rival companies either secretly agreed to fix their charges, or they amalga-mated, that is to say one railway bought up another, and combined its track with its own. It was George Hudson, who began his career as a linen draper in York, who first fully understood the importance of amalgamation as a means of increasing the efficiency of rail-ways. In 1844 he carried through the first big amalgamation in railway history when he formed the Midland Railway from three companies—the North Midland, the Midland

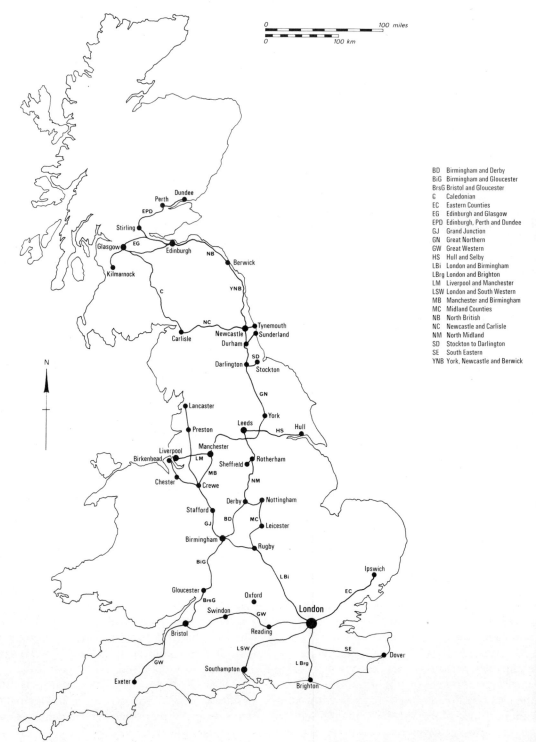

BD   Birmingham and Derby
BiG   Birmingham and Gloucester
BrsG Bristol and Gloucester
G   Caledonian
EC   Eastern Counties
EG   Edinburgh and Glasgow
EPD   Edinburgh, Perth and Dundee
GJ   Grand Junction
GN   Great Northern
GW   Great Western
HS   Hull and Selby
LBi   London and Birmingham
LBrg London and Brighton
LM   Liverpool and Manchester
LSW   London and South Western
MB   Manchester and Birmingham
MC   Midland Counties
NB   North British
NC   Newcastle and Carlisle
NM   North Midland
SD   Stockton to Darlington
SE   South Eastern
YNB   York, Newcastle and Berwick

39 Chief railways in Britain in 1850

Counties, and the Birmingham and Derby Railways. Hudson bought shares in several railways, and effectively founded the North Eastern Railway, so that he eventually controlled much of the railway network in the North and Midlands. *Punch* even pictured Hudson, the speculator and 'Railway King', holding court, but many of his schemes were either unsound or dishonest. He managed to hide the truth for a while by paying shareholders dividends from money raised to promote new companies, but in 1849 his bogus dealings were discovered, and he was disgraced. Yet, although thousands of people who had invested their savings in Hudson's companies were ruined, it should be remembered that he was responsible for many hundreds of miles of railway.

In general Parliament's policy over amalgamation was to allow 'end-on' amalgamations, but to prevent one company from getting a monopoly of transport in an entire region. In 1846–7 several important amalgamations were permitted. The Manchester, Sheffield and

40   *The Battle of Clifton Junction, 1849*
Company employees block the track at Clifton. The quarrel arose over the toll levied by the Lancashire and Yorkshire Railway for allowing the East Lancashire Railway to use part of its track for their Bury to Manchester trains

Lincolnshire Railway was formed from five companies, and the Lancashire and Yorkshire Railway from six. The most important amalgamation was that of the Liverpool to Manchester, the Grand Junction, and the London to Birmingham Railways, to form the London and North Western Railway. Mark Huish, who was appointed manager of the LNWR tried to extend the influence of his railway into what he called 'enemy territory', by using violence, threats, and cuts in rates and fares to force his rivals to submit. Many smaller lines were amalgamated with the LNWR, which became known as 'Huish's Confederacy'.

Parliament's concern with railway development was shown in many other ways. In 1838 the carriage of mails by rail was regulated. An act of 1840 dealt mainly with safety, and in 1842 the Railway Clearing House was set up. This coordinated through traffic over the lines of different companies, and decided upon a fair division of rates and fares. Gladstone's Railway Act of 1844, the Cheap Trains Act, made each company run at least one train daily over its lines, at an average speed of 19 k.p.h. (12 m.p.h.), stopping at every station, and charging a penny a mile. The 'parliamentary trains' were notorious for their slowness and inconvenience, but they still provided a faster and cheaper service than the quickest stage coach. The 1844 Act also made provision for the nationalization, after twenty-one years, of railways built from that date, but the proposal, when it was considered in 1865, was rejected.

In 1845 a government commission inquired into the merits of the two gauges in use, since once railways began to link up with each other a standard gauge was necessary. Brunel emphasized that the GWR's broad gauge of 2 metres (7 feet) permitted very fast speeds with safety. The supporters of the narrow gauge of 1·4 metres (4 feet 8½ inches) stressed its convenience; it was easier to narrow track than widen it, and 3,059 kilometres (1,901 miles) of narrow gauge had been laid, compared

with 441 kilometres (274 miles) of broad-gauge track. The Gauge Act of 1846 prohibited the extension of the broad gauge except in GWR territory. A third rail enabled ordinary trains to use the Great Western lines. The company in 1872 started to change over to the narrow gauge, but the process was not completed until 1892. Railway legislation figured prominently in parliamentary business, and numerous acts dealing with such matters as safety regulations, signalling, and hours and conditions of work appeared at frequent intervals during the rest of the century.

Not only legislation, but also increased competition among the major companies, especially after 1870, influenced railway development in this country. As railway services multiplied and fast average speeds became usual, brakes and signalling were improved. The block system of signalling, whereby the line was divided into sections, and only one train at a time allowed into the block, was introduced in 1840. It was made compulsory in 1899 after a dreadful accident in Northern Ireland. At the same time all trains had to be fitted with continuous brakes. Steel rails replaced iron ones after 1870. As the habit of travelling by rail spread through all classes of society, the railway companies competed for the largest share of passenger revenue by providing greater comfort on their trains. The Midland Railway led the way in 1872 by introducing third-class carriages on its express trains. In 1875 it abolished second-class carriages on its trains, and by making its third-class as good as its old second, forced the other companies to follow suit. Sleeping cars appeared in 1873, luxurious pullmans in 1876, and dining cars in 1880. Steam heating of carriages was introduced in 1884, though this was not general until 1910, and in 1892 corridor trains with toilets came into service.

By the end of the nineteenth century railways were at their peak, and had become part of English life. They offered new jobs such as engine driver, signalman, stationmaster, and porter. In the boom period of construction,

41   *Work in progress on the entrance to Edgehill Tunnel, on the*
Liverpool and Manchester Railway

which really did not slacken until the 1880s, they gave employment to thousands of 'navvies' who dug the tunnels and cuttings, and laid the track. The isolation of the remoter parts of the country was gradually broken down. Farmers benefited from wider markets for their perishable goods. Fresh milk, meat, fruit, and vegetables found a ready sale in the growing towns and cities.

The development of towns in the nineteenth century was due largely to railways. In the 1860s only the wealthy lived in suburbs, but with the introduction of cheap workmen's tickets in 1883 the better paid workmen could live in a suburb, and travel to work by train. The upper and middle classes moved further out into the countryside, so that villages near the major cities grew into towns, and existing towns and cities began to sprawl into the countryside now that large concentrations of

people could be adequately fed, clothed, and housed. Railways could supply all their needs in a way no other form of transport had been able to do.

Railways created new towns and revived old ones. Several towns, such as Crewe, Swindon, and Rugby, grew up at railway junctions, while decayed river ports like Gloucester and Chester were given a new lease of life by the power of the railway to attract commerce and industry. Holiday resorts such as Clacton and Scarborough, Blackpool and Brighton, were creations of the railway for, though the practice of taking seaside holidays preceded railways, it was rail travel which made it possible for large numbers of people to go on day excursions. The practice of taking annual holidays away from home became quite common. Thus social habits were altered by the railway. Even the rise of organized sport, and the growth of the public schools owed much to the ease of travel as a result of the railway network.

Railways created new businesses and destroyed some old ones. Rails, locomotives, rolling stock, and engineering equipment became important exports as British contractors such as the firm of Brassey, contractors to the Grand Trunk Railway of Canada, built railways in four continents. The iron, metallurgical and engineering industries, and coalmining boomed. Between 1840 and 1882 coal and iron production increased five and sixfold respectively. On the other hand the coaching industry soon expired. Within two years of the completion of the Great Western Railway the last stage coach left London for Bristol, and with the disappearance of stage coaches the traditional English inn fell upon hard times until it was revived by the motor car. The canal system decayed, and holders of canal stock found their income dwindling. But in an overwhelming number of cases railways were a boon to industry and trade. Factories no longer had to be located on coalfields when coal could be carried cheaply from the mines. Railways encouraged local specialization by providing good communications between one district and another. Manufacturers found ideal sites by the side of railways for their new factories. Freight rates were lowered, so that costs of production fell, and the competitive position of manufacturers selling goods overseas was strengthened. The conduct of business was accelerated when mail and goods were carried by rail, and traders no longer had to carry large stocks when they were assured of speedy and punctual delivery of orders.

Finally, railways altered the English landscape itself. Impressive bridges spanned rivers. Notable examples are Robert Stephenson's High Level Bridge at Newcastle and the Victoria Bridge at Berwick-upon-Tweed, and Isambard Kingdom Brunel's Royal Albert Bridge across the Tamar from Devon to Cornwall. Main-line terminals like Charing Cross and Cannon Street Stations, built by Sir John Hawkshaw, and Temple Meads in Bristol, added dignity and grandeur to cities. The main routes and branch lines threaded their way across the countryside, like the arteries and veins of the human body, and played a similarly vital role in the nation's life.

REFERENCES

1   *The Creevey Papers* (ed. Sir Herbert Maxwell), Vol. II, quoted from *English Historical Documents 1783–1832*, ed. A. Aspinall and E. A. Smith (Eyre & Spottiswoode, 1969).
2   *The Quarterly Review*, March 1825, quoted from *English Historical Documents 1783–1832*, ed. A. Aspinall and E. A. Smith (Eyre & Spottiswoode, 1969).

CHAPTER 16
Steam Shipping

The early development of the steamship coincided with that of the steam locomotive, but whereas the railway quickly proved its supremacy over other forms of land transport, the steamship's conquest of sea routes took longer. The first steamships consumed vast quantities of coal so that little room was left for passengers or cargo. Refuelling locomotives presented little difficulty, but coaling stations had to be established at strategic points around the world, such as Gibraltar, Capetown, Aden and Singapore, before the supremacy of the steamship was assured. In the meantime, where speed was important in carrying cargoes, clippers, fast, iron-hulled sailing ships which brought the tea crop from China, and Australian wool to London, dominated the ocean routes during the 1850s and 1860s. Where it was unimportant, as in the grain trade, the ordinary sailing ship was widely used until the 1880s. Yet by 1900, as a result of the development of the compound and triple-expansion marine engines, the steamship had virtually ousted the sailing ship from the world's shipping lanes.

The earliest mention of an English steam-driven vessel was Jonathan Hulls's vague specification for a 'machine for carrying vessels or ships out of or into any harbour, port or river, against wind or tide, or in calm'.[1] The next stage in the development of the iron steamship was reached in 1787, when John Wilkinson, a Shropshire ironmaster, launched on the river Severn a boat made entirely of iron. Wilkinson wrote that 'it answers all my expectations and has convinced the unbelievers, who were 999 in 1,000',[2] but his achievement was premature, for little progress was made in developing iron ships for over half a century. In 1788, however,

William Symington, a Scottish engineer, built a wooden boat driven by a Watt steam engine. By 1801, when he launched his *Charlotte Dundas* on the Forth–Clyde Canal, Symington had proved that steam navigation was a commercial proposition, for it towed two barges 31 kilometres (19 miles) at a speed of $5\frac{1}{2}$ k.p.h. ($3\frac{1}{2}$ m.p.h.). Symington's experiment was watched with great interest by a young American, Robert Fulton, who returned to the United States to build steamships. In 1807 his *Clermont*, which plied between New York and Albany, opened the world's first passenger steam service. Meanwhile, Symington had been forced to discontinue his experiment because his patron, Lord Dundas, had withdrawn his financial support when the management of the Forth–Clyde Canal had announced that the wash created by steamships would wear away the banks of the canal. The next steamboat built in Britain was Henry Bell's *Comet*, launched on the river Clyde in 1811. In 1813 several steamships carried passengers between Glasgow and Greenock on the Clyde, and in England the first passenger steamship service began between Bristol and Bath on the river Avon. Steamships made rapid progress now. In 1816 a daily service began operating between Holyhead and Dublin, the journey taking seven hours, and steamships were common sights on many important rivers, and around the coasts of Britain. By 1821 there was a regular cross-Channel service, and in 1827 232 British steamboats were registered.

In 1819 an American steamer, the *Savannah*, made the first Atlantic crossing, but she used her paddles for a total of only $3\frac{1}{2}$ days in a voyage lasting 27 days. The first Atlantic crossing made wholly under steam power was by a Canadian vessel, the *Royal William*, in 1833. The first by a steamship built in England was by the *Sirius* in 1838, which sailed from Cork to New York in 19 days, narrowly beating Brunel's paddle-driven steamship, the *Great Western*, which arrived a few hours later, after a 15-day voyage from Bristol. The achievement of the *Great Western* marked the inauguration of a new, fast, reliable and comfortable method of travel between the Old World and the New, and in the next eight years the *Great Western* crossed the Atlantic 67 times. In 1840 Samuel Cunard won a government contract to carry the mails between England and North America, and he set up a steamship company called the British and North American Royal Mail Steam Packets, which later became better known as the Cunard Line. The *Britannia*, one of four wooden paddle steamers built by the company

under government supervision, became the first *Cunarder* when she set out from Liverpool on 4 July 1840.

So far most steamships had been made of wood. An ironmaster, Aaron Manby, had built in 1822 an iron steamship which he named after himself, but although he built several others which operated successfully on French rivers, his ideas were not adopted in Britain. Iron ships were still in the experimental stage, and shipowners were reluctant to spend large sums on a new kind of ship before it had proved its worth. The superiority of the iron ship, however, became evident in 1844 when Brunel's *Great Britain*, with a displacement of 3,600 tons, became the first iron ship to cross the Atlantic.

Isambard Kingdom Brunel was one of the outstanding engineers of the nineteenth century. Besides constructing docks, harbours,

42   The Great Britain *iron steam ship*
With a length of 190 metres (324 feet), the Great Britain *was 30 metres*
(100 feet) longer than the biggest warship of the time

bridges (notably the Clifton Suspension Bridge spanning the Avon Gorge), and railways, he also built the largest steamships of his time. Brunel was a remarkable man, intensely ambitious, and a visionary. The fact that he was in advance of his time accounts in part for his failures. His atmospheric railway in South Devon, where trains were drawn along at speeds of 115 k.p.h. (70 m.p.h.) by a suction method instead of locomotives, was a costly failure. This railway was worked by stationary engines which pumped the air from a continuous pipe laid along the track. The vacuum created was sufficiently powerful to pull at great speeds a piston which was attached to the train. Rats and sea air, however, destroyed the leather flaps which sealed the gap in the pipe along which the piston travelled, and the system proved unworkable. The docks which he built at Milford Haven also never fulfilled his prophecy that they would rival the port of Liverpool. One vision, however, did come true. When the proposed GWR was under consideration, one of the directors expressed his anxiety over the great length of the route. Brunel countered with the suggestion 'Why not make it longer and have a steamboat go from Bristol to New York, and call it the Great Western?'[3] His suggestion was taken seriously by Thomas Guppy, and the outcome of this remark was the formation of the Great Western Steamship Company.

After the *Great Western* and the *Great Britain* had been successfully completed, Brunel began work on the *Great Eastern*, which was five times larger than any ship afloat. Over 200 metres (680 feet) long, and built entirely of iron, she was driven by screw and paddlewheels, and on her maiden crossing of the Atlantic in 1860, she carried 4,000 passengers at an average speed of 14 knots. Unfortunately, the volume of transatlantic traffic was not enough to make the *Great Eastern* a commercial success, and she was converted into a cable-laying ship. In 1866 she laid the transatlantic cable where an earlier

attempt had failed, and she followed this up by laying a network of cables around the world, from France to America, and from England to India, via the Cape of Good Hope and Aden. Her cable-laying days over, she ended up as a showboat on the river Mersey.

The period 1860–80 was the great age of the iron ship, which had several important advantages over the wooden ship. There was less risk of fire, and the substitution of 13 mm ($\frac{1}{2}$ inch) iron plates for 305 mm (12 inch) oak hulls gave a saving in weight of one-third as well as greater cargo space. After 1880, when cheap steel was available as a result of the inventions of Bessemer and Gilchrist–Thomas (see below, Chapter 18), iron was replaced by steel, which was lighter still. Meanwhile, the shipbuilding industry of the sheltered south coast of England declined as the industry concentrated in the North, especially on Merseyside, Tyneside, Clydeside, and Barrow, where the presence of coalfields, iron and steel works, and their associated engineering trades enabled Britain to maintain her position as the world's chief shipbuilder until after the First World War.

Technical progress was rapid after the middle of the nineteenth century. The inefficient paddle-wheel was replaced by the screw which was always under water, whereas in stormy weather one paddle-wheel was out of the water as the ship rolled from side to side. The introduction of Lord Dundonald's tubular boiler in 1848, and steel boilers in 1856, allowed higher steam pressures to be produced consistent with safety. In 1854 John Elder invented a compound marine engine which required only one-third of the amount of fuel consumed by a simple steam engine. The compound engine was further improved by the development of a triple-expansion marine engine, first used on the *Aberdeen* in 1881. Together with the opening of the Suez Canal (1869), which greatly shortened the voyage from Europe to India and the Far East, but which could not be used by sailing ships because of navigational problems, it assured the triumph of steam over sail. The percentage of steam shipping compared with sail jumped from 20 per cent in 1860 to 70 per cent in 1880; by 1900 it was 90 per cent. The steam turbine engine, which had no pistons or cylinders since it worked on the principle of a jet of steam directed on to rotor blades, was first developed by Sir Charles Parsons in 1884. Ten years later the turbine was used in marine propulsion, when it powered Parson's vessel, the *Turbinia*. The Royal Navy remained sceptical of his achievement until Parsons demonstrated beyond question the superiority of the steam turbine over other forms of marine propulsion. At the Spithead Review celebrating the Diamond Jubilee of Queen Victoria's reign in 1897 Parsons cruised the *Turbinia* at 34 knots between the lanes of battleships. It proved too fast for a destroyer sent to intercept her, and shortly afterwards the Navy adopted the turbine for use in its ships. The diesel engine, invented by a German engineer, was first used in 1912. Oil was a more efficient fuel than coal, and before 1914 the Royal Navy began to convert from coal to oil-burning ships. Steamships also increased in size and speed. In 1850 ships of over 1,000 tons were unusual; by 1914 10,000 tons was common. The passenger liner *Mauretania* weighed 32,000 tons, and the ill-fated *Titanic* over 60,000 tons. The Cunard liners *Queen Mary* and the *Queen Elizabeth*, launched in 1934 and 1940 respectively, each had displacements of over 80,000 tons, a figure which has only been exceeded by oil tankers in very recent years.

REFERENCES

1   Jonathan Hulls, *A Description and Draught of a new-invented Machine for carrying Vessels or Ships out of, or into, any Harbour, Port, or River, against Wind and Tide, or in a calm* (1736).

2   Letter to Stockdale, quoted in Samuel Smiles, *Lives of Boulton and Watt*.

3   L. T. C. Rolt, *Isambard Kingdom Brunel* (Longmans, 1957).

CHAPTER 17
Farming from Prosperity to Depression 1830–80

When Queen Victoria ascended the throne in 1837 there were signs that farming had recovered from the slump that had followed the Napoleonic Wars. Inefficient farmers had been eliminated by the hard times after Waterloo, and agricultural machinery was more widely used. The Royal Agricultural Society, founded in 1838, encouraged more scientific farming. The latest results of scientific research in farming matters were published in its *Journal*, and local branches were formed in many parts of the country. The enclosure of open fields continued, though the enclosure acts of 1836 and 1845 did something to safeguard the few remaining commons and open stretches of countryside. By 1850 the open-field system had almost completely disappeared. In 1834 the Speenhamland system of outdoor relief had been abolished, and the poor rate, paid by owners of land, fell from £7 million to £4 million within three years.

The 1840s saw the beginnings of 'high farming', the golden age of British agriculture, which lasted until the middle 1870s. During this period British farming became the most advanced in Europe. Even the repeal of the Corn Laws in 1846 had little immediate impact. Landowners who prophesied that the end of Protection would ruin agriculture failed to realize that as long as the farmer had the advantage of being close to his market, he could meet the growing demand for wheat, mutton and beef without fear of foreign competition. Railways carried his produce to the towns rapidly and cheaply, and brought his supplies of cattle feed, fertilizer and machinery. As well as employing many thousands of men, the construction of railways stimulated most industries, and farmers benefited from the general rise in prosperity,

as people spent more on buying food.

As agriculture prospered, the farmer became more interested in increasing the milk yield of his dairy herds, the weight of his sheep and cattle, as well as the productivity of his arable land. Livestock was improved by breeders such as Thomas Bates of Kirklevington and Sir Charles Knightley. The Clydesdale cart-horse took the place of teams of oxen, though oxen were still used for farmwork until the end of the nineteenth century. Drainage was used more extensively. The traditional practice of ridging the land so that the furrows acted as surface drains washed away the tilth, while the drainage ditches of Essex and Suffolk were hardly known in other parts of the country. James Smith of Perthshire in 1823 popularized the use of trenches filled with stones and covered over with soil. In 1843 clay pipes were used instead, and two years later Thomas Scragg patented a pipe-making machine which cheapened and increased the output of the kilns.

Justus Liebig, a German scientist, had shown the relationship between plant nutrition and soil composition, and his work was continued by Sir John Lawes and Sir Henry Gilbert of the Rothamsted Experimental Station, built in 1842. They showed that heavy crops could be grown using artificial fertilizers. Peruvian guano, nitrate of soda, and superphosphates came into common usage. This encouraged clean farming, for money spent on manuring badly drained land, or weed-infested land, was wasted. The Gang System, whereby gangs of men, women and children were hired out to farmers, meant cheap and plentiful labour, so that machinery was only slowly introduced, but better ploughs, harrows, drills, reapers, and threshing machines appeared on farms

43   The 'Newbus Ox'
Mere size of animals was highly prized by nineteenth-century farmers

throughout this period. Patrick Bell's reaper, invented in 1826, was improved and in use after 1853. By 1860 threshing machines which dressed and graded grain into sacks were available, and in the 1870s a self-binding device was added to the earliest combine harvester, which developed out of the McCormick reaper. Steam ploughing, pioneered by John Fowler of Leeds, was sometimes used on large fields. Two traction engines placed at opposite ends of the field pulled the plough backwards and forwards. Thus English farming in 1870 compared very favourably with that of continental European countries. The land was more productive than it had ever been, and capital investment in the land, buildings and machinery had been on a large scale.

Yet, if landlord and farmer prospered, one class, the agricultural labourer, failed to share in the rising prosperity. With a rapidly growing population there was a surplus of labour in the countryside, and the poorly paid labourer was forced to exploit the earning capacity of his wife and children, even though he depressed his own wages by doing so. There was neither the need nor the incentive for a farmer to pay higher wages, as the Report on Agriculture in 1867 pointed out. 'It is difficult to expect the landlord to lower his rent in the face of an increasing demand for land, and to expect the occupier to raise wages in the face of an increasing demand for rent.' Rents only fell when agriculture was depressed, and then the farmer could not afford to pay higher wages. In the North, where labourers were hired for a year at a time, wages were relatively high owing to the competition of industry for hands, and the labourer's diet was more varied than in the rural areas of southern England where the staple diet was bread and potatoes. A farm labourer's wife in Somerset told commissioners:

Sometimes when cheap we buy half a pound of butter a week, but most frequently fat which we use with the potatoes to give them a flavour. . . . We never know what it is to get enough to eat, at the end of the meal the children would always eat more.

Farm labourers were unable to exert much influence on farmers to pay higher wages. Trade unions were formed in Buckinghamshire and Hertfordshire in the 1860s, but it was difficult to organize effectively farm labourers scattered over several counties. The clergy often sided with the farmers, and the Poor Law guardians were known to refuse relief to union members. Eventually, in 1872, Joseph Arch succeeded in forming a national union which obtained an increase in wages, but both the union and the increase were destroyed by the depression which hit agriculture after 1875 (see also p. 147).

In 1870 over 5 million hectares (13 million acres) were under tillage, an area never exceeded in the history of British farming. Four-fifths of the food consumed was produced in this country. The farmers anticipated a long period of prosperity for, while the demand for food would rise as the population grew, it appeared that output had reached maximum efficiency, so food prices would rise too. Yet this was not to be. Farming suffered from the periodic slumps which affected the industrial nations of Europe, as well as from bad weather and outbreaks of cattle disease. Several million sheep were destroyed by liver rot in 1879, the wettest summer on record, and there was a terrible epidemic of foot and mouth disease in 1883. Bad weather and cattle disease, however, tended to hide the real reason for the growing malaise of English farming. After the late 1870s farmers no longer profited from shortages. Imported foodstuffs from regions unaffected by bad weather prevented the English farmer from getting high prices for what little he had harvested.

The original cause of the farmer's misfortune was the invasion of grain from North

44 Threshing by steam-driven machinery still required much labour

45   The American grain elevator on the Thames at Woolwich was a symbol of foreign competition for the British farmer

America. This was due chiefly to steam shipping, and the expansion of railways in the United States from 50,000 kilometres (31,000 miles) in 1860, to 150,000 kilometres (94,000 miles) in 1880, which opened up the West to settlement. Wheat was soon grown on a vast scale and at low cost in the virgin prairies, where abundant harvests could be obtained without the use of fertilizers, and farm machinery such as combine harvesters could be used to maximum efficiency. Distance now afforded the English farmer no protection, for the wheat could easily be transported cheaply by rail and steamship to England, where it was allowed in free of duty. The price of home-grown grain tumbled from 56/- a quarter (13 kilograms) in 1877 to 31/- in 1886. By the end of the century English farmers only grew enough grain to meet the population's requirements for two days of the week, and England as a result became dependent on imported cereals.

No sooner had many farmers begun to switch over to pastoral farming than foreign competition was felt as a result of the development of refrigerated sea transport. In 1875 meat chilled by blocks of ice was shipped successfully from New York to London. In 1882 the steamship *Dunedin* docked in London, having brought the first cargo of frozen mutton from New Zealand to Britain. Imports of mutton rose from 9 million kilograms (181,000 hundredweight) in 1882 to 178 million kilograms ($3\frac{1}{2}$ million hundredweight) in 1899, while beef arrived in increasing quantities from Argentina and North America. Fortunately for the English farmer, the effect of meat imports was not nearly so disastrous as grain. Beef prices dropped only $1\frac{1}{2}$d per pound, and mutton by 2d. Refrigeration also enabled farmers in America, Canada, Australia, and South Africa to export fruit to England.

The value of land fell as tenant farmers and landlords struggled to survive. A Royal Commission pointed out that while costs of production had risen, the value of crops had been halved. The standard of English farming remained high, but confidence had been shaken, and enterprise was lacking. Capital investment in the land slowed down. Fences, ditches, and buildings were neglected. Rents fell, and the wages of farm labourers were depressed. During the decade 1871–81 92,000 fewer labourers were employed in farming, which ceased to be the largest industry. By 1911 there were more coal miners than farm workers, as within a generation 300,000 men deserted the countryside. In a second crisis (1891–4), the price of grain dropped to 23/- a quarter (13 kilograms), and the acreage of wheat declined still further.

The downfall of English farming was the price paid for Britain being the workshop of the world. Parliament could do little to restore farming to its earlier prosperity so long as it refused to protect agriculture. The town workers, who were in a majority, had been given the vote in 1867, and neither of the great political parties was willing to ignore their desire for cheap food. Nor did factory owners wish to see pressure for wage increases grow as a consequence of dearer food. When the farm labourer won the vote in 1884 it was too late to alter the attitude of the Government.

On 1 May 1851 troops and 6,000 extra police stood by in London awaiting an expected invasion of the capital, as the first of 6 million people flocked to see the Great Exhibition in Hyde Park. For a real fear existed that the crowds of ordinary working folk brought by railways from the grimy, overcrowded cities of the industrial North and Midlands would be so angered by all the signs of wealth they saw about them, that they would end up by pillaging the residential areas of the rich in and around Hyde Park.

There were objections too from sources other than those who feared disturbances. It was Prince Albert, the President of the Royal Society of the Arts, who had suggested that an exhibition of manufactures similar to those which had taken place in Paris, be held in London. But Prince Albert's German background, and the unpopularity of the Monarchy at the time, drew down criticism upon the scheme. An exhibition, where all countries could display their products, would be good propaganda for the Free Traders, and it was therefore opposed by the Protectionists. Not least, there was much argument over the

46 'Going to the Exhibition'

proposed site and design of the building which would house the exhibition.

Parliament finally approved the site in Hyde Park, but two hundred and forty suggested designs were rejected by the Royal Commission responsible for organizing the exhibition before Joseph Paxton's plan of a huge, glass, domed palace was accepted. Paxton was the talented chief gardener at Chatsworth House, the stately home of the Duke of Devonshire. He was quite a remarkable man, with varied business interests in railways and engineering. One day, when Paxton was in London discussing railway matters with a Mr Ellis, an M.P., he expressed his doubts whether the proposed building for the Great Exhibition would be suitable, and spoke of his own ideas. Ellis, who was involved in the planning stages of the exhibition, at once took him round to see Lord Granville, the chairman of the Commission, whereupon Paxton was given ten days' grace in which to present his plans.

Paxton's design was highly original. The building, which was to be called the *Crystal Palace*, was really a giant, prefabricated greenhouse. It had the merit that the thousands of standardized parts could be manufactured in different places, and assembled quickly on the spot. The work of construction took only four months to complete.

The framework of the building, which could be seen from afar by visitors as they approached, was made of iron, the metal of the age. The walls and roof were composed of nearly 90,000 square metres (1 million square feet) of glass, which protected the exhibits from the weather. Inside the building, for the price of 1/-, visitors could see the finest products of British manufacturers and craftsmen, as well as exhibits from the empire and many other parts of the world. There were over 14,000 exhibitors, whose goods illustrated the manufacturing ingenuity of Man. Every variety of textile was on display. Wedgwood pottery, Black Country metal goods, artistic glassware mingled with jewelry,

Persian carpets, French lace and tapestry, precious metals, and Canadian timber and furs. Nasmyth's steam hammer, manufacturing machinery of all kinds, and a thirty-ton locomotive capable of travelling 95 k.p.h. (60 m.p.h.) illustrated the development of steam power. From the United States came the McCormick reaper, the Colt revolver, and mining prospectors' equipment from the recently discovered goldfield in California. The latest products of science, such as Ross's great telescope, Wheatstone's telegraph, aerial balloons, and photographic equipment, pointed towards a continuing era of scientific discovery and achievement.

The Exhibition was an outstanding success. It was estimated that 17 per cent of the population visited it. There were none of the feared disturbances. The *humbler orders*, as *The Times* referred to the working classes, paid their shillings, viewed the exhibits, many of which they themselves had helped to make, and left London quietly, well satisfied with their day's trip. For the Victorian middle classes, the Exhibition symbolized the immense confidence they had, not only in themselves, but in Britain's future as a manufacturing nation.

The date of the Great Exhibition coincided almost exactly with the middle of a period of about half a century (1830–80), when Britain could unquestionably be called the *Workshop of the World*. What had made this possible?

Britain had good supplies of coal and iron, the two most important commodities of the age. Her working population was skilled and adaptable, and the industrial developments of the previous century had put her well to the fore in the race towards industrialization. Her banking facilities were the best in the world. Concentration upon the production of basic necessities such as clothing, the means of transport (ships and railway rolling stock), coal (the essential fuel of the age), and iron (the most important metal), all contributed to her success as a manufacturing and trading nation. When this was combined with staggering advances in the quantity and quality of the

47 View of the Exhibition

goods she produced, Britain was easily able to exploit the world demand for her products by underselling all her competitors. From Britain's shores flowed a steady stream of manufactures and coal, in return for which she received foodstuffs and raw materials.

The rapid expansion of Britain's economy during this period was also aided by the improvements in internal transport, which speeded up the distribution of goods, encouraged the growth of towns and local specialization, and cheapened the costs of production. Britain in 1850 had 10,000 kilometres (6,000 miles) of railway, a figure which was more than doubled in the next twenty years. Railway construction in Europe, America, and India also provided ample opportunities for investment, and exports of locomotives, rolling stock, and rails.

International trade was growing rapidly. This meant that more ships and shipping services were needed, both of which Britain was in an excellent position to provide. The gold discoveries in California in 1849, and Australia in 1851, increased the world's supply of money, thereby promoting trade. Britain's pursuit of a policy of Free Trade also prompted the expansion of world trade, by encouraging other countries to lower their customs barriers. Gladstone's tariff reforms of 1853 and 1860 left only fifteen important duties, and British manufacturers applauded .the idea of equal trading opportunities for all nations, knowing that this would secure Britain the lion's share of world trade. In addition, the empire and colonies readily accepted one quarter of Britain's exports. The manufacturers also had a large home market as a base from which to operate, due to a rising population, whose purchasing power, except in brief periods of depression, grew each year.

Britain's industrial supremacy in the nineteenth century was based upon four major industries: iron and steel, engineering, textiles, and coal. During this period the iron and steel industries underwent great technical changes. The larger blast furnaces built to meet the growing demand for iron in the first half of the century required more powerful draughts of air to bring about efficient combustion of the fuel. In 1828 John Neilson (1792–1865), the manager of Glasgow Gas Works, persuaded the Clyde Iron Works to give his idea of a hot blast a trial. It was at once discovered that a pre-heated blast of air halved the amount of coal used in the furnace. Later, the hot waste gases from the furnace were used to heat the blast, thus making a further saving in fuel. Scottish pig iron production rose dramatically. In England, where coal was very cheap, there was less interest shown in adopting the process, until ironmasters had learned from the experience of their Scottish counterparts.

Another milestone in the development of the iron industry was the invention of the steam hammer in 1839 by James Nasmyth (1808–90), a Scottish engineer. When Brunel was building his revolutionary steamship, the *Great Britain*, it was found that the traditional

48   *The steam hammer*

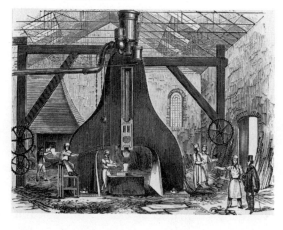

tilt hammer used for large-scale forging was not powerful enough to forge the paddle shaft. Nasmyth's advice was asked, and he designed a steam hammer. It could deliver such tremendous blows that a special pad had to be provided to prevent structural damage to the building which housed it, but was so accurate in its operation that it could just crack an eggshell. The large-scale manufacture of the great iron bars and girders needed for bridges, steamships, and railways was now possible.

Progress in the iron industry, however, was far outweighed in importance by successive discoveries of methods of making steel cheaply and in quantity. In spite of increasing demand, steel manufacture had lagged behind, and no major improvement had replaced Huntsman's crucible process until the introduction of Bessemer's converter.

Henry Bessemer (1813–98) was a professional inventor. He designed a perforated stamp impossible of forgery, a sugar press for use in Jamaica's plantations, and he invented plate glass and velvet. During the Crimean War he devised a new kind of artillery shell which required an exceptionally long gun barrel of great strength. But, until the price of steel had been reduced, the cost of producing it was prohibitive, even in wartime. In 1856 Bessemer came up with a very simple solution to the problem. Molton iron was poured into a large, pear-shaped converter where it was heated to a very high temperature. A blast of air was driven upwards through the converter, which oxidized (burned) the impurities in the iron. This part of the process lasted about twenty minutes, and produced a most impressive fireworks display, with twenty-foot long flames leaping from the top of the converter. The converter was then tipped on its side, and the molten steel was poured into a ladle. The quality of the steel was improved by the addition, before the *blow*, of a calculated quantity of iron ore rich in magnesium. This was a suggestion of Robert Mushet, and Bessemer acknowledged his debt to him by paying Mushet's widow a handsome pension.

49 *Bessemer steel shop*

The price of top-grade steel dropped from £55 to £30 per ton, and the Bessemer process established a new industry in Britain—steelmaking. Steel was soon being substituted for iron in a wide variety of articles. Railways and shipbuilding in particular benefited considerably from cheap steel. From 1860 the railway companies began to convert their wrought iron rails to steel ones. Steel was also ideal for ships' boilers and plating, and from about 1880 it began to replace iron completely in shipbuilding.

The port and town of Barrow-in-Furness was the result of Bessemer's process, and the discovery of local deposits of iron ore. In 1850, H. W. Schneider, a German who became a naturalized British subject, discovered a rich ironstone deposit on the Duke of Devonshire's estates in the Furness peninsula of north-west Lancashire. He persuaded the duke to build a railway from his estates to the tiny, isolated village of Barrow, which then had 150 inhabitants. Docks were built, and soon thou-

sands of tons of ironstone were being shipped out weekly. In 1859 Schneider founded a huge steelworks in Barrow. Three years later, the Furness railway, in which Joseph Paxton had one thousand shares, was linked to the east coast smelting districts, and 500,000 tons of ore were being mined annually. James Ramsden, the manager of the Furness railway, built a shipyard at Barrow, which was later bought by the massive armaments firm of Vickers, and it was at Barrow that many of Britain's Ironclads and Dreadnought battleships were built. By 1870 Barrow's population was 20,000.

Another method of making steel was discovered in 1864 by William Siemens and Emile Martin. This was the open hearth process. Superheated air was passed over the iron-ore and scrap iron, which lay in a hearth, or trough. The impurities were burned out by the flame striking the metal, for no fuel was allowed to come into contact with the metal. The hot waste gases from the furnace were passed through regenerative chambers at each end of the hearth, where they heated a large honey-comb of bricks. By blowing air alternately through one chamber, and hot waste gases through the other, the temperature in the chambers was regenerated, and a considerable saving in fuel costs was effected.

Unfortunately, in neither the Bessemer process, nor the open hearth process, could steel be made from ores containing phosphorus. Non-phosphoric ores could only be obtained from the Cumberland–Furness area, Spain, Sweden, and the Lake Superior iron-ore fields in the United States. The use of phosphoric ores only became possible after the invention of the Gilchrist-Thomas process in 1879.

Sidney Gilchrist Thomas was a police court clerk who was keenly interested in steel making. He and his cousin, Percy Gilchrist, an analytical chemist, discovered a way of making steel from phosphoric ores on a commercial scale. They found that if the Bessemer converter was lined with dolomite limestone, the impurities in the ore collected in the slag, which could be run off, leaving good quality, basic steel. The process was successfully demonstrated at a Middlesbrough steelworks, and within days the news had been tele-graphed around the world. The process brought about a fresh expansion of the British steel industry in Scotland and the North-east of England. But, although Britain benefited from this discovery, her chief industrial rivals, Germany and the United States, with their huge deposits of phosphoric ores, gained im-measurably more. The introduction of the Gilchrist–Thomas process was one sign that the period of Britain's undisputed industrial supremacy was coming to an end.

The tremendous surge in the production of iron and steel called for a great advance in metal-working techniques. Steam-powered machinery required very accurate, smooth working parts, and as iron machinery became more complicated, and more widely used, new specialist skills and machine tools, had to be developed. New occupations such as fitters, turners, and 'steam engine makers', were

created by the Industrial Revolution, and a new industry, that of making tools to make machines, came into being.

Eighteenth-century craftsmen had been familiar with a wide range of tools, including slide rests, drills, punches, and templates. But the early iron machines were made by carpenters and millwrights, who were more accustomed to working with wood than metal. The nuts and bolts were made separately, and when a machine broke down, the individual parts had to be handmade to repair it. Not surprisingly, the early iron machines were clumsy and unreliable. Even James Watt had been satisfied when the pistons of his engines fitted their cylinders to within the 'thickness of an old shilling'. The great difference be-tween the eighteenth century and the nine-teenth century in the use of machine tools was that in the latter they were used to ensure *standardization* of parts, which were inter-changeable. The importance of this develop-ment for industrial progress can hardly be overemphasized. Henry Bessemer, for ex-ample, found that he could have identical machinery made quite independently in London, Manchester, and Glasgow.

Engineering became mechanized after 1830 largely as a result of the achievements of two generations of toolmakers. Henry Maudslay (1771–1831) designed a micrometer accurate to within one-thousandth of an inch, and developed the lathe into a factory tool for manufacturing machine parts. Maudslay set up his own business near Oxford Street in Lon-don, and later built an engineering works in Lambeth.

Maudslay acquired his skills working for Joseph Bramah (1748–1814), who invented a patent lock which was almost thief-proof, the water-closet, and the pullover tap found on the bars of many public houses today. Joseph Whitworth (1803–87), and James Nasmyth (1808–90), gained their early experience of machine design in Maudslay's workshops, be-fore they migrated to Manchester in the 1830s. Whitworth developed the screw-cutting lathe, and produced the first standardized screws. He also made accurate gauges, drills, planing and slotting machines, and a slide-rest accurate to within one-millionth of an inch. Nasmyth developed a whole range of tools, which he stocked in standard sizes, and sold from catalogue descriptions.

The expansion of the textile industries continued, but rather more slowly than in the heyday of the early nineteenth century. Great engineering firms such as Dobson and Barlow, started up in Bolton in 1790, and Mather and Platt, founded in Salford in 1830 to manufacture bleaching and calico-printing machinery, supplied the textile industries with the machinery upon which their supremacy in world markets was based. The introduction in 1830 of an automatic version of Robert's self-acting mule made cotton spinning a genuine steam-power process. Shortly afterwards, *ring spinning*, whereby the spindles were made to revolve at very high speeds, was introduced from America. All the major processes were speeded up, and between 1845 and 1875 output per worker almost doubled in the cotton industry.

Mechanization in the woollen industry, however, took place at a slower rate. Wool-combing machines were invented by Samuel Lister and James Noble in the 1850s. But at this time there were still very few power looms in the woollen industry, where most weavers were outworkers. It was only by 1870 that power-loom weaving triumphed, as it had done in the cotton industry in the 1840s. After 1850 the hosiery and lace trades began to feel the effects of the introduction of machinery, but only after 1880 were stocking frames driven by steam power.

By 1850 the textile industries were concentrated in particular areas. Nearly all the English cotton workers lived in South Lancashire and North-east Cheshire. The woollen industry was slightly more scattered, though even so it was mainly concentrated in the West Riding. But within each area there was further specialization. Thus Nottingham specialized in cotton

hosiery, Leicestershire in woollen hosiery. Bolton and Manchester spun only fine yarns; Oldham and Ashton only coarse yarns. Halifax and Huddersfield concentrated on worsteds, Dewsbury on shoddy, while Leeds concerned itself less with manufacturing woollen goods, and more with marketing and tailoring.

The output of the coal industry also rose fast during this period, but muscle, rather than machine, power was the key to increased production. Miners at the coal face still hewed the coal from the ground with picks and shovels. In the 1850s, after Robert Galloway had proved Faraday's theory that dry coal dust caused pit explosions, steam-driven air pumps and exhaust fans, already widely used on the Continent, were introduced into British mines. Metal cages carried the coal to the pithead, and took miners up and down the mine shafts. Wire rope for winding machinery was introduced from Germany in 1850. But, apart from these changes, there was little technical progress in the coal industry until the twentieth century.

There were great advances in communications, which benefited merchants, industrialists, and ordinary folk alike. The development of railways and steamships has already been described in detail (see Chapters 15 and 16). Horsedrawn omnibuses were common in large towns, though country areas were still largely without a proper form of public transport. The telegraph, invented by Charles Wheatstone in 1837, was first used in the same year by the London and North Western Railway. One of the first messages to be transmitted resulted in the capture of a murderer, who fled from London by train, but was arrested when he alighted at his destination. In 1869, when the telegraph came under the control of the Post Office, telegraph poles were a common sight alongside roads. The invention of the telephone by Graham Bell, in 1876, slowly came into use in Britain during the 1880s. But one of the greatest forces for social and economic change was the introduction of the Penny Post in 1840.

Sir Rowland Hill (1795–1879), who published his pamphlet *Post Office Reform* in 1838, is usually given the credit for the idea of a penny postal service and pre-paid letters bearing an adhesive stamp. But for several years Robert Wallace, M.P. for Greenock, had been campaigning for a cheap postage rate regardless of distance, and as far back as 1680 William Dockwra ran a private penny post in London, when he conveyed at a profit letters and packets anywhere in London and Westminster for one penny. Rowland Hill's suggestions were adopted by the Government and after 1840 a letter could be carried anywhere in Britain for the cost of one penny. An efficient, cheap postal service was of great importance to businessmen and exporters. It also encouraged the spread of literacy, and enabled families to communicate cheaply and quickly with distant relatives. The original penny black postage stamp has become world famous and nearly every country in the world has adopted the idea of the adhesive stamp for pre-paid mail. Even today, British stamps have the distinction that they bear no mention of the country of origin, a tribute to the fact that they were first in the field. Pillar boxes, probably the idea of Anthony Trollope, a Post Office surveyor in the Channel Islands, first appeared in London in 1855. Soon they were in use throughout the country. For a long time, however, it was customary to pay the postman one halfpenny for each delivery at the house, and it was only in 1897, to mark the Diamond Anniversary of Queen Victoria's reign, that postal deliveries were made free.

Revolutionary though many of the changes described above were, they nevertheless affected directly only a small part of the population. In 1831 the typical Englishman was a countryman, and the typical worker a handicraftsman. Even in 1851, when more people lived in towns than in the countryside, the small workshop was still the most usual form of industrial unit, and only at the end of the century had the factory won undisputed supremacy in most manufacturing industries. In the 1830s there were over 50,000 men, women, and children who sweated for their daily bread in the production of hand-made nails, and even in 1866 there were still 20,000. In Willenhall and Wolverhampton 5,000 locksmiths toiled in the back premises of their dwellings. In neighbouring Walsall and Bloxwich, the 'small master' was predominant in the saddlery trades. A similar picture was to be found in the boot and shoe industry, the pottery and cutlery trades, and most other industries. The factory was really only to be found in cotton manufacturing.

Most businesses in Victorian times were small family partnerships. The great trading firms, the railways, shipping lines, and some banks, were joint stock companies. Other exceptions were to be found in the iron and steel industries, and shipbuilding, which required considerable amounts of capital and large labour forces. But factories with more than 200 workers were uncommon; less than 100 was usual. The passing of Limited Liability Acts in 1856 and 1862 made little difference to the size of firms until after 1870. Until the device of limited liability a shareholder was responsible for the entire debt of a firm which went bankrupt. As a result of these acts investors could buy shares in companies and be liable only for the amount of the shares they held. This eventually encouraged the growth of very large firms, with thousands of shareholders, and boards of directors managing the companies' affairs.

Thus there was a large class of employers ranging from merchants, bankers, ironmasters and factory bosses, down to backstreet craftsmen who employed one or two people in their workshops. Together with others such as lawyers and shopkeepers, they made up what is (rather inaccurately) called the middle class. It was the existence of a large, ambitious, and hard-working middle class which was the driving force for social and economic change in Victorian England. When one looks back on the achievements of this period, it is to this class, its activities, and the rewards its members received for their endeavours, that one's attention is usually drawn.

The well-to-do prospered greatly during this period. They built themselves substantial houses on the outskirts of industrial towns, away from the soot and grime expelled by the factories. They filled their living rooms with heavy furniture, and elaborate ornaments. They employed two or three domestic servants to cater for their daily needs. Their sons were sent to public schools, and their daughters had governesses. A carriage and pair were the trappings of wealth and respectability.

The typical middle-class household was well ordered. The father was the head of the family; his word was law, at least in public. His wife bore him many children, and since fewer died in infancy, families with ten children were common. They were brought up to know their place, and to speak only when spoken to. Every girl with a decent upbringing was expected to be able to play the piano, an essential social accomplishment of the age. Leisure hours in the home were usefully occupied with reading, knitting, and embroidery. Above all, an air of respectability had to be maintained. Attendance at church every Sunday was a ritual. Entertaining guests to dinner was done with strict etiquette, and visits to the theatre were both expensive and formal occasions, frowned upon in some quarters. A sense of decorum was even maintained during the customary annual seaside holiday, when a secluded beach was desirable, and bathing costumes which covered the greater part of the body the rule.

What of the poorer classes? If few houses belonging to the wealthy had bathrooms, the amenities and the furnishings of working-class homes were very meagre indeed. They were usually concentrated in the centres of towns, near the places of employment. A communal tap in a courtyard was the usual source of water. Soap was cheap, but few people bothered to wash themselves completely, though some enterprising local authorities opened public baths and washhouses. Some towns had public parks, but the countryside was still usually within walking distance of the town centre. The railway companies ran cheap day excursions, and in 1867 the first bicycles appeared.

The average worker in the second half of the nineteenth century consumed more meat, tea, sugar, cheese, milk, and tobacco than his predecessor fifty years earlier. Wages in general had more than kept pace with prices, partly as a result of the activities of the trade unions and cooperative societies. Skilled workers such as engineers saw a great advance in their real wages, and even farm labourers, among the most lowly paid groups, saw a 50 per cent increase in their wages, though much of this gain was surrendered when depression hit English farming after 1875.

It is wrong, however, to think of the ordinary workman living in a kind of golden age of Victorian prosperity. The threat of unemployment was always present. Sharp bouts of trade depression threw many workers out of their jobs. The American Civil War (1861–5) cut off supplies of cotton from Lancashire, and Lancashire people suffered great hardship. The working classes had few defences against the results of being out of work. There were no social benefits beyond the cold comfort afforded by the workhouse. Even when fully employed, the working man had little opportunity of building up some savings to fall back upon in hard times. In the absence of old age pensions, the end of his working days often meant poverty. Although the nation's wealth was being accumulated on a vast scale, it was unevenly spread through the population. More than half the total income went to less than 10 per cent of the population, while approximately one-quarter of the population lived at or below the poverty line, not earning sufficient to keep themselves physically fit. Nevertheless, it remains true that the standard of living for the majority of people in England greatly improved, as a rising tide of exports was exchanged for foodstuffs obtained from many parts of the world.

PART II

CHAPTER 19
Law and Order

It is time now to consider in more detail the changes which took place in living and working conditions during the Industrial Revolution. In days when towns were few and far between, and the means of communication poor, villagers had little contact with the rest of the country, and village life and politics revolved round the parish church. The Church was a stabilizing influence in society, and from its pulpits were preached not only the Scriptures, but the doctrine of civil obedience. Most people knew their place in the social order and were prepared to accept it.

The natural leaders of village society were the squire and parson. The parson was normally the chairman of the parish vestry which controlled the affairs of the village. The squire represented authority; more often than not, he was chief landowner, employer, judge and administrator rolled into one. The justices of the peace were usually recruited from the squirearchy, and the government of the country was largely in their hands. With the help of the parish vestries and those borough authorities which were under their control, the justices saw to it that roads, bridges, and public buildings were kept in good repair. They appointed overseers of the poor, licensed fairs, markets, and public houses, dealt with minor offences against the law, heard appeals in quarter sessions, and were generally responsible for the maintenance of good order. Occasionally the J.P. was a lawmaker, as when the Speenhamland System of poor relief was introduced by a group of Berkshire magistrates in 1795. The towns also conducted their affairs with very little interference from the Government in London. Preoccupied with trivial matters, they were ill-equipped to deal with important ones.

The relative simplicity of this village and town life was destroyed as the Industrial and Agrarian Revolutions gathered momentum. Many villages were transformed either by enclosures or by the growth of industry. As new industrial towns grew, the evils of overcrowding and bad housing were intensified. The social problems created by an expanding population, and an increasingly urban society, were met in a variety of ways. The development of education was promoted first by the Churches and private individuals, and after 1833 also by the state. Numerous working-class organizations gained improvements for their members in the form of better opportunities, wages, and conditions. New administrative machinery improved public health and amenities in towns. Finally, the Government slowly accepted the responsibility for protecting the people from the more harmful results of industrialization.

If the eighteenth century was in many ways an age of stability, it was also an age of violence and disorder. Riots against high food prices and low wages, turnpike tolls, unpopular ministers of the Crown, and Methodist preachers, were part of a way of life. Murders were common, and footpads and thieves made even town centres in daylight places where travellers went equipped to resist violent assaults on their persons and property. Society's only answer in this century to the threat of increasing crime, a savage criminal code, was ineffective. As Thomas Buxton, a law reformer, remarked in 1821: 'We rest our hopes on the hangman, and in this vain and deceitful confidence in the ultimate punishment of crime, forget the very first of our duties—its prevention.'[1]

50 'Gin Lane' by William Hogarth

51   Scene of hanging eleven felons at Newgate

Many writers attributed the lawlessness of England in the second quarter of the century to the growing habit of drinking cheap gin.

There is not only no safety of living in the town but scarcely any in the country now; robbery and murder have grown so frequent. These accursed spirituous liquors which to the shame of our Government are to be so easily had and in such quantities drunk, have changed the very nature of our people, and will if continued to be drunk, destroy the very race [wrote one pamphleteer].[2]

In the 1740s it was calculated that the annual consumption of gin reached 8 million gallons, and that one in six of London's houses sold the stuff. Gin drinking declined after an Act of 1751 taxed spirits heavily, but the social conditions in which this demoralizing habit had flourished continued to breed its quota of crime. Unemployment and low wages were only partially relieved by private charity and the Poor Law. The crime rate grew as the population increased, especially in the towns which developed with amazing speed during the Industrial Revolution. Vice and crime were spawned in the squalid, overcrowded conditions in factory towns and villages. Many sports and pastimes were cruel and brutalizing, while executions and barbaric punishments in front of huge crowds accustomed people to the sight of violence and cheapened human life. Even the severity of the criminal code created more crime, since it encouraged criminals to commit worse crimes in order to escape the consequences of a lesser one, because they could only be hanged once.

Smugglers enjoyed the silent, if not open, approval of the public; many respectable people bought contraband tea, brandy, and other goods, though they did it secretly at night. Armed clashes between smugglers and revenue officers did not always result in a triumph for justice, while the mob's sympathy was usually with the smuggler about to be hanged for his activities. In 1736 an Edinburgh mob rioted at the execution of a popular smuggler, and Captain Porteus, who was in charge of the proceedings, ordered his troops to fire on the crowd. Porteus was tried and convicted for murder. He was reprieved by George II, but was lynched by an infuriated mob, which broke into the prison before his release. In some coastal areas, especially Cornwall, wreckers lured ships to destruction and, since under a statute of Edward I no ship could be accounted a wreck if a man, cat or dog escaped alive from it, sailors who struggled ashore might be despatched by the villagers to remove all traces of their crime.

In a society plagued with the problem of lawlessness, there were few means for solving it. Some English counties in the early part of the eighteenth century still retained the principle of communal responsibility for crimes so that, if a victim of robbery could prove his loss to the sheriff before sundown, he was re-imbursed. This elementary method of making people concern themselves with the prevention of crime was impracticable, however, and harsher punishments, as well as rewards for those who brought criminals to justice, were generally adopted. The reward for catching a highwayman was £40, together with the highwayman's horse and equipment, provided they had not been stolen. Thief-taking for reward was open to anyone, and common informers sometimes became rich on the proceeds. The most notorious thief-taker was Jonathan Wild, who built at the same time his own underworld network of crime. He was eventually hanged in 1725 for receiving stolen property.

Most large towns had trained bands of citizens whose purpose was to maintain law and order. They might be aided by vigilante squads, special constables, and watchmen, nicknamed 'Charlies', or 'Hour bawlers'. The latter were usually old and feeble, armed only with a staff, and were easily frightened away, or bribed, by gangs of desperate criminals. In 1748 Henry Fielding opened an office in Bow Street, London, from which his famous runners tracked down criminals. On his death

in 1754 the organization was developed by his blind brother John Fielding. By 1772 detailed descriptions of wanted men were issued, and the runners, dressed in scarlet waistcoats, were a familiar sight in the city. They were too few, however, to make much impact upon the crime rate, and they were certainly incapable of dealing with large-scale disturbances. When mobs got out of control, the magistrates were often compelled to call on the yeomanry or troops to restore order.

It was the Gordon Riots in London which prompted the formation of the earliest police force. In 1780 Lord George Gordon, head of the Protestant Association, petitioned Parliament not to relax certain details of the existing

52 *'Past one o'Clock' by Thomas Rowlandson*

anti-Catholic laws, and stirred up the mob's prejudices against Catholics. In the four-day riots which followed 700 people lost their lives, and hundreds of houses were burned to the ground. Order was only restored with difficulty after George III himself had called in the army. Five years later the Government tried to place responsibility for keeping the peace in the City of London, Westminster and Southwark, in the hands of three Police Commissioners, who were empowered to recruit constables. Fierce opposition forced Pitt to abandon the idea, but a similar scheme was operating by 1792. The results, however, were not very successful. The Commissioners refused to cooperate outside their own areas, so that the system merely drove criminals into neighbouring parishes which had no efficient police forces.

The idea of a state-controlled police force still aroused hostile feelings. It was attacked as a 'French' innovation, and a threat to the Englishman's liberty. Oliver Cromwell's experiment of maintaining law and order by dividing England into twelve military districts, each under a major-general, had produced a lasting suspicion of the army as a means of keeping public order. Yet, when public opinion accepted the softening of the criminal code, a police force became inevitable.

This arrived with the Metropolitan Police Act of 1829, introduced by Sir Robert Peel as Home Secretary in the Duke of Wellington's government. The new force had its headquarters in Whitehall Place, overlooking Scotland Yard. The constables were civilians, and were armed only with truncheons. They wore a distinctive uniform of top hat and frock coat, and were paid 19/- per week. They were not concerned with the punishment of crime, only its detection and prevention. At first the police were unpopular, and magistrates showed a marked sympathy for those accused of assaulting them, but it soon became clear that the streets were quieter at night, and robberies were less frequent.

If London's crime rate went down, that of the provinces went up, because many criminals, helped by the improvements in transport, left London to operate elsewhere. A Royal Commission on Constabulary Forces in 1839 commented that criminals

migrate from town to town, and from the towns where they harbour, and where there are distinct houses maintained for their accommodation, they issue forth and commit depredations upon the surrounding rural districts; the metropolis being the chief centre from which they migrate.[3]

A national network of police forces cooperating with each other became essential.

Thus the Police Act of 1839 encouraged J.P.s to appoint special constables, and to inform the Home Secretary of what police forces were necessary in their areas, but they were slow to adopt the new system. By 1853 only twenty-two counties had taken advantage of the act. The 1856 Police Act therefore made it compulsory that 'in every County (or part of a County) in which a Constabulary has not been already established . . . the Justices of the Peace shall proceed to establish a sufficient Police Force for the whole of the County'. Local authorities were encouraged to form efficient police forces by a system of monetary grants from the central government, which also served the purpose of developing the power of Whitehall. A further change was made in 1888. Boroughs with a population over 10,000 were to retain their own police forces, controlled by the Local Watch Committee. Elsewhere they became the responsibility of the newly formed County Councils.

During the nineteenth century the British policeman became a symbol of law and order, and of kindly efficiency. The police remained unarmed, even though on occasions like the Chartists riots in the 1840s, or the miner's lockout in Yorkshire in 1893, their ability to cope with disorder was severely strained, and troops were called in to assist them. Britain became an orderly country, a process aided by the spread of education, a rising standard of living, the influence of the Churches, but one in which the police played a crucial part.

During the second half of the eighteenth century the list of capital offences was greatly lengthened, so that by 1800 there were over two hundred. They included, apart from very serious crimes like treason, piracy, murder, and attempted murder, many quite trivial offences: picking pockets, stealing goods worth five shillings from a shop, impersonating a Chelsea Pensioner, damaging Westminster Bridge, and cutting down a tree in any avenue, garden or orchard. The fact that the numbers hanged, though high, bore little relation to the number liable to execution, showed that the penal code, far from being a deterrent, was absurd as well as inhumane. Imposing the death penalty for minor offences encouraged criminals to commit further crimes to escape capture, private individuals not to prosecute, and juries to refuse to convict. Transportation, which had started as a means of providing cheap labour for the plantations in America and the West Indies, was used increasingly as an alternative to the death penalty. After 1787 convicts were transported to New South Wales and Tasmania. Many prisoners died on the long sea voyage, and in Australia their task was often clearing the bush in chain gangs. Few ever saw their homeland or family again. The practice finally ceased in 1853.

Lord Holland and William Eden suggested penal reform in the eighteenth century, but it was not until Romilly took over the leadership of the movement that any progress was made. Sir Samuel Romilly (1757–1818), the son of a Huguenot immigrant from France, became a brilliant barrister, and was eventually appointed Solicitor General in 1806. Romilly realized that reform would be slow in the face of strong opposition, since Parliament regarded the protection of property as a sacred duty. In 1808 he persuaded the Commons to substitute transportation for life instead of hanging for pickpockets, but failed to abolish the death penalty for stealing five shillings from a shop. Nevertheless there was a growing public opinion that the criminal code as it stood belonged to a bygone age.

53 *Taking turns on the treadmill*
'The machine is a wheel which, lying horizontally, is worked by the prisoners holding a rail and, stepping upwards upon one of the treadles, by a simultaneous movement press it down; when they step upon the next, and so on, keeping the wheel in constant motion. To lessen the labour, however, each steps off, and returns again in rotation' (quoted from W. H. Pyne, Lancashire Illustrated [*1827*])

Sir Robert Peel, who became Home Secretary in 1822, was influenced by the law reformers Thomas Buxton and Sir James Mackintosh, who led the movement after Romilly had committed suicide in 1818, but he was too practical and cautious to satisfy the more adventurous demands of the reformers. Nevertheless, Peel's achievements were impressive. In addition to his prison reforms, he codified over three hundred different statutes into four understandable Acts, abolished the death penalty for one hundred offences and, except in the case of murder, allowed the courts to exercise mercy. By making the punishment more appropriate to the crime, Peel made justice more certain, since juries would now convict prisoners. Yet the criminal code still retained some inhuman features. Until 1834 'the scarecrow remains of poor wretches who had long since expiated their crimes' could be seen hanging on gibbets in the Port of London, and the pillory was only abolished in 1838. In 1837 a boy of nine years was hanged at Chelmsford for setting fire to a house. By 1841, however, the number of capital offences had been further reduced, and after 1838 and for the rest of the century nobody was hanged except for murder or attempted murder. The last public execution in England took place in 1868.

The substitution of long-term imprisonment for capital punishment, and after 1853 for transportation, focused attention on prison conditions and administration. Conditions inside prisons were unbelievably bad. No distinction was made between hardened criminals, vagrants, young offenders, and prisoners awaiting trial; they were herded together in cramped, insanitary quarters, where epidemics of 'gaol fever' (typhus) frequently swept off the inmates. The gaolers, who were unpaid, extorted what money they could from the prisoners for the necessities of life. George Ellis, later an M.P., visiting Newgate Prison in 1816, declared that the scenes of depravity were beyond description.

We went all over Newgate, which is dreadfully crowded, and the prisoners were not properly classed. The infirmary was quite horrid; a moderate sized room and so hot, with twelve persons in it, and two dead ones. Saw the boys' school. There is one boy named Leary of thirteen who has been in Newgate twenty times, and been four times under sentence of death.[4]

Buxton wrote in 1818 of the cruelties and degrading life a prisoner underwent. No useful work was done, and no instruction provided.

54   *John Howard visiting an English prison*

The moment he enters the prison irons are hammered onto him; then he is cast into a compound of all that is disgusting and depraved. At night he is locked up in a narrow cell, with perhaps half-a-dozen of the worst thieves in London, or as many vagrants, whose rags are alive and in actual motion with vermin. . . . He is habituated to idleness and familiarized with crime. In short, by the greatest possible degree of misery, you produce the greatest possible degree of wickedness; because he is too bad for society, you return him to the world impaired in health, debased in intellect, and corrupted in principles. [5]

The campaign for prison reform can be traced back to the Society for the Promotion of Christian Knowledge, which investigated London prisons in 1702, but no notice was taken of its proposals. In 1729 General James Oglethorpe, a philanthropist, reported on the *State of the Gaols in this Kingdom*, but no improvements followed the enquiry. Perhaps the most famous prison reformer was John Howard (1726–90), a Bedfordshire landowner, who devoted most of his life to investigating English prisons. His account of what he had seen, *The State of Prisons in England and Wales*, published in 1777, shocked public opinion. Howard proposed that prisoners should be classified according to their sex, age, and offence; that wholesome food, hospital facilities, proper clothes and sanitation be provided; prisoners should be given religious instruction, gaolers paid, and inspectors appointed to ensure that these measures were carried out. Although some of the proposals were written into the Penitentiary Houses Act of 1779, its terms were generally evaded. Howard died in 1790, and the French Revolution delayed further reform for another generation.

Elizabeth Fry (1780–1845), a Quaker, carried on Howard's work. She visited prisons and publicized the need for reform. Aided by Romilly she influenced the prison reforms Peel introduced as Home Secretary. Prisons were to be organized along the lines laid down by the Home Office, and regularly inspected; gaolers were to be paid; women prisoners were separated from the men, and were supervised by women warders; prisoners received regular visits from the chaplain and the doctor, and were taught to read and write.

Other improvements gradually followed. The imprisonment of debtors, who owed quite trivial sums, came to an end in 1844, when imprisonment for debts under £20 was abolished. Following a report in 1853 prisoners were kept in separate cells, and where possible they were given useful work during the day. Public opinion at the end of the century was prepared to accept further reforms, and the Prison Act of 1898 relaxed the rigid rules of prison discipline. The Liberal governments of 1906–14 passed several important measures. The Probation of Offenders Act (1907) allowed magistrates to place first offenders on probation instead of sending them to prison, where they might be converted into fully fledged criminals. In 1908 imprisonment of children under fourteen was stopped; instead young offenders were sent to Borstals. Hardened criminals could be sentenced to preventive detention, long terms of imprisonment in order to prevent them from committing further crimes. In 1914 the Criminal Justice Administration Act instructed that reasonable time be allowed for the payment of fines.

REFERENCES

1 T. F. Buxton, speaking in House of Commons, quoted by Basil Montagu, *The Mitigation of the Punishment of Death*.
2 Letter of Bishop Benson, quoted by E. Cadogan, in *Roots of Evil* (Murray).
3 Report of the Constabulary Force Commissioners, *Parliamentary Papers*, 1839.
4 Diary of George Ellis, September 1816, quoted in *English Historical Documents 1783–1832*, ed. G. M. Young and W. D. Hancock (Eyre & Spottiswoode, 1970).
5 T. F. Buxton, *An Inquiry whether Crime and Misery are produced or prevented by our present System of Prison Discipline* (1818).

Religious ideas and beliefs have always influenced men's thoughts and actions. Even in our own materialistic age the Christian religion still has a part to play in many people's lives. The purpose of this chapter is to show how some of the more important religious movements of the eighteenth and nineteenth centuries influenced everyday life in England.

By 1720 the country was settling down to a period of religious calm after the disturbances of the previous century, when people had argued and fought over the way in which God should be worshipped. During Oliver Cromwell's rule as Lord Protector of England (1653–8) Anglican ministers had been deprived of their livings. When Charles II became king in 1660 these were restored to them, and in the reaction against the Protectorate the Nonconformists (i.e. those who did not conform to the teachings of the Church of England) were persecuted. Parliament did its best to strengthen the position of the Established Church, and to discourage Dissenters. The Corporation Act (1661), the Act of Uniformity (1662), and the Test Act (1673) between them banned Dissenters from becoming members of town corporations, from holding any kind of civil or military office under the Crown, and from admittance to the universities of Oxford and Cambridge. Heavy fines were imposed for non-attendance at Anglican services, and by the Five Mile Act (1665) Nonconformist ministers were forbidden to live within five miles (eight kilometres) of any place where they had acted as a minister.

The severity of the Clarendon Code, as these Acts were called, was only reduced after 1689, when the Act of Toleration granted Protestant Dissenters freedom to worship in their own ways. It did not officially apply to Roman Catholics, but in practice they too were allowed to worship as they pleased. Many Dissenters took Anglican communion occasionally so that they could hold office, but from 1728 this was not necessary. From that year an annual Indemnity Act was passed, granting an official pardon to all who held office without attending an Anglican service, though Roman Catholics were excluded until 1793.

There are no reliable figures for the numbers belonging to the various religious groups in 1700, but the great majority of people were members of the Church of England. There were four main groups which had broken away from the Established Church. The largest was the Presbyterians, whose first English church had been founded in Wandsworth in 1572. The Congregationalists, who also started in Elizabethan times, believed that church membership should be open only to those who had dedicated themselves to the service of Christ. The third group, the Baptist Church, started as an offshoot of the Congregationalists, and was founded by John Smythe in 1609. Baptists maintained that only adult believers should be baptized, and thereby received into the body of the Church. Finally there were the Quakers who believed in nonviolence. The Dissenters varied in the details of their organization and beliefs, but they all had an earnestness and enthusiasm for their faith which was lacking in the Church of England. Nevertheless, even the Dissenters shared with the Anglicans in the general decline of religious fervour in the early eighteenth century.

The Church of England had serious weaknesses. It was powerful but complacent, and had acquired a rather worldly reputation.

When William III became king in 1689 after James II had fled the country, only a few Anglican clergy resigned because they said that their oath of obedience to James meant that they could not serve under William. They were called the Non Jurors. Those who remained, and their successors, tended to favour a comfortable living and a quiet life.

A high position in the Church was greatly coveted, and much canvassing occurred when a good living or a bishopric fell vacant. Often bishops were appointed for political rather than religious reasons, as a reward for faithful support of the government. Many church livings were given by landowners to a younger son or brother in order to give him a career, irrespective of his religious convictions. Pluralism was common—that is, a clergyman often had more than one living, and therefore more than one income. When he was absent from

55 'The Sleeping Congregation' by William Hogarth

his benefice it was looked after by a poorly paid curate. The Church was out of touch with the ordinary people, although much good work was done by conscientious churchmen up and down the country. But many parsons, while they mixed easily with the gentry, had little contact with their parishioners, who did not understand their learned sermons. In particular, the needs of growing industrial areas were neglected, for new parishes were rarely created. The gravest fault of the Church was its failure to convey any kind of lasting spiritual message or hope to the great masses of working class men, women and children.

Into this easy-going age came a man who started a religious revival. John Wesley was born in 1703, in the Lincolnshire village of Epworth. He was the son of an Anglican clergyman. His mother, who was deeply religious, brought her children up strictly. John was ordained in 1725, and became a fellow of Lincoln College, Oxford. In 1729 he and his brother Charles formed a Bible study group. They organized, or 'methodized' every hour of the day. They visited Oxford prison, and helped the poor. They were soon known as the 'Holy Club', or 'Methodists'. In 1735 the Wesleys went to Georgia, in America. On board ship they met members of a religious group called the Moravians. Wesley was deeply impressed by them, for they seemed to have the strong faith he felt he himself lacked. But on 24 May 1738, a few months after his return to England, Wesley attended a service in Aldersgate, and experienced the religious conversion he longed for.

Wesley was convinced that anyone who turned to Christ would be saved. This was the message he preached for the next fifty years. When he was refused permission to preach from Anglican pulpits Wesley followed the example of another member of the 'Holy Club', George Whitefield, and preached in the open air. In this way he was able to preach to many people, such as the coalminers of Kingswood, near Bristol, who normally never

56   George Whitefield preaching at Moorfields, 1742

went to church. One important aspect of the Wesleyan movement was the stirring hymns written by his brother, Charles Wesley. They include 'Christ Whose Glory Fills the Skies', 'Soldiers of Christ Arise', and 'Hark the Herald Angels Sing'.

Wesley gave many of his listeners hope of a better life to come, and he encouraged them to be honest and hard-working. He formed groups of Methodists who met regularly for private prayers. Members who did not live up to a strict code of moral conduct were expelled. In 1743 Wesley noted the following reasons for the expulsion of sixty-four members

Two for cursing and swearing. Two for habitual Sabbath-breaking. Seventeen for drunkenness. Two for retailing spirituous liquors. Three for quarrelling

and brawling. One for beating his wife. Three for habitual, wilful lying. Four for railing and evil speaking. One for idleness and laziness. Twenty-nine for lightness and carelessness.[1]

The enthusiasm of the Methodists was at first greatly disliked, and few of the regular clergy joined the movement. Methodist preachers were denied the use of church pulpits, so they preached in the open air. Many were brutally assaulted, or driven out of the neighbourhood by 'Church and King' mobs. But gradually, as employers found that Methodists tended to be industrious and sober, this hostility towards Wesleyanism died down.

Wesley himself had no wish to separate from the Church of England, and indeed he did not do so, but as Methodism developed its own distinctive features and organization a break became inevitable. This came about when, in 1795, four years after Wesley's death, the Methodist Conference declared that Methodists had no need to attend the Anglican Church in order to receive communion; instead they could receive it at the hands of their own ministers.

The example of Methodism inspired a more spiritual approach to religion within the Church of England itself. The Evangelicals who, unlike the Methodists, remained part of the Established Church, also believed in leading strict and virtuous lives. The Clapham Sect, or the 'Saints', led the way. In the late eighteenth century Clapham was a high-class suburb of London, where William Wilberforce and some of his associates lived. They and John Venn, the rector of Clapham, led lives of self discipline at a time when moral standards were low. They adopted the custom of family prayers and saying grace before meals, and they insisted on the strict observance of the Sabbath. As time went on their ideas were widely adopted by the wealthy, and they became the typical outlook of the middle-class Victorian family.

But the Evangelicals did more than live virtuous lives—they led useful ones too. Wilberforce and his friends campaigned against the slave trade which was finally outlawed in 1807, and in 1833, largely as a result of their efforts, all slaves in the British Empire were freed. Thomas Buxton devoted his life to the cause of law reform, and Hannah More to the Sunday Schools movement. The Evangelicals formed societies for promoting education at home and abroad, and for improving the condition of the industrial masses. The Church Missionary Society was founded in 1795 to preach the Gospel abroad. The British and Foreign Schools Society was formed in 1803 to bring education within the grasp of the poor. Evangelicals were also in the vanguard of the movement for factory reform. Their chief spokesman in Parliament, Lord Ashley (later Earl of Shaftesbury), worked for the protection of child and female labour in the mines and factories. The Factory Acts of the 1840s, and the Mines Act (1842), were in part due to his persistence.

The Industrial Revolution, with its growth of population, and the concentration of that population in fast developing industrial regions also caused many people to look at the Established Church and feel a need to reform it. An Act of 1836 altered the diocesan boundaries and created the bishoprics of Ripon and Manchester to cater for the industrial North. New parishes were created, and churches were built in industrial districts which before had been left entirely to the Nonconformists. An Ecclesiastical Commission, composed of the two Archbishops, the Bishop of London, and several laymen, was set up to administer Church finances. In 1838 another Act dealt with the question of pluralism. It was decided that no clergyman could hold more than one living if they were more than three kilometres (two miles) apart, if either had a population over 3,000, or if the additional stipend was more than £1,000. An Act of 1840 restricted the number of canons in every cathedral chapter. The money saved by this was used to increase the income of the lower clergy.

Several Acts were passed which granted religious toleration to the Nonconformists and Roman Catholics. In 1828 the Test and Corporation Acts were repealed, and in the following year the Catholic Emancipation Act was passed. Ever since the Act of Union between England and Ireland in 1801, the mainly Anglican Parliament at Westminster had been responsible for ruling several million Roman Catholics. The Act of 1829 gave Catholics civic equality, for they could become M.P.s, and hold any public office except those of Lord Chancellor, Viceroy of Ireland, and the Monarchy itself.

In 1836 a Marriage Act was passed. Roman Catholics and Nonconformists could now be married in their own churches, provided the registrar was notified. Hitherto, only Church of England clergy could legally marry people.

In 1852 part of every public cemetery was set aside as 'unconsecrated ground' for Dissenters, where burials could take place with Nonconformist rites. (In 1880 Nonconformists were permitted to use consecrated ground.) In 1854 Oxford University allowed Nonconformist students to read for the B.A. degree, and Cambridge University followed in 1856. The Universities Test Act (1871) opened the universities of Oxford, Cambridge, and Durham on equal terms to Anglicans and non-Anglicans alike. In 1882 college headships and fellowships were opened to Nonconformists. The other universities, of course, were non-sectarian from the start. In 1858 Jews could become M.P.s, and in 1874 a Jew, Benjamin Disraeli, became Prime Minister. Thus slowly but surely non-Anglicans were accorded equal rights with Anglicans.

These changes occurred partly because Victorian England, at least until near the end of the nineteenth century, was a deeply religious country. In addition to Evangelicalism and the growth of the Nonconformist Churches, there were several other important religious movements. The High Church Movement, or Oxford Movement (so called because its leading exponents were Oxford University dons), was a reaction against the influence of the Free Churches. Four Fellows of Oriel College, John Newman, John Keble, Edward Pusey, and Richard Froude, published pamphlets called *Tracts for the Times*. Many people thought that the ideas expressed in them were too close to the teaching of the Roman Catholic faith for the comfort of the Established Church. In 1840 Newman wrote *Tract 90* in which he tried to prove that Anglican and Roman Catholic beliefs could be reconciled. He became more and more attracted to Catholicism, and in 1845 he joined the Roman Catholic Church, and later became a cardinal. Some of Newman's associates, much to the dismay of many of his friends, followed his example. The High Church Movement certainly inspired a new interest in the Catholic Church and, at the

same time, a revival of prejudice against it. There were loud protests against the action of Pope Pius IX in 1850 in appointing Catholic bishops in England. An Ecclesiastical Tithes Act was passed in 1851 which forbade Catholic clergy from accepting tithes already held by the Church of England.

If the Oxford Movement concentrated on intellectual issues, the Christian Socialists tried to be of practical help to the poor. Their leaders were Frederick Maurice, Professor of Divinity at King's College, London, Charles Kingsley, a country clergyman, and author of *The Water Babies*, and Thomas Hughes, who wrote *Tom Brown's Schooldays*. They wanted a classless, Christian society, and the movement developed links with Chartism, Cooperation, and trade unionism. However, Christian Socialism was largely unsuccessful, and it never really reached the great mass of the poor it set out to help.

The Salvation Army, on the other hand, formed in 1878 by 'General' William Booth (1829–1912), had a far more popular appeal. As a boy Booth had been apprenticed to a pawnbroker, and he never forgot the poverty he saw in those days, when people had been forced by hunger to pawn their meagre possessions in order to buy food. Booth became a Methodist lay preacher in the worst slums of the East End of London. He was so successful that he had to call upon his converts for help in controlling the vast crowds which came to hear him. Booth then began to organize his movement, which he called the Christian Mission, renamed in 1878 the Salvation Army. Eventually, the Army had a chain of command stretching down from the General himself, who acted in the same way as a Head of a Church, to the officers who did the field work in the towns. Uniform was worn as 'an outward and visible sign of an inward and spiritual grace'. Booth was convinced that there was no need of sacraments for the salvation of souls. The Salvation Army was not content with indoor church services, but preached the gospel on the street corners. The services were kept simple and informal, with free prayer, public repentance, hand clapping, and hymn singing accompanied by the Salvation Army bands. In carrying out his aim of practical Christianity Booth established 'colonies' where the destitute could be given work, shelter and food. Help was given to discharged prisoners, and legal aid was provided for the poor. Missions were sent overseas, the first one going to the United States in 1880, and the Salvation Army rapidly developed into the worldwide organization known today.

Originally, the Salvation Army set out to bring the Christian message to the vast throng of ignorant, unchurched workers of the big towns. For, although Victorian England was outwardly pious, the influence of the Churches was limited to so-called respectable folk. Even this hold was to be relaxed, however, as the century wore on. A turning point came in 1859 when Charles Darwin published his book *The Origin of Species*. Darwin's theory of evolution flatly contradicted the first chapter of Genesis, and seemed to prove that time was on the side of the apes rather than the angels. This put many members of the clergy and general public, who had been brought up to believe in the Bible literally, in a dilemma. Some people turned away from the Church and became atheists or agnostics, and many others, who felt the need for a strong faith, turned to Roman Catholicism.

New inventions, the increasing pace of industrialization, the rise of new professions and opportunities, and the way in which Man was changing and beginning to control his environment, all led to a decline in organized religion. By the last quarter of the nineteenth century religion was no longer the backbone of English society, and church-going no longer occupied a central place in the lives of many people. Even in villages a falling off in church worship had become noticeable by the end of the century, though it was nothing like as much as in the twentieth century. It was to help meet the increased urban demand for Sunday recreation that the National Sunday League was formed. It organized cheap rail excursions, and in 1896 succeeded in getting museums and art galleries opened to the public on Sundays.

The Nonconformist Churches suffered a smaller drop in the number of their regular worshippers than the Anglican Church, partly because the more ritualistic form of service provided by the latter did not appeal to the majority of its members, and so its congregations diminished. In order to counter the swing away from church going the Nonconformist Churches organized P.S.A.s (Pleasant Sunday Afternoons). These were meetings held in the chapel, when a hymn was sung and a prayer said, but apart from this, the meetings were not directly concerned with religious activities. Often an outside speaker, such as a local trade unionist or socialist, would be invited to address the meeting.

Nevertheless, Sundays in the Edwardian era, though far more relaxed than they had been fifty years earlier, were very strict compared with today. Upper and middle-class folk still walked to church, rather than infringe upon the rest period of their grooms. Most hotels and restaurants did not open on the Sabbath, and there was a strong prejudice against Sunday newspapers.

REFERENCE

1 *Journal of John Wesley* (Epworth Press, 1940).

CHAPTER 21
Education

For many centuries education in England and Wales had been closely associated with religion. From the introduction of Christianity into England in A.D. 597 to the Reformation in the sixteenth century the Church, apart from a few schools run by the gilds for training apprentices, provided and controlled all forms of education—from the chantries and song schools for the very young, to the colleges of Oxford and Cambridge. In medieval times an important duty of the humble parish priest was to keep a school in which the elements of Latin grammar were taught. Thus bright boys of poor parents sometimes received a free education which gave them the opportunity to enter the Church or royal government, since in those days Latin was the universal language spoken and written by churchman, scholar and official alike. The state took little or no interest in education, regarding it as the proper business of the Church, so that the progress of education at any time depended almost entirely upon the efforts of interested private individuals. These two influences, the tradition of classical learning, and the role of the Churches in education, have had a marked effect upon the development of the English educational system right up to the present day.

Because anyone, no matter what his qualifications (or lack of them), could set up a school, there existed in England at the end of the eighteenth century a great variety of schools. Most towns had old established grammar schools, which provided what we should today call secondary education. Samuel Bamford has left us a description of the schooling he received at Manchester Free Grammar School, which may be regarded as fairly typical of the better grammar school.

Each class sat on a strong oaken bench, backed by a panel of the same, placed against the wall, with a narrow desk in front, so that all sat around the school in regular gradation. The boys of each class were placed according to their proficiency, and the first and second boys of the class experienced considerable authority over the others. The school hours were from 7 to 8.30 at morning, from 9.30 to 12 at noon, and from 2 till 5 afternoon. The master was seldom more than five minutes beyond the time. Every boy who afterwards entered the school, was bound to go up to the table and present his shoulders for correction. The mustering and flogging being over, the classes went through their lessons; the boys who in spelling and reading could readiest make out a word when those above him were at fault, moving up to their places, and thus the quickest spellers and readers were always towards the upper end of their class. When a boy had been at the head of his class some time, and especially if he happened to have some acquaintance amongst those of the next class above him, and they wished to have him amongst them, their head boy would take him by the hand, and leading him to the master would say, 'If you please, sir, must —— (mentioning the surname) go into my class?' when a brief intimation, as a nod, a 'yes' or 'no' would decide the application.[1]

The learning consisted chiefly of committing to memory long passages from Greek and Roman authors, but the training did at least provide the opportunity to enter one of the two universities in England, or the professions.

Many grammar schools, however, had lost sight of their original purpose of giving a free education to poor but able children. Occasionally the master and perhaps his assistant lived comfortably on the endowment while teaching one or two pupils only. Other schools, while retaining a narrow emphasis on the teaching of Latin and Greek, no longer enjoyed a sufficient income to offer free places, and had become mainly fee-paying schools for the sons of the rich. These were the future public schools. Until their reform under the influence of famous headmasters like Dr Thomas Arnold, headmaster of Rugby from 1828 till his death in 1842, and Edward Thring, headmaster of Uppingham from 1853 to 1887, life in these schools was often brutal and unpleasant. Masters and boys regarded each other more as natural enemies than teachers and pupils. The boys were unruly and discipline was enforced by floggings. Riots were not unknown. On two occasions, in 1793 and 1818, soldiers had to be called in to restore order at Winchester School, when the boys revolted, and held the school against all comers, while a riot at Marlborough in 1851 lasted nearly a week.

For those parents who could not afford to send their sons to a public school there were other private schools from which to choose. They were often owned by a clergyman, and some even offered 'useful' instruction such as arithmetic, history and geography. Probably the best type of education was given by the dissenting academies, which had a four year curriculum including modern subjects such as science. The education of girls was neglected, since it was thought more important that girls should learn social graces such as dancing and deportment rather than knowledge.

A variety of schools provided some form of elementary education. Common day schools imparted a little learning to the older sons of tradesmen, mechanics and the like, who could afford the fees of a few pence each week. Charity schools, established by the Society for the Promotion of Christian Knowledge, were free. The society was formed in 1698 to provide every London parish with a school, but the movement soon spread to the provinces, and by 1754 over 2,000 schools had been established. In them children were taught reading, writing, arithmetic, and the Anglican catechism, which had to be learned by heart. 'Dame schools' were hardly more than places where mothers parked their infants for the day while they worked. As the name implies they were usually run by a woman who earned a few coppers a week child-minding. The schoolroom might be a living room, a cellar, or a draughty attic. Schools of industry were places of drudgery for young children, who were taught 'useful' crafts such as sewing and weaving. Sunday schools had existed since the early eighteenth century, but the movement became widespread at the end of the century because so many children worked in mines and factories that they never attended weekday schools. In 1780 the Sunday School Union was started by Robert Raikes who opened a school in Gloucester in order to check hooliganism on the Sabbath, following the closure of the local factory. The children were taught to read the Bible, show respect to their social superiors, and accept their position in life without complaining.

The Sunday School movement led to the formation of two church societies which provided an elementary education for poor children, the British and Foreign Schools Society, and the National Society. In 1801 Joseph Lancaster (1778–1838), a Quaker, opened a school in Borough Road, London, where he taught children by the monitorial system. By this method the teacher first taught a small group of the older, more intelligent children. When they had learned the lesson thoroughly, each monitor returned to his group and taught the others in the class. Thus one teacher was able to teach many children by mass production methods hitherto associated with the new factories. This system had obvious benefits when teachers were in such short supply, but unfortunately it reduced learning to a dull, mechanical process, since everything had to be learned parrot fashion. In 1808 Lancaster fell into debt and his school was taken over by Joseph Fox and William Allen who founded the British and Foreign Schools Society. Three years later Andrew

57 Model Lancasterian School, Borough Road, London

Bell (1753–1832), a Church of England clergy-man, who also claimed to have invented the monitorial system in his mission school in Madras, set up a rival organization, the National Society. The two societies competed furiously to establish schools, especially in the growing industrial towns where the need was greatest, and as a result of their labours some 20,000 schools were founded.

Yet in spite of these efforts, few children of poor parents received any worthwhile instruction. A parliamentary committee reported in 1818 that 'a very great deficiency exists in the means of educating the poor, wherever the population is thin and scattered over country districts. The efforts of individuals combined in societies was almost wholly confined to populous places'.[2] But the position in many large towns was hardly more encouraging. Mr W. F. Lloyd, Secretary of the Sunday School Union, who gave evidence before another committee in 1834, believed that a major obstacle to educating the poor was

the enormous extent of the parishes. In the eastern districts of London the populations of some of the parishes amount to 60,000. The utter impossibility of any clergyman, or any set of gentlemen, undertaking to provide funds for a comprehensive system of education, under such discouraging circumstances, must be evident.[3]

Where schools were available many children did not attend. Parental indifference to schooling and abject poverty were equally to blame. According to William Gurney, Vicar of St Giles in London, many children never went to day schools because their parents sent them out to beg, and 'on a Sunday they get more by begging than they do on any other day in the week, because more people are out and about',[4] so they did not attend Sunday School either.

Many parents were too poor to buy decent clothing for their children, or to afford a few coppers a week to pay the teacher. Often they relied upon the earnings of their children to supplement the family income. Thus in London *there are a vast number of children employed in selling matches, sweeping the streets, and various other low employments, whose parents are very careless of their instruction; they will not put themselves to any trouble to procure decent clothing for their attendance at school; many of the families are so poor as to be unable to procure clothing; in one family, consisting of six children, there was only one suit of clothes, which each child was obliged alternately to use when he went out into the street.*[5]

Gurney tried the experiment of giving the poorest children clothes in order that they might attend school decently clad, but he found that they came once or twice, and then disappeared, 'and the clothes disappeared also'.

Clearly much more was needed than the efforts of well meaning individuals and voluntary organizations. If children were to be properly educated elementary schooling had to be universal, compulsory, and financed largely, if not wholly, by the state. Yet those who tried to provide more schools through government action met much opposition. Some people argued that educating the poor was very costly, wasteful, and possibly dangerous for society.

It would teach them to despise their lot in life, instead of making them good servants in agriculture and other laborious employments to which their rank of society had destined them; instead of teaching them subordination it would render them factious and refractory, as was evident in the manufacturing counties; it would enable them to read seditious pamphlets, vicious books, and publications against Christianity. Besides, it would burden the country with an enormous expense.[6]

An even greater stumbling block to educational progress was the attitude of the Chur-

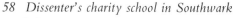

58 Dissenter's charity school in Southwark

ches. Neither the Roman Catholics nor the Nonconformists were prepared to allow public money to be spent on schools run on Anglican lines, and the Anglicans were not prepared to tolerate any other kind. In 1807 Samuel Whitbread's bill to provide every parish with a school maintained, if need be, by a local rate was wrecked by the opposition of the Anglican clergy. Therefore, in 1820, Henry Brougham, a champion of popular education, proposed to give control of parish schools to the Church of England, but his bill was attacked by the Dissenters and defeated.

An important step forward was taken in 1833. Brougham proposed that all children between the ages of six and twelve years should attend school. After some debate the House of Commons dropped the bill, but it was clear that the matter could not be left there. So the sum of £20,000 was voted for the purpose of building schools, provided that half the cost had been raised by voluntary subscriptions. The money was to be divided between the National Society and the British and Foreign Schools Society in proportion to the amount contributed by each society.

In 1839 the grant was increased to £30,000, and inspectors were appointed. At the same time the first central authority for education was created—the Committee of the Privy Council for Education. Its chief purpose was to establish day training colleges for teachers. The first Secretary of the Committee was Dr James Kay-Shuttleworth. Dr Kay had been a successful doctor in Manchester. He had been shocked by the unhealthy conditions in which the Manchester poor lived, and he published a pamphlet called the *Moral and Physical Condition of the Working Classes employed in the Cotton Manufacture in Manchester*. His revelations disturbed many people and made him a nationally known figure, so that when the Poor Law Amendment Act of 1834 was passed Kay was appointed assistant commissioner for East Anglia. Kay's interest in education was aroused when he came across a thirteen-year-old boy in a workhouse school successfully

teaching a class in the absence of the master. This led Kay to set up an experimental school at Norwood, in London, for the training of pupil teachers. It was as a result of this work that Kay was appointed in 1839.

In 1840 Kay opened a teacher training school in an old manor house at Battersea. But he had little official support, and when the school ran into financial difficulties he handed it over to the National Society. By 1845 the society had started another 21 colleges containing over 500 students. The pupil teacher scheme was enlarged in 1846 when certain schools which were reported as efficient by H.M. Inspectors were allowed to train students. During the 5-year apprenticeship (between the ages of 13 and 18 years) the trainees received a yearly grant of £10 rising by instalments to £20. At the end of the course an examination was held, and successful candidates were given grants to enter a training college.

The 1850s and 1860s were a time of growing concern over the state of education in this country. Both France and Prussia had efficient, national systems of elementary education which England lacked, and it was generally realized that some form of education for the mass of the people was vital. At least one-third of the population could neither read nor write. Yet the need for skilled men at every stage of production, from shop floor to management, was becoming greater as more and more industries adopted mechanical methods of production. As other nations built up their industries, British industries had to become more efficient if they were to keep their lead over foreign competitors. Ultimately, the nation's economic and social progress depended on the quality of its educational system. In these circumstances, the belief that the country was not getting the best return for the money it was spending on education became a matter for government concern.

In 1858 a Royal Commission headed by the Duke of Newcastle was appointed to inquire into the state of education and to recommend ways in which elementary schooling could be extended cheaply and efficiently. The chief proposal of the Newcastle Commission was Payment by Results, whereby the government grants to schools, and teachers' salaries, would depend upon the results of their pupils in an examination. This system was introduced in 1862 by Robert Lowe, the Vice-President of the Department of Education set up in 1856. Lowe promised that 'If it is not cheap, it shall be efficient; if it is not efficient, it shall be cheap'. By the system every child who passed the examination in the three 'R's gained for the school a grant of eight shillings; for general merit and attendance the grant was four shillings. Payment by Results quickly justified itself on the grounds of cheapness but in other directions its effects were bad. It encouraged teachers to find ways to defeat the inspectors. Often absentees were marked as present in the registers to boost attendance figures. On the day of the examination some of the failures were sent to another school so that the percentage of passes would be improved. The teachers tended to concentrate on the duller children in order to get them through the examination, and brighter children were neglected. Learning became 'cramming' as children were forced to memorize certain texts, and some inspectors on their rounds came across children reading fluently from books held upside down. Subjects like geography, music and cookery often disappeared from the timetable, so that more time could be devoted to the three 'R's.

The extension of the vote to the town worker in 1867 made educational reform a matter of urgency, for as W. E. Forster, the author of the 1870 Education Act, remarked, 'Now that we have given them political power we must not wait any longer to give them education.' Hitherto the attempts of various governments to provide at least a minimum of education for all children had been haphazard and ineffectual. The early Factory Acts had marked the first hesitant steps towards a system of compulsory education. The 1802 Factory Act stated that apprentices were to be 'instructed in some part of every working day . . . in the usual hours of work in reading, writing and arithmetic . . . by some proper person'.[7] The 1833 Factory Act was more explicit. All factory children in cotton and woollen manufacturing between the ages of 9 and 13 were to have two hours' schooling every day except Sundays. One of the duties of the factory inspectors, who were appointed for the first time, was to see that this was properly carried out. But most manufacturers did not think it was their job to provide schools, and only a few made even half-hearted efforts to carry out the intention of the law. Besides, schooling took the children away from the machines, and parents objected to the reduction in their children's earnings. Often no teacher was available and the millowner could hardly be blamed for this.

The church societies were unable to provide sufficient school places and teachers for the school population, which was estimated in 1870 at over 3 million. Since there was accommodation for only 2 million children school attendance was not compulsory. But even in areas well endowed with schools many children went only when there was no work available and, of those who did attend school, over half went for fewer than one hundred days a year. Not surprisingly, nearly three-quarters of the children left school unable to write a letter properly, add up a bill, or even knowing the whereabouts of the chief countries of the world. It was to remedy these gaps in education that the 1870 Education Act was passed.

This Act established a national system of elementary education in England and Wales. In areas where there were not enough schools the church societies were given six months in which to provide them. If they failed to do so local school boards, with powers to build and maintain schools, and to levy a local rate, were to be elected by ratepayers. The school boards could make education in their area compulsory, though few did so. The problem of religious instruction was overcome by the

59 Interior of London Board school
The children (left foreground) are lifting little weights

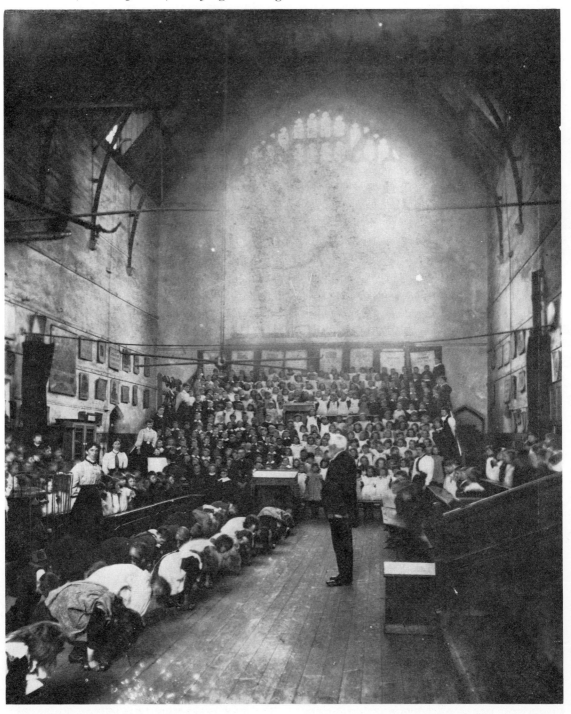

Cowper–Temple clause in the Act, which stated that religious education in board schools was not to be biased in the direction of any one particular denomination. Parents were given the right to withdraw their children from scripture lessons and school assemblies if they wished. Parents still had to pay a few coppers each week to provide for the education of their children, though this payment was waived in cases of hardship. But both free and compulsory education came about within the next twenty years.

Lord Sandon's Act (1876) laid down that no child under 10 years was to be employed, and no child under 13 who could not reach a certain standard in reading, writing and arithmetic, unless a certificate of regular school attendance was produced. Mundella's Act (1880) made education compulsory to the age of 10, and laid the responsibility for attendance on the school board. The school board man became a familiar sight in many neighbourhoods as he went on his rounds looking for truants from school. In 1893 the school-leaving age was raised to 11, and in 1899 to 12 years. Elementary education was made free in 1891. The system of Payment by Results was abandoned in 1897.

Secondary education, on the other hand, was neglected, for the 1870 Act dealt only with elementary schools, and successive governments concentrated on 'filling the gaps' in the system. Furthermore, the value of secondary education was not recognized, and the Government found it easier to follow public opinion than lead it. Thus when the Clarendon Commission (1864) on public schools, and the Taunton Commission (1868) on secondary schools other than public schools, recommended a complete overhaul of secondary education, hardly anything was done. Later, in 1881, a royal commission on technical education reported that Britain lagged behind continental countries in the provision of secondary and technical education. For a country such as Britain, whose strength and prosperity largely depended upon selling manufactured goods abroad, to neglect scientific and technical education was most unwise. Yet the only result was a Technical Instruction Act of 1889 which levied a penny rate to aid technical instruction. In 1890 local authorities were allowed to establish some form of technical instruction using some of the revenue raised from increased duties on wines and spirits. This was the so-called *Whisky money*.

Thus by the end of the century English education was in a hopeless muddle. Five separate authorities existed for secondary schools; the Education Department, the Science and Art Department, the Board of Agriculture, the Charity Commissioners, and the local authorities. There was similar confusion at local level too, with school boards, school attendance committees, boards of managers, boards of governors, and the county and county borough councils, all with overlapping duties.

Long overdue reform came when Balfour's Education Act was passed in 1902. This was partly the result of a legal decision called the *Cockerton Judgment* (1900). Many board schools had been in the habit of providing what was in effect a form of secondary education in the top classes of their schools. In addition many ran evening classes for older children who had left school but wished to carry on with their education. Mr Cockerton, a district auditor, contested that the school boards were acting beyond their powers, and his view was upheld by the courts. Thus illegality was added to confusion in the educational system, and parliamentary action could not be avoided.

The 1902 Act was largely the work of a civil servant, Sir Arthur Morant. It placed control of elementary, secondary, and adult education, as well as the training of teachers, in the hands of education committees of the county and borough councils, which were to be known as local education authorities (l.e.a.s). The 2,500 school boards were abolished, and were replaced by 330 l.e.a.s. In this way education became one of the social services for which local authorities were responsible, and one of the chief charges on local rates. The Act also strengthened secondary education. Hitherto, only the children of wealthy parents could hope to benefit from a grammar school education, but from 1907 'free places', or 'scholarships', to grammar schools were paid for by the l.e.a.s. The number of these scholarships grew from 47,000 in 1907 to 143,000 in 1927, and by this means some poor but clever children were able to make their way to university.

The growth of the universities

For the greater part of the period that this book covers, however, a place at university was an attribute of wealth rather than ability. At the beginning of the nineteenth century there were only two English universities: Oxford and Cambridge. These were the preserves of the very wealthy, and only Anglicans could attend them. Far from being places of learning they were really exclusive clubs for aristocrats. There were few public lectures, and teaching was done mainly by private tutors. The examination system had fallen into disuse, and scientific studies were neglected, as Classics held pride of place. Change came gradually. Cambridge led the way in widening the fields of study by making Mathematics and the Natural Sciences degree courses. Oxford introduced a proper system of examinations. By the University Tests Act of 1871 the two universities were opened to candidates of any religion, and they ceased to be the monopoly of Anglicans.

Of greater importance was the creation of new universities. In 1828 University College in Gower Street, London, was established by a group of Nonconformists who wanted to have a university of their own, free from religious tests. This was quickly followed by King's College in 1831, opened by a group of Anglicans in reply to the 'Godless institution in Gower Street'. In 1836 the two colleges were incorporated into the University of London, with the power to confer degrees. The University of Durham was created in 1837. In 1851, a college of higher education was founded by John Owens, a rich merchant, in Manchester. This, together with colleges in Liverpool and Leeds, became Victoria University in 1880. In 1904 Victoria University was divided into the three separate universities of Manchester, Liverpool and Leeds. Meanwhile, other universities were established; the University of Wales (1893), Birmingham (1900). Sheffield (1905), and Bristol (1909).

The new universities attracted students mainly from their own neighbourhoods, and they developed strong local traditions. As might be expected they laid emphasis on scientific studies related to the industrial activities of their own regions, for example, the various branches of engineering. Most of their students came not from public schools but from grammar schools, and because most of the undergraduates lived cheaply at home or in lodgings, they became available to a wider class of people.

REFERENCES

1   Samuel Bamford's recollections of Manchester Free Grammar School, *Early Days*, ed. H. Dunckley (1893).
2   Report of Parliamentary Committee into the Education of the Lower Orders of the Metropolis (1818), quoted from J. Stuart Maclure, *Educational Documents of England and Wales 1816–1967* (Chapman and Hall, 2nd ed., 1968).
3   Report of Parliamentary Committee on the State of Education (1834), quoted from J. Stuart Maclure, op. cit.
4   Report of Parliamentary Committee into the Education of the Lower Orders of the Metropolis, quoted from J. Stuart Maclure, op. cit.
5   Report of Parliamentary Committee into the Education of the Lower Orders of the Metropolis, quoted from J. Stuart Maclure, op. cit.
6   Mr Giddy, M.P., Parliamentary Debates, July 1807.
7   *Health and Morals of Apprentices Act* (1802).

Free, universal education has changed the manners and outlook of every class in society. Thomas Carlyle considered education 'a prime necessity of man', and the intelligent working man has always been interested in education as a means of achieving a better position in life. The mechanics institutes of the early nineteenth century were organized by working men to improve their economic prospects. Men like Francis Place and Robert Owen, who fought for the right of working men to organize themselves into trade unions in order to win better conditions, shorter hours, and higher wages, were equally interested in promoting the education of the working classes. But, though education ultimately proved the stronger force for social change, of all forms of working-class self-help, trade unions had the deepest roots in the past, and in the nineteenth century they proved of greater benefit to the workers.

The need for trade unions developed first in those industries controlled by capitalists or where change was rapid. So long as industry was rural, domestic, and small-scale, there was little social distinction between master and man when they worked side by side. But new processes such as the application of steam power and the growth of the factory system placed the workman at a disadvantage in his relationship with his employer. Consequently, trade clubs were formed to take the place of the decayed craft gilds, which had formerly protected the interests of the craftsman.

Trade clubs acted as friendly societies. They insured their members against sickness, unemployment, and death. They met in public houses, where the boxes containing their funds were opened and checked. A typical friendly society was the Journeyman Shoemakers and Tailors in a parish near the Tower of London. Formed in 1780, its eighty members paid a 2/6 entry fee, and monthly subscriptions of 1/3. When a member fell sick he received 7/- per week when the box was above £20, and 4/- otherwise, while £7 was given for the burial of a member and £5 for his widow.

Many trade clubs, however, extended their activities. They restricted the entry of apprentices into their craft and thereby made their labour more valuable. They also went on strike to defend their wages and thus acted as a combination. William Pike, giving evidence in 1726 before a House of Commons committee on combinations of workmen in the West Country woollen industry declared

that his own Weavers would willingly have worked for him at the Wages he gave, but that the Club threatened, if they did so, to pull them out of the house, and coulstaff them [i.e. beat them with stout sticks used for carrying tubs of butter], *upon which he was forced to pay them the Price demanded, to save his work from being cut; and has known several that have been coulstaffed.*[1]

As a result of this inquiry an Act of Parliament, one of many passed during the century, made combinations (or unions) of workmen in the woollen industry illegal, and anyone belonging to a combination could be sentenced to three months' hard labour on the evidence of one witness before two magistrates. Consequently, many combinations formed for the purpose of striking for higher wages pretended to be friendly societies and proved very difficult to suppress, especially after the Friendly Societies Act of 1793 protected their funds and gave them legal recognition.

By the end of the eighteenth century Parliament had become very concerned about the number and strength of combinations. No doubt Parliament thought it unwise that its laws regarding conspiracies in restraint of trade should be so openly ignored. But the chief motive for suppressing combinations was the Government's fear of public disorder at a time of war and revolution abroad, for they could easily be a disguise for societies with revolutionary aims. The final years of the century were critical. The French were preparing to invade England; the navy, England's first line of defence, mutinied in 1797; and a rebellion in Ireland, which was supported by French troops, was only put down with difficulty. Thus the Government was in the mood to listen favourably to the petition of the master millwrights in London against the activities of a combination of their journeymen.

The Combination Acts of 1799 and 1800 prohibited combinations of both workmen and employers to regulate wages and hours. The effects of the Acts were controversial. Their novelty lay in the provision of summary trial of offenders, not in the severity of the penalties laid down, which were mild in comparison with other crimes. Many workmen were imprisoned for trying to raise their wages, but not one successful prosecution of an employer is recorded, although some employers combined to depress wages. Yet in spite of the Combination Acts many trade unions operated quite openly without interference by the authorities. Others were driven underground, where they became secret societies whose chief weapons were 'turnouts', threats, and violence. Frame-breaking, or Luddism (see p. 82), was common during the early years of the nineteenth century. A Declaration of the Framework Knitters issued in 1812 vowed that 'all frames of whatsoever description the workmen of whom are not paid in the current coin of the realm will invariably be destroyed'.[2] Strikes sometimes resembled miniature civil wars rather than industrial disputes. Thus in many ways the Combination Acts were ineffective, and may even have contributed to violence.

Their repeal in 1824 was mainly the achievement of two men, Francis Place, a Charing Cross Road tailor, and his ally in the House of Commons, Joseph Hume, a radical M.P. Place believed that wages tended to find their own level through the operation of economic laws of supply and demand, and therefore once the Combination Laws were repealed trade unions would tend to disappear of their own accord. With the gradual return of prosperity the Government was prepared to consider a relaxation of restrictive laws, and a select committee was appointed to inquire into the operation of the Combination Laws. Place carefully instructed the workmen who appeared before the committee as to the sort of answers they should give, and himself gave evidence that the laws tended to aggravate the hostile relations between employer and workman. In its report the committee concluded

That the laws have not only not been efficient to prevent Combinations, either of masters or men; but, on the contrary, have in the opinion of many of both parties had a tendency to produce mutual irritation and distrust, and to give a violent character to the Combinations, and to render them highly dangerous to the peace of the community.[3]

The result of the repeal, however, was a violent increase in trade union activity, and a second, more restrictive Act was passed in 1825. Trade unions were still permitted, but they were to confine their activities to peaceful bargaining on wages and hours, and the provisions about 'molesting', or 'obstructing' fellow workmen were made stricter. Thus there was considerable doubt about the legal position of trade unions, since their members could still be prosecuted under Acts against conspiracy in restraint of trade, and much depended upon how judges would interpret vague phrases like 'intimidate' and 'obstruct'.

The failure of unionism in 1825 showed the need for larger unions which could effectively organize their members over a wide area. John Doherty formed a national Spinners' Union, which became the nucleus of the

60 Contemporary ridicule of the trade union movement, 1834

National Association for the Protection of Labour. Both these organizations collapsed in 1831, however, because the introduction of spinning machinery was weakening the operatives' bargaining powers. The movements towards large unions culminated in 1833 when Robert Owen (1771–1858) formed the Grand National Consolidated Trades Union which soon had a membership of half a million. The aim of the 'Grand National' was a general strike which would force the government and employers to surrender control of production to the workers.

Yet within a year the union lay in ruins. It tended to attract only the wilder elements of the working classes, since the skilled craftsmen · valued their own societies too much to join it. The four most important unions, the potters, builders, spinners and clothiers, refused to join,

while most factory workers gave their support to the rival Ten Hours' Movement. The GNCTU was too large and unwieldy, and it was impossible to please all groups of workers in so many different trades. The funds were squandered in local, ill-coordinated strikes which the employers were able to crush easily. Many employers forced their workers to sign a document declaring that they did not belong to the Union, and sacked those who refused. Strikes were answered with lockouts: that is to say, the factory gates were shut until the workers agreed to return to work on the employer's terms. The final blow to the GNCTU came when six farm labourers from the village of Tolpuddle, in Dorset, were prosecuted for administering unlawful oaths when enrolling new members, and were sentenced to seven years' transportation to

Botany Bay. This savage sentence reflected the determination of the Government to suppress the trade union movement.

The collapse of the GNCTU checked but did not destroy trade unionism, though Chartism, a political campaign which aimed at improving wages and conditions by getting working-class men into the House of Commons, the Cooperative movement, and the Ten Hours' Movement for factory reform, were alternatives to which many workers turned. In 1842, a grim year of distress, there took place in Lancashire the 'Plug Plots', when the plugs were removed from factory boilers, bringing work to a standstill. In the same year the Miners' Association, with 70,000 members, was formed with its headquarters at Wakefield. Alongside trade unions friendly societies such as the Oddfellows and Foresters flourished, while the Journeyman Steam Engine Makers, founded in 1826, pointed the way with its centralized control of funds to the New Model Unionism of the 1850s and 1860s.

The foundation of the Amalgamated Society of Engineers in 1851 was a landmark in trade union history. The ASE had high subscriptions of a shilling per week, a full-time paid secretary who administered the funds which were kept at central headquarters in London, and a cautious, responsible policy. Unlike Robert Owen, William Allen, the Engineer's leader, accepted the capitalist structure of industry, and believed that the worker's interests were best served by co-operation with the employers. Strike action was to be avoided wherever possible. The financial strength of the ASE, and its sickness and unemployment benefits, made it a model for other unions, such as the Amalgamated Society of Carpenters and Joiners, formed in 1860, and the Tailors in 1866. These years also saw the beginnings of national leadership of the trade unions. Several important unions had their headquarters in London, and their leaders, William Allen, Robert Applegarth of the Carpenters, Edwin Coulson of the Brick-

layers, George Odger, a Shoemaker, and Daniel Guile of the Ironfounders, formed the London Trades Council which claimed to be representative of trade union opinion. These five men were nicknamed by their opponents the *Junta* (from the Spanish word for council), but they did much to make trade unionism a respectable part of Victorian society, guiding unionism along prudent lines, and influencing Parliament and public opinion on important matters such as the extension of the franchise. In 1868 the Trade Union Congress, representing a wide cross-section of unions, was formed. In 1871 the Congress appointed a small 'Parliamentary Committee' to lobby M.P.s on trade union matters, and the TUC later became the central organization of the whole movement.

Nevertheless, the growth of trade unionism was thrice threatened during this period: by trade depression in 1866–7, the Sheffield Outrages of 1866, and the legal case of *Hornby* v. *Close* in the following year. The slump of 1866–7 was short-lived, but it enabled opponents of trade unions to attack them on the grounds that they harmed British exports. In Sheffield two rival unions of cutlers waged gang warfare against each other, and several murders were committed, supposedly in the name of trade union solidarity. In October 1866 a workman's house was blown up with gelignite. These acts of terrorism resulted in a government inquiry into the whole structure of the trade union movement. The leaders of the New Model unions were anxious to convince public opinion that the violence in Sheffield had nothing to do with them, and the report of the Commission did indeed make it clear that responsible unions such as the Engineers were far more typical of trade unionism than the cutlers of Sheffield.

In the case of *Hornby* v. *Close* the Boilermakers' Society sued a local official for the recovery of £24 which he owed the society. But the judge ruled that the Friendly Societies Act of 1855, which protected their funds, could not apply to trade unions because, unlike friendly societies, they were organizations which tended to act in restraint of trade. Therefore, a trade union, being an illegal though not a criminal organization, could not recover embezzled funds through the law courts. This legal decision jeopardized the whole future development of the trade union movement, and its leaders immediately mounted a campaign to get it reversed.

Gladstone's Trade Union Act of 1871 helped the unions by giving full legal protection to their funds, but the recent Sheffield Outrages had made the government sensitive on the question of intimidation of workers. The Criminal Law Amendment Act which accompanied it made 'watching and besetting', and similar practices associated with strikes, illegal, thus contradicting an Act of 1859 which had permitted peaceful picketing. This Act was bitterly resented by the unions since it could be a useful weapon in the hands of unsympathetic judges, as was shown in the Gas Stokers' strike of 1872 when harsh prison sentences were inflicted upon the leaders. Thus the trade union movement probably owed more to Disraeli's legislation than to Gladstone's. The Master and Servant Act (1867) softened the harshness of the old law whereby breach of contract by a workman was a criminal offence punishable by hard labour, while his employer was liable only to civil proceedings. But the sentence of twelve months' hard labour passed on the London Gasworkers showed that further change was necessary. The 1875 Employers and Workmen Act made contract a civil matter with both parties equal. The Conspiracy and Protection of Property Act of the same year legalized peaceful picketing, and stated that the law of conspiracy was not to apply to trade disputes unless what was done during a strike was actually a criminal offence if done by a private individual.

The hitherto unorganized, unskilled workers now took a keen interest in trade unions, whose membership grew from about 1 million in the early 1870s to 4 million on the eve of the Great War. The first of the New Unions was Ben Tillett's Tea Workers' and General Labourers' Union, followed by the Gas Workers in 1872. Joseph Arch, a Methodist lay preacher, created an Agricultural Labourers' Union in Warwickshire. Its aim was

to elevate the social position of the farm labourers of the country by assisting them to increase their wages; to lessen the number of ordinary working hours; to improve their habitations; to provide them with gardens or allotments; and to assist deserving and suitable labourers to migrate or emigrate.[4]

This soon became the National Agricultural Labourers' Union which within weeks had over 100,000 members. But the union soon collapsed, for British farming was hit by severe depression after 1875, caused by imports of cheap grain from North America, and refrigerated mutton and beef from New Zealand and Argentina. Farmers could not afford to pay even existing rates of pay, let alone higher ones, and so farm labourers lost all their bargaining powers.

New Unionism became important after 1889, when it spread throughout the London area and the northern industrial towns. The New Unions, in contrast to New Model Unions, represented the unskilled, poorly paid workers, and were organized along the lines of whole industries rather than separate crafts. Their leaders, with no craft skills to defend, were chiefly concerned with wages and the right to work. They wanted state-guaranteed employment or maintenance, a minimum wage, and an eight-hour day. Strike action was their chief weapon. A small but significant strike took place in 1888 when the match girls of the London firm of Bryant and May, who worked in atrocious conditions dipping matches into phosphorus (many suffered from a dreadful form of cancer called 'phossy-jaw' as a result), stopped work. They were led by Mrs Annie Besant and won. In May 1889 the London Gas Workers got a cut in the basic working day from 12 hours to 8.

These victories were infectious, and the London Dockers struck for a minimum wage of 6d an hour. They were led by John Burns, Tom McCarthy, Ben Tillett and Tom Mann, and the Port of London was paralysed for nearly a month. Each day thousands of dockers paraded in orderly fashion through the City of London, and their determination, as much as the hardship they and their dependants suffered, won them much support. Over £80,000 was subscribed to maintain the dockers' families. Large contributions also came from Australia, just at a time when strike funds and the dockers' morale were running low. This proved decisive and the dock owners were forced to grant the 'docker's tanner'. Elsewhere, in the major industrial cities, the Gas Workers were winning an eight-hour day. These strikes proved that unskilled workers could organize themselves effectively and win better pay and conditions.

In the next twelve months there were over 1,000 strikes, and the growing power of the trade unions, together with the violence of their strikes, caused many employers to close their ranks in resistance. The great engineering dispute of 1897 was seen by many people as part of a deliberate campaign by the employers to smash the Federation of Engineering and Shipbuilding Trades. Several legal decisions would have undermined the trade union movement if the principles they laid down had been generally accepted. In the case of *Lyons* v. *Wilkins* Lyons, a leather goods manufacturer, succeeded in winning a court injunction to prevent the Fancy Leather Workers' Trade Society from picketing his premises, though there had been no question of violence being used. In 1896 the London Building Trades Federation was forced to pay damages to a firm for putting them on a 'black list' of 'unfair' employers. The question of the unions' legal liability could not have been more confused. The crucial test cases, however, came with the Taff Vale Judgment of 1901, and the Osborne Case of 1909.

In 1900 a short strike took place on the Taff

Vale Railway in South Wales. The railway company sued the Amalgamated Society of Railway Servants for damages in order to recover the revenue lost during the strike, and it was awarded £23,000. This meant that strike action became a very doubtful asset for a union, since holding a strike might involve a union in paying ruinous costs. This decision convinced the unions of the need for an independent political party which would promote the trade union cause in Parliament. Within a year, membership of unions affiliated to the Labour Representation Committee rose from 469,000 to nearly 1 million in 1906. At the same time the unions demanded that Parliament change the law, and this was done when the Liberals gained power in 1906. The Trades Disputes Act (1906) stated that trade union funds were not liable for civil wrongs, i.e. if a union withdrew the labour of its members, thereby breaking their contract with the employers, the union could not be held liable for damages.

The Osborne Case arose out of a decision of the TUC in 1903 to raise a fund for the payment of Labour M.P.s by means of a compulsory levy on the unions. In 1907 W. V. Osborne, a Liberal, who belonged to the Amalgamated Society of Railway Servants, objected to the contribution to the Labour Party made by all the larger unions. In 1909 the House of Lords ruled that trade unions were like corporations, and were therefore governed by Acts of Parliament. The 1876 Trade Union (Amendment) Act had defined a trade union as a combination 'for regulating the relations between workmen and masters, or between workmen and workmen, or for imposing restrictive measures on the conduct of any trade or business'. No mention was made of political activity, so that using union funds to support M.P.s was beyond the powers of a trade union, and therefore illegal.

This was a great blow to the Labour Party, which relied upon the political levy to finance working-class M.P.s, who would otherwise have been unable to sit in the House of

Commons, and sixteen Labour M.P.s were deprived of their salaries. The Payment of M.P.s in 1911 helped to solve the difficulty, but the unions still agitated for a complete reversal of the Osborne Judgment. In 1913 the Trade Unions Act legalized the political levy provided it was supported by a majority of the members. An individual who did not wish to pay was allowed to 'contract out', but in practice few workmen took advantage of this clause, since it made them unpopular with their workmates.

The period 1889 to 1914 was one of extensive industrial unrest. With wages lagging behind prices after 1900 the unions showed a new militancy, and an extremist section was prepared to use any weapon to force the hand of the Government. Syndicalism, a French and American inspired movement, preached the gospel of a general strike to bring industry to a standstill, and compel society to accept the workers' demands. Relations were especially bad in the coal-mining and shipbuilding industries. In 1910 there were strikes in the coal mines of the North-east, and in South Wales troops had to be called in to restore order. In 1911 a successful seamen's strike sparked off a series of strikes in the docks. In 1914 steps were taken to form a Triple Industrial Alliance consisting of the Miners' Federation, the National Union of Railway-

men, and the Transport Workers' Federation (formed in 1910 by Tom Mann and Ben Tillett) whose aim was a general strike 'to deliver a straight left to the chin of Fat'. In the opinion of the social historians, Sidney and Beatrice Webb, 'British trade unionism was in the summer of 1914 working up for an almost revolutionary outburst of gigantic industrial disputes'. The country was saved from the spectre of massive industrial strife only by being involved in a far greater conflict, for on 4 August Britain entered the First World War.

REFERENCES

1   Report of Committee of House of Commons on Combinations of Workers in the West Country Woollen Industry (1726), quoted from *English Historical Documents 1714–1783*, ed. D. B. Horn and Mary Ransome (Eyre & Spottiswoode, 1969).
2   *The Declaration of Framework Knitters* (1812), quoted from *English Historical Documents 1783–1832*, ed. A. Aspinall and E. A. Smith (Eyre & Spottiswoode, 1969).
3   Report of the Select Committee on the Combination Laws (1824), Hansard, *Parliamentary Debates*.
4   Joseph Arch, *The Story of His Life, by Himself* (1898).

CHAPTER 23
Chartism

Trade unions ultimately derive their strength from dissatisfaction, either with existing rates of pay and conditions, or with the guarantees that they will be maintained. Their aims and methods are *economic*, though they sometimes resort to *political* means of achieving their wishes. Chartism on the other hand, whilst its driving force was economic discontent, aimed directly at the reform of Parliament. Only when the working classes were fully represented in the House of Commons, it was thought, would an improvement in their standard of living become possible.

In its simplest terms Chartism was a mass movement which pressed Parliament to accept the *People's Charter*. This contained six demands: votes for all men over twenty-one, vote by secret ballot, a general election every year, payment of M.P.s, each member of Parliament to represent the same number of people, and M.P.s no longer to be required to own property. The acceptance of these ideas would have enabled the workers to return members of their own class to the House of Commons. Social and economic reforms to improve the people's condition could then be more readily achieved.

Chartism had many causes. The working classes were bitterly disappointed by their failure to secure the vote in 1832. After the collapse of Robert Owen's huge trade union in 1834 they turned eagerly to a movement which promised to win them the vote. The Poor Law Amendment Act, which abolished outdoor relief, caused great resentment, especially in the North of England in the winter of 1838–9, when widespread unemployment forced many families to enter the hated workhouses. Chartism was largely a 'knife and fork' question; behind the Charter's demand for

parliamentary reform lay hunger and misery. Thomas Attwood, introducing the 1838 petition in the Commons, declared that workers

only sought a fair day's wages for a fair day's work; and that if they [the House of Commons] *could not give them that, and food and clothing for their families, they then said they would put forward any means which the law allowed, to change the representation of that House.*[1]

The 1842 Charter stated that many families had to live on $3\frac{3}{4}$d per head per day, while Parliament had shown no desire to 'curtail the expenses of the state, to diminish taxation, or promote general prosperity'.

The strength of Chartism came from two main types of worker. The keenest supporters were those in the old, declining crafts such as handloom weaving, wool-combing, frame-knitting, and nail making, where wages were sinking to starvation level. The second main group consisted of skilled workers in traditional crafts such as cabinet making, shoe-making, printing, and tailoring, still largely untouched by technological change. These crafts contained the elite of the old working class, who were accustomed to association in their trade unions and friendly societies, and had a political awareness far in advance of most workers. They were typical of the London Working Men's Association, founded in 1836 by William Lovett with the aim of drawing 'into one bond of unity the intelligent and influential portion of the working classes in town and country. To seek by every legal means to place all classes of society in possession of equal political and social rights'. It was the London Working Men's Association which drew up the original Charter in 1838, the battle-cry of the Chartists.

Thus Chartism was a reaction against those aspects of the Industrial Revolution which, at a time when the government took little interest in regulating working conditions, wages and hours, led to the exploitation of labour. The main centres of Chartist disturbances were in areas of decaying industries like the outworking villages of Lancashire, Yorkshire, Nottinghamshire and Leicestershire, where the last survivors of domestic spinning and weaving were to be found, and in medium-sized industrial towns like Bolton and Bradford, which grew with astonishing speed in the first half of the nineteenth century. Large towns such as Birmingham, Bristol, Leeds and Manchester had many Chartists, but they were often less militant, while the country villages and market towns supplied few recruits to the movement.

The Chartist leaders were drawn chiefly from the ranks of the working classes. William Lovett, a tall, melancholy man, was born in Penzance in Cornwall, where he was brought up as a Methodist. After migrating to London in 1821 he became a journeyman cabinet maker, and in 1836 he founded the London Working Men's Association. Its aim was the reform of Parliament, and in 1838, with the help of Henry Hetherington and Francis Place, Lovett drew up the famous Charter. Lovett wished to persuade Parliament to accept the Chartists' demands through the 'moral force' of their arguments. His support came mainly from London, and from Wales and Scotland, where religious nonconformity gave the Chartist agitation a strong moral force tone. The North of England, with its tradition of mass agitation, provided more aggressive leadership, and the popular support on which demagogues like Feargus O'Connor relied. O'Connor was convinced that the Charter would only become law if the government was frightened into accepting it, and he used his position as editor of the Leeds *Northern Star* to preach 'physical force' Chartism. O'Connor was a brilliant orator who could arouse a crowd to a pitch of enthusiasm, but he was too

erratic to provide good leadership. His extremism was to alienate a section of the middle classes which allied itself to the Chartist cause under Thomas Attwood. Attwood, a banker, founded the Birmingham Political Union to press for currency reform which he believed would cure the country's ills. Others who played important parts were Joseph Stephens, John Fielden and Richard Oastler, both keen factory reformers, and John Frost, who led the miners in the Newport Rising.

Signs of coming violence were visible during the winter of 1838–9. Widespread drilling took place in the North, and huge torchlight meetings were held. Signatures for the petition were collected, and delegates to a Chartist Convention elected. The Convention met in London on 4 February 1839, to coincide with the opening of Parliament which it claimed to supersede. Its task was to decide what steps should be taken if the petition was rejected, but almost immediately it split into two factions. Lovett attacked the violent language of the northern Chartists: 'The whole physical force agitation is harmful and injurious to the movement. Muskets are not what are wanted, but education and schooling of the working people'. When the petition containing $1\frac{1}{4}$ million signatures was rejected in the Commons by 235 votes against 46, the Convention proclaimed a 'sacred month', or general strike, together with a refusal to pay any rent, rates or taxes.

The Government, however, took firm action. Lovett and several hundred Chartists were imprisoned. Sir Charles Napier was placed in command of the Northern District with 6,000 troops and artillery. The choice of Napier was a wise one. He sympathized with many of the Chartist demands, but he utterly opposed the use of illegal force. He invited the leaders of the northern Chartists to a gunnery demonstration, where he informed them that he

would never allow them to charge him with their pikes, or even march ten miles, without mauling

61 *Chartist Revolt, 1839*
Chartists, led by John Frost, attempt to capture the Westgate Hotel,
Newport

them with cannons and musketry, and charging them with cavalry when they dispersed to seek food; finally, that the country would rise on them and they would be destroyed in three days.[2]

There was no Chartist rising apart from John Frost's tragic attempt to seize Newport. The march was quickly broken up by a few troops as the Chartists entered the town; fourteen Chartists were killed, while their leaders were rounded up and transported. Thus ended the first phase of the Chartist movement.

In 1842 a second petition containing 3 million signatures was presented to the Commons. It was again decisively rejected by 287 votes to 49. Strikes and scattered riots followed, especially in Lancashire, where many men were out of work. But once again the high hopes of the Chartists came to nought, and Lovett abandoned the movement to devote his energies to the cause of working-class education.

Two further developments remain to be considered; O'Connor's Land Scheme, and the third petition. O'Connor hated industrialism, and in 1845 he created the National Land Company which was to buy land for resettling workers on three-acre smallholdings. The money was to be raised by the sale of shares costing 26/- each, and lucky shareholders were to be selected by ballot. A Land Bank to finance the operations of the company was formed in 1846, and by 1848 five estates had been established. In 1849, however, the scheme collapsed. Many of the settlers were townsmen, with little knowledge of farming. Arrears of rent piled up. Finally the Government declared that the company was not registered according to the law. O'Connor, who had worked hard to ensure the success of his venture, suffered great financial loss when the company went bankrupt.

In 1847 trade slumped and food prices rose; bread riots flared up as discontent grew and enthusiasm for the Charter mounted. O'Connor's election as M.P. for Nottingham was hailed as a good omen by the Chartists, and the revolution in Paris added to the mounting political excitement. A new petition was organized, and signed by an estimated $5\frac{1}{2}$ million people. The leaders planned to hold a massed meeting of Chartists on Kennington Common, whence they would march on Parliament, in order to present the petition. The Government, which was seriously alarmed by the threat, took elaborate military precautions, enrolling over 100,000 special constables, and forbidding the marchers to cross the Thames. The petition, therefore, weighing over five hundredweight, was taken in three cabs to Parliament, where a committee discovered that it contained only 2 million signatures, as well as many fictitious names such as 'No Cheese', 'Pug Nose' and 'Flat Nose'. Both Queen Victoria and the Duke of Wellington were included some fifteen or sixteen times. On one sheet was written the words 'We could not get paid for any more today'. Parliament refused to discuss the petition, which was laughed out of existence. Chartism was a spent force from this time onwards, though it lingered on until 1858.

Chartism failed because many of its ideas looked back to an age that was fast disappearing, while its political demands were too revolutionary for the times. The clock could not be put back to an age of domestic industry, and the middle classes, only recently given the vote, joined the landowning aristocracy in resisting any extension of the vote to the working classes, who were themselves not united in seeking it. Rival movements such as the Ten Hours' Movement for Factory Reform, the Cooperative Societies, and even the Anti-Corn Law League, which offered hopes of a reduction in price of bread, attracted many workers away from Chartism. The driving force of Chartism was economic and social discontent and, as wages gradually rose and unemployment fell, interest in the movement waned. The Factory Acts of 1844 and 1847, and the Mines Act of 1842, provided better conditions for textile workers and coal miners, who were the backbone of the movement. Lastly, Chartism lacked a coordinating purpose and strong, united leadership. Both the aims and the tactics of the movement were often the subject of bitter argument. The more responsible trade unionists stayed outside, so that Chartism attracted the wilder elements of the working classes, which alienated not only the middle classes and Lovett's supporters, but enabled the Government to take effective steps to neutralize the agitation.

Even though Chartism failed it is not lacking in importance. Though it would be wrong to say that Chartism frightened the Government into passing social reform, the fears aroused by Chartism helped push Parliament more quickly along the path of social reform. By channelling the expression of discontent into peaceful petitioning, it acted as a safety valve in a period when most European countries experienced revolutions. In its reliance on great principles instead of great men Chartism played its part in educating the working classes for a more democratic system of government, and in its strengthening of class consciousness it contributed something to the later development of socialism. Finally the Six Points were not outrageous demands; only the request for annual parliaments never became law. The property qualification for M.P.s was abolished in 1858; secret ballot was introduced in 1872; M.P.s were paid after 1911; universal manhood suffrage arrived in 1918, and a series of reform Acts have created a system of roughly equal electoral districts.

REFERENCES

1 Hansard, *Parliamentary Debates*, 1839.
2 W. Napier, *The Life and Opinions of Sir Charles Napier*, Vol. II, 1857.

Whereas the Chartist movement was noisy in order to impress the Government, the cooperative societies wished to be left alone, and asked nothing of the law except protection. Dr William King, who formed the Brighton Cooperative Trading Association in 1827, emphasized the strong element of self help in the movement, and the way in which the working class was beginning to seek respectability and independence.

The principle of the society is—the value of labour. The operation is by means of a common capital. An individual capital is an impossibility to the workman, but a common capital is not. The advantage of the plan is that of mutual insurance; but there is an advantage beyond, viz that the workman will thus get the whole produce of his labour to himself, and if he chooses to work harder or longer, he will benefit in proportion.[1]

William Lovett, who was storekeeper of the London Cooperative Society, opened in 1826, described the methods of the early societies.

The members subscribed a small weekly sum for the raising of a common fund, with which they opened a general store, containing such articles of food, clothing, books, etc. as were most in request among working men, the profits of which were added to the common stock. As their funds increased, some of them employed their members, such as shoemakers, tailors, and other domestic trades; paying them journeymen's wages, and adding the profits to their funds. Many of them were also enabled by these means to raise sufficient capital to commence manufactures on a small scale, such as broadcloths, silk, linen, and worsted goods, shoes, hats, cutlery, furniture etc. . . . I was sanguine that those associations formed the first step towards the social independence of the labouring classes . . . and that

the gradual accumulation of capital by these means would enable the working classes to ultimately have the trade, manufactures, and commerce of the country in their own hands.[2]

By 1831 there were over 300 societies scattered over the country. In that year 3,000 members from 56 societies met in Manchester, where they formed the North-West of England United Cooperative Company with its wholesale warehouse in Liverpool. Robert Owen developed a similar scheme whereby the workers in each trade exchanged their products with those of another. The chief difficulty was the disposal of the workers' products, and Labour Exchanges, or Exchange Bazaars, were set up as central depots where goods were exchanged according to the amount of labour involved in making them. But the Exchanges were quickly glutted with goods for which there was little demand, and they soon disappeared.

The cooperative movement owed a great debt to Owen, who accepted industrialization but detested capitalism. Owen wished to establish 'Villages of Cooperation' where capitalism, competition, and the profit motive would be replaced by cooperation. Each village would have about a thousand people who would be self-sufficient, producing goods priced not in terms of money but in labour hours. Owen made several attempts to establish such communities, notably at Queenswood, and 'New Harmony' in America, but all failed. The schemes involved great expense in establishing the villages, and the difficulties of keeping them going soon proved insurmountable. The villages could not compare favourably with towns in terms of production, culture and social activities, while the restrictions imposed by communal living were almost intolerable. Thus there were two kinds of cooperation. The first involved the buying and selling of goods without the intervention of middlemen and the profit motive. The second involved the ownership of the means of production, and ultimately the land itself. All the early attempts at cooperation failed, but these two aspects of the cooperative movement later merged successfully in the Co-operative Wholesale Society.

The Cooperative Movement revived in 1844 when seven weavers formed the Rochdale Society of Equitable Pioneers, with 28 members and a working capital of £28, half of which was spent in renovating and stocking an old warehouse in Toad Lane which was to serve as their shop. The aims of the Society were:

The establishment of a store for the sale of provisions, clothing, etc. The building, purchasing, or erecting a number of houses, in which those members, desiring to assist each other in improving their domestic and social condition, may reside. The manufacture of such articles as the Society may determine upon, for the employment of such members as may be without employment, or who may be suffering in consequence of repeated reductions in their wages.[3]

The success of the Rochdale Pioneers was founded on the principle of dividend upon purchase. Part of the profit made by the society, that is the difference between the retail price and the wholesale price of the articles sold, was ploughed back into the business; the rest was returned to the customer in proportion to the amount he had purchased. The Rochdale Society grew rapidly. Within twenty years it had over 5,000 members, and a share capital of nearly £80,000.

In 1846 the cooperative societies were granted legal protection, and in 1852 they obtained the right to sue. Their growth was further encouraged by the Limited Liability Acts of 1856 and 1862, whereby shareholders became liable only to the extent of the shares

they held in the society, instead of the full amount of any debt incurred by the society. Cooperative stores appeared all over the North and Midlands, and in 1872, when they joined together to form the Cooperative Wholesale Society, the movement had nearly ½ million members.

The next stage in the development of the CWS was the production of its own goods. Its first venture was to open a biscuit factory at Crumpsall, near Manchester, in 1872. Soon its activities ranged from providing its own banking and insurance facilities, to the manufacture of boots and shoes, soap, textiles, furnishings and furniture, paint, hardware, and glass. A cooperative dairy society was established at Drumcollogher, in Ireland, in 1889, and a creamery at Castlemahon. Bacon factories were opened in Denmark (1900), and Tralee, in Ireland (1901), while the Society purchased its own tea plantations in Ceylon (1902). In 1917 the movement brought out its own newspaper, and formed its own political party, the Cooperative Party, which worked closely with the Labour Party.

Today the range of services provided by the CWS is extensive. There are cooperative travel agencies and funeral directors, opticians and chemists, ballrooms and catering, in addition to ordinary shops and supermarkets. Throughout its history the movement has tried to keep to its principle of producing 'a better class of goods; things made to wear and not to sell. Cooperators ought to take a pride in making their "brand" an acknowledged sign of superiority'. Yet there is little doubt that the CWS is finding difficulty in keeping its idealism and pioneering spirit, and it is regarded by most members and outsiders merely as another gigantic commercial undertaking in a world of Big Business.

The rise of the Labour Party

Like Chartism and Owenism, many of whose demands it renewed, socialism aimed at changing the whole social and economic order in the interests of the working classes, who made up the great mass of the people. Like those movements too, it was a direct product of the Industrial Revolution which had created a wide gulf between the capitalists who owned the means of production and distribution, and the workers who merely worked for wages. William Morris, a socialist who wanted a return to self employment, attacked the system of 'wage slavery' when he wrote, in 1885:

The 'manufacturer' aims primarily at producing, by means of the labour he has stolen from others, not goods but 'profits', that is the 'wealth' that is produced over and above the livelihood of his workmen. Whether that 'wealth' is real or sham matters nothing to him. If it sells and yields him a 'profit' it is all right. . . . It is this system, therefore, which we must be resolute in getting rid of, if we are to attain to happy and useful work for all. The first step towards making labour attractive is to get the means of making labour fruitful, the Capital, including the land, machinery, factories, etc., into the hands of the community, to be used for the good of all alike.[4]

The most extreme doctrine of socialism was developed by Karl Marx (1818–83), a German Jew, who lived for much of his life in exile in England on account of his political beliefs. In 1847 Marx was co-author with Friedrich Engels of the *Communist Manifesto*. In his monumental work *Das Kapital*, published in 1867, Marx explained how his study of history had led him to his theory of class war. He believed that just as the middle classes, in replacing the agrarian framework of society by an industrial and commercial one, had usurped the supremacy of the old nobility, so the middle classes in their turn would be overthrown by the proletariat. Competition, which was unavoidable in a capitalist society, meant that the rich got richer, and the poor got poorer. But by concentrating wealth in fewer and fewer hands, and workers in large factories and

towns, capitalist societies were digging their own graves. When the working classes had been exploited beyond the limits of their endurance, violent revolution would lead to the establishment of the dictatorship of the proletariat, and the creation of a classless society, as all means of production, distribution and exchange came under public ownership. Though Marx never ceased to dream that socialist revolution in England was near at hand, the development of British socialism was hardly influenced by Marxist theories. Whereas in several European countries there developed well organized socialist parties which aimed at seizing power by revolutionary means, in England it was not until near the end of the century that the working classes became seriously interested in the creation of a special working-class party, and then its objective was to acquire influence by legal, parliamentary means.

There were several reasons for the slow growth of socialism. The Chartist outbursts had been followed by a long period of relative prosperity, in which the working classes had shared. The extensions of the franchise had increased the electoral importance of the workers. The Second Reform Act of 1867 almost doubled the electorate by giving the vote to the town artisan, while the Third Reform Act of 1884, which enfranchised the agricultural labourer, increased the number of men who could vote from $2\frac{1}{2}$ million to 5 million. Both major political parties adopted programmes of social reform, for neither of them could afford to alienate the working-class vote. Furthermore, the trade union movement had succeeded in improving the standards of living of its members. There were also, after 1867, a number of working class M.P.s. In some industrial areas the concentration of workers in one particular industry, such as coalmining, enabled them to return their own 'labour' candidates, though they were 'Labour' only in the sense that they were labouring men; they usually acknowledged membership of the Liberal Party, hence their nickname 'Lib-Labs'. All this meant that there was no compelling urgency for a party to represent solely the interests of the working classes.

Yet by the end of the century the workers were becoming more aware of the need for a Labour Party. The long period of prosperity had come to an end, and wages drifted behind prices as Britain's industrial supremacy was challenged by more efficient, newly industrialized nations such as Germany and the United States. The very success of New Unionism in organizing unskilled labour created stronger resistance on the part of employers to the workers' demands, a process which seemed aided and abetted by the courts. Several important legal decisions, by questioning the legality of strikes and picketing, dealt heavy blows to trade unionism. In 1886 the Liberal Party split over the issue of Home Rule for Ireland, and in the next few years Gladstone's governments concentrated on conditions in Ireland to the neglect of those in England. Lastly, there was greater familiarity with socialist ideas as a result of the increasing activity of local and central government in the daily life of the people. The 'Gas and Water Socialism' of some major cities like Birmingham popularized the idea of public ownership of certain essential services and industries.

The first socialist organization since Chartism appeared in 1861, when Henry Hyndman founded the Democratic Federation. Mainly a middle-class body, its programme included the original Chartist demands for payment of M.P.s, equal electoral districts, and votes for all men. Among other things it also demanded the Right to Work, free education, and the nationalization of the land, railways, mines and banks. Renamed the Social Democratic Federation in 1884, it organized large-scale demonstrations such as that held in Trafalgar Square on 'Bloody Sunday' in November, 1887, when a workman was shot by the police, but it never succeeded in converting the working man to a liking for revolutionary activity. Two of its most prominent members

were John Burns, one of the leaders of the dockers' strike in 1889, and William Morris. Meanwhile, in 1884, a group of middle-class intellectuals had formed the Fabian Society. The Fabians, who included the social historians Sidney and Beatrice Webb, and the playwright George Bernard Shaw, put their faith in achieving socialism through the 'inevitability of gradualness', after the example of the Roman general Fabius, who defeated Hannibal by his delaying tactics and his refusal to fight pitched battles until victory was certain. The Fabians had considerable influence through their lectures, and the publication of *Fabian Essays*, which were factual analyses of contemporary conditions in support of socialist ideas.

The initiative for the formation of the Labour Party lies with James Keir Hardie. Born in Holytown, in Lanarkshire, Hardie was a coalminer from the age of ten years to the day when he was dismissed for acting as the miners' spokesman in resisting a reduction of their wages in 1879. He took up journalism, and devoted his life to helping the miners' cause, becoming a socialist in the process. In 1887 and 1888 he published a small journal *The Miner*, and in the latter year took part in forming a Scottish Labour Party. In 1892 Hardie was elected member of Parliament for West Ham, and created a minor sensation when he appeared at Westminster in a cloth cap instead of the customary top hat. Shortly afterwards, in January 1893, he was chairman of a conference of trade union delegates and representatives from the various socialist groups which met at Bradford and formed the Independent Labour Party. But in the general election of 1895 the party failed to secure the return of even one of its 28 candidates, so that the continuous history of the Labour Party may be said to have begun in 1900, when the Labour Representation Committee, more simply known as the Labour Party, was born. Its chairman was Keir Hardie, and its first secretary, James Ramsay MacDonald, a future prime minister.

Hardie's socialism was uncomplicated and direct, like his speeches, and sprang from a Christian desire to help the poor. 'I myself have found in the Christianity of Christ', he admitted later, 'the inspiration which first of all drove me into the movement and has carried me on in it.'[5] Hardie never understood Marxism, and never tried to. 'I am not guided so much by a consideration of policy, or by thinking out a long sequence of events, as by intuition and inspiration. I know what I believe to be the right thing, and I go and do it.'[6] A pacifist, he made himself unpopular by opposing both the Boer War and the Great War, declaring that he would rather see his own son in the grave than fight his fellow workers. In Parliament he fought on behalf of the miners, the unemployed and the distressed. Unlike some of his more extremist socialist brethren, who wished to overthrow the state as a capitalist institution, Hardie did not regard the state as an enemy of Socialism. He once told an audience:

The State itself is neither capitalist nor anticapitalist. The State is simply a good old donkey that goes the way its driver wants it to go. When the capitalists rule, of course the State serves the capitalists. When the workers get sense enough to stop sending capitalists, and send Socialists drawn from their own ranks to represent them, then the State becomes your servant, and not the servant of the capitalists.[7]

The growth of the Labour Party astounded contemporaries. In 1900 63,000 men voted Labour and returned two Labour M.P.s: Keir Hardie for Merthyr Tydvil, and Richard Bell for Derby. In 1906 323,000 men did so, and 29 Labour M.P.s took their seats in the Commons, a number which was increased to 42 in the second election of 1910. After 1911 the Labour Party even had its own newspaper, the *Daily Herald*. Nevertheless, Labour had not achieved power and, as Hardie declared in 1914, though 'The past twenty-one years have been years of progress, we are only at the beginning. The emancipation of the worker has still to be achieved'.[8] Before the First World War the Labour Party could only play a small role in Parliament, giving its support to social reforms such as the Eight Hour Day for Miners, and Old Age Pensions. Even when Ramsay MacDonald headed two Labour governments in 1924 and 1929–31, he achieved very little, for Labour did not have an absolute majority over the other two major parties, and it took office in difficult circumstances. Thus the nationalization of several vital industries, and the creation of the 'Welfare State', longstanding socialist ambitions, were only realized between 1945 and 1951, when a Labour government under Clement Attlee was in office with the majority needed to carry out a socialist programme of legislation.

REFERENCES

1   Dr King to Henry Brougham MP, quoted in T. W. Mercer, *Dr W. King and the Cooperator 1828–1830.*
2   William Lovett, *The Life and Struggles of William Lovett* (1876).
3   G. J. Holyoake, *The History of the Rochdale Pioneers* (1857).
4   William Morris, *Useful Work v Useless Toil* (1885).
5   W. Stewart, *J. Keir Hardie* (Cassell, 1925).
6   W. Stewart, op. cit.
7   W. Stewart, op. cit.
8   W. Stewart, op. cit.

CHAPTER 25
The Reform of Factories, Workshops and Mines

The nineteenth-century working-class movements were a response to the Industrial Revolution which had created a new environment and changed the lives and occupations of many people. As human power, which was characteristic of the domestic system of industry, was replaced first by water power and then by steam power, the family as the most common unit of production was destroyed, and the factory took its place. In the eighteenth century large units of production were already found in a few industries such as silk manufacture, shipbuilding, and the metal industries, but during the course of the nineteenth century they became the typical organization of firms. Great misery was caused before the material benefits they brought outweighed their ill effects. Thus several independent movements, in which the workers set out to help themselves, came into existence, and these worked alongside charitable organizations and Parliament in gradually making life better for most people.

It was only as fear of revolution receded after 1815, and after the reform of Parliament in 1832, when the landowner's influence in the House of Commons was reduced, that Parliament really began to legislate on social problems. The dominant economic ideas of the early nineteenth century emphasized the importance of a vigorous individualism and 'laissez-faire', a policy of 'leave well alone'. This meant that the duty of the government was to ensure the free play of economic forces in society, and to interfere with them as little as possible. In general it was sincerely believed that success was the reward of adaptability, self-denial and hard work, and that if more men practised these qualities human misery would be greatly reduced. Secondly,

charity was regarded less as a duty of the state than of the individual. Many industrialists fulfilled their obligations, providing generous benefits and facilities for their workpeople but, whereas in former times the village squire and parson, and the local justices of the peace, had been adequate safeguards for seeing that the poor did not suffer intolerable misery, the need for government intervention to help the less fortunate in society was made painfully clear in the nineteenth century by the sheer scale and complexity of the problems which arose.

Industrial conditions in early Victorian England were chaotic. Factories had started up in dilapidated sheds and buildings, and had spread out to the moors, hillsides and villages as the financial circumstances of the owners permitted. The most publicized evils of the factory system were usually found in the old and small mills, where machinery was so crowded together that passageways were not clearly defined, and where accidents occurred most frequently from machinery not being boxed in. Ceilings were sometimes so low that it was difficult to stand upright, while lighting, ventilation, and drainage were inadequate. It was in these mills that the worst cases of child cruelty were found. Many of the large mills, however, were beautifully situated in the countryside, with their internal arrangements made, so far as possible, with a view to the comfort of the workpeople, though such mills were in a minority. The report of one factory inspector called Horner in 1837 makes it clear that no generalization is possible on the evils of the factory system. He wrote:

I have often wished that those who so thoughtlessly

believe and give currency to tales of the miseries of the factory worker, and of the cruelty and hard-heartedness of their masters, would go to some of the mills to which I could send them, and judge for themselves. They would then see how greatly they have erred in their general condemnation of what they term the factory system, and how much virtue, intelligence, comfort and happiness are to be found among the workers in a well regulated mill.[1]

Great contrasts also existed in coalmining and iron manufacturing. An official account of the miners and ironworkers of Merthyr Tydvil describes how

Their houses are ranged round the works in rows, sometimes two to five deep, sometimes three stories high. They rarely contain less than from one to six lodgers in addition to the members of the family, and afford most scanty accommodation for so many inmates. It is not unusual to find that ten individuals of various ages and sex occupy three beds in two small rooms. The surface of the soil around is frequently blackened with coal, or covered with high mounds of refuse from the mines and furnaces. The road between the rows is so imperfectly made as to be often, in wet weather, ankle deep in black mud. Volumes of smoke from the furnaces, and the rolling mills and the coke hearths are driven past according to the direction of the wind.[2]

Here 'The boys are taken into the coal or iron mine at eight or nine years old, often earlier. The value of the labour of the youngest is about 6d a day. Their occupation consists in opening and shutting air-doors, in throwing small pieces of coal or ironstone into the trams, or in handing implements to the men at work.'[3] Where coal seams were not very thick, these children spent their days in what amounted to solitary confinement in darkness, for they had to be in the pit as soon as work started, and they could not leave before the end of the day's shift. Their wages were spent mainly on gambling, drinking and smoking. Skilled workers and coal hewers could earn very good wages of up to £3 or £4 a week, and evidence of material wealth could be seen

inside their cottages, each of which had an 'abundant store of provisions, substantial and costly furniture, together with an ample store of good clothing with which themselves and their families are furnished'.[3]

Yet fearful accidents were common in the mines. They were caused mainly by inadequate ventilation and drainage, and by the practice of entrusting air-doors underground, and winding machinery at the top of the shaft, to young children. Pit-falls too were frequent. Mining was also an unhealthy occupation. One of the conclusions reached in the *Mines Report* of 1842 was that mining 'deteriorates the physical constitution; the limbs become distorted; and in general the muscular powers give way, and the workpeople are incapable of following their occupations at an earlier period of life than is common in other branches of industry'.[4]

But the most distressed sections of the population in the early nineteenth century were the handloom weavers and knitters. The invention of power spinning had created a brief period of prosperity for them, but high wages and the ease with which the occupations could be learned, had attracted too many people into them, so that wages were depressed. In Lancashire the influx of Irish who were willing to accept low wages, which were better than they could hope to obtain in their own country, made matters worse. In the South-west of England and East Anglia the major cause of their distress was the loss of their industry to the north. In Lancashire, once power weaving became general, the hand weavers were cast on the industrial scrap heap. Their misery was prolonged because manufacturers found them a useful reservoir of labour which could be tapped when trade was brisk, but handweavers were the first to be laid off when business slackened, while the fact that they worked in their homes put them in a weak bargaining position with their employers.

Their plight was made worse by the difficulty of finding other work. Trade unions restricted entry into their particular crafts, so that it was not easy for unskilled labourers to find jobs which offered them some sort of security. Mobility of labour was restricted by the Settlement Laws which prevented a man from leaving his village unless he had a certificate stating that his parish accepted full responsibility for him, so that he would not become a burden on the rates of another parish. In 1795 the laws were altered to the extent that a man could only be sent back to his own parish when he became chargeable on the rates, and not immediately he appeared in a parish not his own. The Settlement Laws did not finally disappear until the Union Chargeability Act of 1865. Families too were reluctant to tear up their roots in a village to seek employment in an unfamiliar town, especially when moving about the country was difficult before the spread of railways.

The efforts of humanitarians and social reformers were at first concerned with checking the exploitation of young children who were unable to help themselves. The early spinning mills, which were water powered, were often built in remote parts of the countryside, so that labour had to be imported. Many of these mills obtained their apprentices aged 6 to 12 years from foundling hospitals and the workhouses of large towns like London and Birmingham, which were relieved of the costs of maintaining them. Sometimes the children lived in special apprentice houses, as at Quarry Bank Mill, at Styal, in Cheshire, or sometimes they had their sleeping quarters on the top floor of the mill, above the machines they tended by day. During their so-called apprenticeship the orphan children worked without pay, the millowner merely providing food, clothing, and shelter. Children were employed in preference to adults wherever possible, because they could be paid lower wages, and they were also more easily controlled than adult male labour—an important consideration for a millowner when large numbers of workers were gathered under one roof. Moreover, the simplicity and smallness of early spinning machinery meant that they could be tended by children, whose supple fingers could perform the intricate repairs to snapped threads.

The first Factory Act was the Health and Morals of Apprentices Act (1802), introduced by Sir Robert Peel the Elder. It applied to textile mills only, and limited the hours of apprentices to 12 hours daily between 6 a.m. and 9 p.m. Night shifts were forbidden, and education was to be provided in some suitable part of the building. The manufacturers evaded this law, however, by employing 'free' children, i.e. children whose parents had consented to allow them to work. A Factory Act of 1819 prohibited the employment of children under 9 years old, and limited the hours of those under 16 years to 12 hours a day. But the 1819 Act applied to cotton mills only, and both the 1802 and 1819 Acts failed to provide for proper inspection, so that they were largely ignored by millowners.

Fortunately, factory conditions slowly improved, though they remained terrible by today's standards. With the spread of steam-driven machinery most of the early mills were either enlarged, or were abandoned by wealthy owners and rebuilt. In the early mills it had been difficult to combine the high temperature needed with an adequate supply of fresh air. The use of steam pipes, which gave out calculated quantities of heat overcame this problem. An even temperature could be maintained, and windows could be opened for ventilation. Machinery could be laid out in rows in spacious rooms. Cleanliness was cultivated. Iron machinery and floors were easier to clean than wooden machinery and floors, which soaked up the oil. At the same time the fire hazard was reduced. Gas lighting instead of candles was another improvement. Much of the dust and fine cottony down which had clogged the atmosphere of the older mills disappeared with new methods of cleansing the cotton.

Wages in the mills were comparatively high compared with other occupations—they had to be to attract labour. Fine-yarn spinners earned 25/- to 30/- per week, and coarse spinners up to 21/-. Weavers, chiefly young women and girls, could expect 10/- to 16/- a week, and children 3/6 per week. But the early age from which millworkers were employed, and the long hours of monotonous work in unhealthy surroundings impaired their health. Workers in cotton factories usually rose at 5 o'clock in the morning and worked in the mill from 6 a.m. to 8 a.m. when they returned home for half an hour for breakfast. Breakfast generally consisted of tea or coffee with a little bread, and sometimes oatmeal porridge. They then returned to the mill until midday, when an hour was allowed for lunch—usually of boiled potatoes covered with melted lard or butter, with sometimes a few pieces of meat or fried bacon in addition. The working day ended at 7 or 8 p.m., unless overtime was demanded. It was these excessively long hours, especially for children, which provided the chief target for factory reformers.

In northern industrial districts a strong agitation for factory reform grew up, led in Lancashire by John Fielden, a millowner, and in Yorkshire by Richard Oastler, an estate agent with a gift for political agitation. In 1830 Oastler published a series of letters called *Yorkshire Slavery,* which shocked public opinion. In them he denounced

the cruelties which are inflicted personally upon the little children, not to mention the immensely long hours which they are subject to work, are such as I am very sure would disgrace a West Indian plantation. On one occasion I was in the company of a West Indian slave-master and three Bradford spinners; they brought the two systems into fair comparison, and the spinners were obliged to be silent when the slave owner said, 'Well, I have always thought myself disgraced by being the owner of black slaves, but we never, in the West Indies, thought it was possible for any human being to be

so cruel as to require a child of 9 years old to work 12½ hours a day; and that, you acknowledge, is your regular practice.'[6]

Michael Sadler, a Tory M.P., sponsored the cause of factory reform in Parliament by introducing a bill demanding a Ten Hours' working day, but he failed to secure its passage.

In the 1832 general election Sadler lost his seat, and Ashley Cooper, who later became Lord Shaftesbury, took over the leadership of the factory reform movement in Parliament. The 1833 Factory Act was the result of Ashley's cooperation with Viscount Althorp, the Home Secretary, after whom the Act was named. It applied to all textile mills except silk and lace. No child under 9 was to be employed; children aged 9–13 could work a maximum of 9 hours a day and 48 a week. Young persons between 13 and 18, and children under 13 had to attend school two hours daily. Four inspectors were appointed to enforce the Act, which became the model for factory legislation for at least a quarter of a century. In 1836 an Act making compulsory the Registration of Births, Marriages and Deaths was passed to enable factory inspection to be carried out efficiently.

In 1844 Peel's government passed another important factory Act which reduced the hours of work for children in textile mills. Children between the ages of 8 (not 9 as formerly) and 13 were not to work more than 6½ hours a day. Young persons, and women (included for the first time) were limited to 12 hours a day. Dangerous machinery was to be fenced in, and accidents reported to doctors. Certificates of age and school attendance were made compulsory.

But neither the 1833 Factory Act, nor that of 1844, satisfied factory reformers, whose aim was the restriction of adult labour to ten hours a day. The 1833 factory commissioners were convinced that 'the interests of the children are, of all other considerations, that which appears to enter least into the councils of the operative agitators'.[7] It was generally assumed or admitted that the restriction of child labour would also limit the hours of adults; in textile mills children and adults 'must always go together; they can't do without one another'. The Ten Hours' Movement finally achieved its aim with the passage of the 1847 Factory Act. This limited the hours of work in textile mills to 58 a week, or the equivalent of a ten-hour day. The relay system, whereby children began and stopped work at different times, had made inspection difficult. An Act of 1850, which clearly defined the limits of the working day, put an end to this practice. With this Act the spotlight was taken off the textile industries, and subsequent factory legislation applied increasingly to other industries.

Coalmining was regulated by Parliament. The Mines Act of 1842, introduced by Lord Ashley, forbade the employment of women and children underground. No child under 10 was to be employed, and no child under 15 could be put in charge of winding machinery. Hours, however, were unrestricted. A further Act in 1850 provided for government inspection of mines, and owners were compelled to submit plans of the workings of their collieries.

But outside textiles and coalmining, industrial conditions were almost untouched by legislation. Karl Marx found that in brick and tile making 'Work from five in the morning until seven in the evening is considered "reduced" and "moderate". Both boys and girls of six, and even four years of age, are employed. They often work longer than adults.'[8] In straw plaiting children often started work at 4 years old. Terrible conditions existed in Sheffield's industries, and in the Black Country trades such as chain and nail making, and in the clothing trades, notorious as 'sweated industries'. Sweating was defined as 'a condition of industry under which workers are practically compelled to work at starvation wages for excessive hours and under insanitary conditions'. In parts of the East End of London, and in some provincial towns,

62 Brick-makers

nearly every house contained sweating dens. One member of the Children's Employment Commission (1864) described sweated labour in Nottingham thus:

It is not at all uncommon to find 14 to 20 children huddled together in a small room, perhaps not more than twelve feet square, and employed for 15 hours out of 24 at work that of itself is exhausting from its weariness and monotony, and is besides carried on under every possible unwholesome condition.[9]

In 1860 bleaching and dyeing establishments were brought under the Factory Acts. An Act of 1861 regulated conditions in lace-making where it was done by machinery. The Factory Act of 1864 was the first attempt to extend factory regulations to trades and industries, such as pottery, not carried on in conventional factories. Two related Acts of 1867, the Factory Extension Act, and the Workshop Regulation Act, applied the principles of previous factory laws to foundries, copper mills, printing and book-binding, and the manufacture of paper, glass and tobacco, but relaxed the definition of a normal working day. Male young persons could be put on night shift in blast furnaces, iron and paper mills, and others, provided they were not employed on the day before, or the day after. The Workshop Regulation Act provided for inspection of premises where more than fifty people were employed, but in order not to overburden the factory inspectorate, this responsibility was placed upon the local authorities. This experiment, however, did not prove successful, and in 1871 the duty of inspection was transferred from the Poor Law Boards of Guardians to the inspectors.

In 1876 the working day in textile factories was reduced by half an hour. The Factory and Workshop Act of 1878, in Disraeli's second Ministry, was important because it consolidated all existing factory legislation into one Act. Special rules for white lead works and bakehouses were introduced in 1883. Factory Acts in 1891 and 1901 raised the minimum age of child labour from 10 years to 11, and from 11 to 12 years respectively. A parallel series of Acts was also passed governing conditions in mines. A safety Act of 1855 brought in a code of General Rules for collieries. The Coalmines Regulation Act (1860) prohibited the employment of children under 12 years unless they had a certificate proving they had reached a certain standard of education. An appalling series of accidents brought about the Coal Mines Act of 1872 which compelled colliery managers to possess certificates of technical competence. Pits were to be inspected daily to ensure that they were safe.

One of the most notable campaigns for social reform in the nineteenth century concerned climbing boys, the assistants of chimney sweeps. Their plight was perhaps one of the most haunting evils of the Victorian age. An Act of 1788 had failed completely to protect chimney sweep apprentices. These wretched creatures spent their childhood sweeping chimneys and flues which sometimes were only seven inches square. If they were frightened or unwilling to climb the chimney, pins were forced into their feet by the boy who followed them up, or lighted straw was used for the same purpose. Their knees and elbows were rubbed with brine to harden them. They seldom washed, and by living and working in sooty conditions, many con-

tracted an unpleasant disease, 'sooty cancer'. Their cause was championed by Lord Shaftesbury and the novelist, Charles Kingsley. An Act of 1834, which made it a misdemeanour to send a boy up a chimney while the fire was still alight, and another of 1840, had done little to abolish the evil, for twenty-three boys were suffocated in chimneys during the next twenty years. In 1863, in an attempt to arouse the public conscience. Kingsley published the *Water Babies*. The next year, Parliament passed an Act prohibiting sweeps from employing children under 10 and from using children under 16 for actually cleaning the chimneys. In 1875 sweeps were compelled to take out annual licences, and the difficult task of enforcing the law was handed over to the police. Fortunately, the spreading use of machinery, which practically supplanted human labour in sweeping, meant that future legislation on this subject was of trifling importance.

REFERENCES

1   *Parliamentary Papers*, 1837/XXXI, p. 93.
2   Seymour Tremenheere's description of the mining village of Merthyr Tydvil in 1839, in Report to the Committee of the Council for Education, Appendix II: *Parliamentary Papers*, 1840/XL, pp. 208–9.
3   Seymour Tremenheere, op. cit., p. 212.
4   Seymour Tremenheere, op. cit.
5   *Reports from Commissioners: Children's Employment (Mines)*, XV, p. 258.
6   Richard Oastler, *Yorkshire Slavery*, in *Report on the Bill to regulate the Labour of Children in Mills and Factories*, 1832.
7   *Report of Commissioners on the Employment of Children in Factories: Parliamentary Papers* 1833/XX p. 49.
8   Karl Marx, *Das Kapital* (London ed., 1938).
9   *Children's Employment Commission* (1864).

CHAPTER 26
Medical Advance, Public Health, and Local Government

This chapter tells of the remarkable progress in the conquest of disease, and in the general health of the British people. This was brought about firstly by medical advance, which meant that disease and injury no longer killed so many people; secondly, by social changes such as better houses, food and clothing, which made for healthier living; and thirdly, and perhaps most important of all, by the development of public health, when the Government concerned itself directly with protecting the nation's health.

Most Englishmen living in the early eighteenth century had a fatalistic attitude towards disease, assuming either that it was a punishment for sin, or that it was an unavoidable accompaniment of life. Although the plague had not reappeared after 1665, smallpox was a terrible scourge of all classes, carrying off one in thirteen of those who died, and disfiguring where it did not kill. Epidemic diseases claimed each year their heavy toll of victims. Even minor ailments such as the common cold and influenza caused great discomfort in an age when scientifically developed drugs were unknown. Surgery was primitive; complicated operations were almost impossible without anaesthetics, and where major surgery was attempted the patient usually died from the shock to his nervous system, or as a result of blood poisoning. The death rate, especially among infants, was appallingly high. Nearly half the children born died before reaching the age of two years. In London during the 1730s 35 out of every thousand people died each year, compared with 11 today.

Progress in medicine was handicapped by the traditional belief that diseases were due to impurities in the blood or other fluids, when

63 Leech finders in Yorkshire
The leeches attached themselves to the women's feet and legs, from which they were transferred to a small barrel, or keg of water slung around the waist. The leeches were used by doctors for bleeding their patients

treatment consisted of removing the impurities by bleeding, vomiting, purging, or sweating, and that other disorders in the human body were caused by undertension or overtension of particular organs, in which case the treatment consisted of stimulating or relaxing them with alcohol or opiates. Diseases were not properly classified. Dissection of the human body was forbidden by law, and disapproved of by public opinion. The medical profession itself was divided into three groups, physicians, surgeons and apothecaries, each jealous of its rights and status. Physicians usually had a degree in medicine, but their knowledge was acquired from books rather than contact with the sick. It was common practice for them to prescribe treatment for patients they had never seen, but whose symptoms had been described to them by apothecaries. Surgeons could operate on the exterior of their patients, but were not allowed to give internal medicines. Until 1745 when the surgeons broke away from the barber's gild, a man might be both a barber and a surgeon. Apothecaries, whom nowadays we should call chemists, were mere compounders of drugs. Since they did not charge fees for their diagnosis, the poor went to them for treatment, and there was much jealousy between apothecaries and physicians.

Yet important changes were beginning to lay the foundations for progress in medicine. Several London hospitals were founded in the early eighteenth century. The Westminster Hospital was built in 1719, St George's in 1733, and St Bartholomew's, a very old hospital, was rebuilt in 1729. Thomas Guy, a bookseller, built Guy's Hospital in 1721, and Thomas Coram, a sea captain, who had been saddened by the wretchedness of many children living in the slums of London dockland, founded a hospital for abandoned babies in 1740. Dispensaries were started where the poor could receive free treatment. The relationship between dirt and disease was slowly understood when doctors began to realize that cleanliness mattered. Cheap cotton clothes, more and cheaper soap, better food, cast iron water pipes instead of wooden ones, were only some of the beneficial results of the Agrarian and Industrial Revolutions.

Doctors were infected by the scientific spirit of enquiry of the second half of the eighteenth century. John Hunter (1728–93) through his anatomical research did much to make surgery an experimental science. William Smellie's methods in training London doctors and midwives led to a significant fall in that city's death rate. The most important development, however, came in 1798 when Edward Jenner (1749–1823) substituted vaccination for inoculation in the fight against smallpox. Inoculation, which induced a mild attack of smallpox in order to avoid a severe one, had been introduced into England from Turkey by Lady Mary Wortley Montagu, a famous traveller, but it was risky. Jenner

noticed that milkmaids were generally immune from smallpox, and he safeguarded his patients from smallpox by giving them the harmless cowpox. In France the Revolution freed French medicine from the paralysing grip of tradition. Many diseases were classified, thus facilitating their treatment. Physicians and surgeons began to cooperate more readily, and clinical procedures improved; patients were examined, not merely observed. Laennec invented the stethoscope in 1819, and in 1835 the value of the clinical thermometer was popularized by Bequerel and Breschet. All these new techniques were soon adopted in England.

Without anaesthetics, however, major surgery was almost impossible; without antiseptics even successful operations usually resulted in death as a result of blood poisoning. It was their discovery which revolutionized surgery and saved millions of lives. Sir Humphry Davy first discovered the pain-killing effects of nitrous oxide, or 'laughing gas', in 1800, and Michael Faraday in 1818 showed that ether produced insensibility to pain, but their experiments were not followed up at once. Even as late as 1839 Velpeau, a great French surgeon, declared: 'The avoidance of pain while operating is an idea for a fairy tale. . . . The cutting of the knife and pain are two aspects of surgery which cannot be separated, rather must the patient be logical and accept that they go together.' The use of ether as a reliable anaesthetic was pioneered by two Boston dentists, William Morton and Charles Jackson, in 1846, during an operation before an assembly of distinguished surgeons. The following year a Scottish surgeon, James Simpson (1811–70), used chloroform, and soon his example was followed by many others.

Unfortunately, in nearly half the operations, successful surgery was only a prelude to death, as gangrene usually set in. Simpson himself admitted that 'The man who is stretched on the operating table in one of our surgical hospitals is in far greater danger of dying, than was the English soldier on the battlefield of Waterloo'. It was well known that the chances of recovery from an operation were better in a private house than in a hospital. Hygiene in hospitals was almost entirely lacking, for the relationship between bacteria and disease had not been discovered. Surgical instruments were not sterilized, and surgeons performed operations in coats stiff with dried blood; indeed, the more senior and experienced the surgeon, the dirtier his coat. All too frequently the patient died of the dreaded 'hospital disease', blood poisoning. Semmelveis, a doctor in Vienna, discovered in 1847 that the number of cases of childbed fever in mothers in lying-in hospitals was reduced when doctors and nurses washed their hands in chlorinated water before approaching their patients, but his claim met a sceptical reaction, and it was left to Joseph Lister (1827–1912) to prove beyond all doubt the value of antiseptic surgery. Lister was Professor of Surgery in Glasgow. He used a weak solution of carbolic acid to spray the air while an operation was in progress, and he insisted that instruments and assistants' hands were scrupulously clean. At first Lister was ridiculed, but it soon became clear that his methods made operations safer, and they gradually became standard practice in hospitals.

After 1870 remarkable advances in medical knowledge brought about a sharp decline in the death rate from infectious diseases. Louis Pasteur, a French chemist and physicist, and Robert Koch, a German doctor, developed the science of bacteriology. They discovered that microscopic living organisms which they called bacilli caused diseases in animals and men, and that each disease was caused by one particular microbe or bacillus. Pasteur pioneered the practice of immunization, whereby protection from a particular disease was given for a limited length of time. In 1885 he discovered his famous cure for hydrophobia, a dreadful disease caused by the bite of a mad dog. Soon tetanus and diphtheria had been virtually conquered, and by the early twentieth century most organisms which caused disease had been identified.

Great advances were also made in radiology and in the development of new drugs. The German physicist Röntgen discovered X-rays in 1895, which came to be used not only for diagnosis but also for treatment in many cases. Radium, discovered by Madame Curie, is used in the treatment of some types of cancer. Vitamins, substances vital for health, were found in 1911, and after 1922 insulin saved the lives of many sufferers from diabetes. Another momentous achievement was Alexander Fleming's discovery of penicillin in 1928, now used in the treatment of many illnesses. In 1935 a group of new drugs known as sulphonamides, which killed many harmful organisms, was developed, and there seems to be no end to the products of science in combating disease.

Not all these discoveries were made in Britain, but the British people benefited immensely from them. The improvement in the nation's health was also aided by social change. As the standard of living rose, so life became more comfortable and enjoyable. Housing and public health were improved as a result of parliamentary legislation. Working hours were reduced, making more time available for recreation and leisure, and seaside holidays became more common for all classes of people. First the railway, then the bicycle, motor car, and motor coach replaced alcohol as the quickest way out of an industrial city. The beginnings of the Welfare State were seen in the greater concern shown to children. It has been claimed that the opening of children's clinics, and the medical inspection of school children, started in 1907, have saved more lives than were lost by Britain in the Great War.

The improvement in public health

Judged by the public health standards of today, eighteenth-century English towns were deficient in all the amenities we take for granted. Supplies of drinking water were often impure, sanitation and drainage inadequate, and unpleasant smells abounded. But there had been much town improvement in the latter half of the century, and not all towns were dismal, squalid places. Westminster was paved in 1762, Portsmouth was both paved and drained in 1769, while Liverpool, Birmingham and Bristol were civic minded. Southampton and Oxford were noted for their fine buildings, and watering spas such as Harrogate, Weymouth and Brighton were famous for their cleanliness. Bath, with its population of 30,000 was perhaps the most fortunate, for according to the Reverend Whitwell Elwin Bath was

surrounded by hills which pour down a vast

quantity of water into reservoirs. Pipes are laid from the reservoirs to every part of Bath and, as the springs from which the water rises are as high up on the hills as the roofs of the houses, water can be carried into the attics without the application of a forcing pump; thus no machinery is employed. The only water works are the pipes which convey the water. . . . In addition to these private supplies the corporation provides five public pumps which are open to all the inhabitants free of expense.[1]

Unfortunately, the efforts of many enterprising corporations were swamped when the towns multiplied in size and population. The early nineteenth-century industrial towns created grave problems of public health because their growth was so rapid and uncontrolled. Any ideas of town planning were

64   Cowgate in Edinburgh in 1840

swept aside as factories and houses sprang up in higgledy-piggledy fashion, and many factory towns grew as blots on the landscape. The families of labouring folk in manufacturing towns lacked most amenities.

They rise early, before daylight in winter time, to go to their work; they toil hard, and they return to their homes late at night. It is a serious inconvenience, as well as a discomfort, to them to have to fetch water at a distance out-of-doors, from a pump or the river on every occasion that it may be wanted. . . . The minor comforts of cleanliness are of course foregone, to avoid the immediate and greater discomfort of having to fetch the water.[2]

In many towns water was bought by the bucketful from water carriers. Investigations by energetic reformers like Dr Southwood Smith and Dr James Kay-Shuttleworth in several London neighbourhoods revealed shocking sanitary arrangements. Virginia Row was typical of many.

In the centre of this street there is a gutter, into which potato parings, the refuse of vegetable and animal matters of all kinds, the dirty water from the washing of clothes and of the houses are all poured. In a direct line from Virginia Row to Shoreditch, a mile in extent, all the lanes, courts, and alleys in the neighbourhood pour their contents into the centre of the main street, where they stagnate and putrefy. Families live in the cellars and kitchens of these undrained houses, dark and extremely damp. In some or other of these houses fever is always prevalent.[3]

Benjamin Disraeli, later prime minister, in his novel *Sybil* drew on contemporary conditions to describe an industrial town.

Wodgate had the appearance of a vast, squalid suburb. As you advanced, leaving behind you long lines of little dingy tenements, with infants lying about the road, you expected every moment to emerge into some streets and encounter buildings bearing some resemblance in their size and comfort to the considerable population swarming and busied around you. Nothing of the kind. There

were no public buildings of any sort. No churches, chapels, town halls, institute, theatre; and the principal streets in the heart of the town in which were situate the coarse and grimy shops, though formed by houses of a greater elevation than the preceding, were equally narrow and if possible more dirty. At every fourth or fifth house, alleys seldom above a yard wide and streaming with filth, opened out of the street. These were crowded with dwellings of various size, while from the principal court often branched out a number of smaller alleys, or rather passages, than which nothing can be conceived more close and squalid and obscure. Here during the days of business, the sound of the hammer and the file never ceased, amid gutters of abomination and piles of foulness and stagnant pools of filth; reservoirs of leprosy and plague, whose exhalations were sufficient to taint the atmosphere of the whole kingdom and fill the country with fever and pestilence.[4]

Such conditions, even if somewhat exaggerated, had demoralizing effects on the poor who were condemned to live in back-to-back houses with no through circulation of air. It was in the early nineteenth century that there began to develop a good 'west end' in cities, and a poor 'east end', for, though improvements were made in the districts where the wealthy lived, little was done to improve the poorer areas. The marked difference in health between industrial and agricultural workers, not to mention upper, middle and working classes, was notorious. The average age of death of mechanics, labourers and their families in Manchester and Rutlandshire was 17 and 38 years respectively. In 1839 in Bethnal Green (population 62,018) the average age of death, by classes, was as follows:

Number of deaths	Occupation	Average age of deceased
101	Gentlemen and persons engaged in professions and their families	45 years
273	Tradesmen and their families	26 years
1,258	Mechanics, servants and labourers and their families	16 years

The need for reform was urged not only by the medical profession but by the Poor Law Commissioners, who proved that there was a close relationship between pauperism and bad living conditions.

In general all epidemics and all infectious diseases are attended with charges immediate and ultimate on the rate. . . . The amount of burthens thus produced is frequently so great as to render it good economy on the part of the administrators of the Poor Laws to incur charges for preventing the evils, where they are ascribable to physical causes.[5]

It was the action of the Shoreditch Poor Law Guardians, who exceeded their powers in spending money on sanitary improvements in an effort to stamp out a bad outbreak of fever, which gave birth to the public health agitation. The expenditure was criticized in an official audit of the accounts, and the outcome was an inquiry in 1838, made on the insistence of Edwin Chadwick, the Secretary of the Poor Law Commissioners. Chadwick (1800–90) had become deeply interested in public health since one of his duties as Secretary was to visit slums in order to report on the conditions in which the poor lived and worked. Soon afterwards Chadwick was asked to conduct a nation-wide survey concerning all aspects of public health, and in 1842 he produced his Report *The Sanitary Condition of the Labouring Classes.* For several years no action was taken on its recommendations except the appointment of a Royal Commission to investigate the *State of Large Towns and Populous Districts,* which reported in 1844 and 1845. This was partly because the administrative problems were so complex that it took time to draw up an adequate bill, and partly because Parliament found itself fully occupied with the famine in Ireland and the campaign for the repeal of the Corn Laws. In 1848, however, the Public Health Act was passed. This set up a General Board of Health consisting of three members, Lord Morpeth, Lord Shaftesbury and Chadwick himself. Local boards of health could be established on the request of the General

Board in areas where the death rate exceeded 23 per 1,000 (the national average being 21 per 1,000), or where one-tenth of the inhabitants petitioned for one. The local boards had powers to borrow money and levy a rate to finance sanitary improvements. They could also deal with nuisances such as unpleasant smells, and control offensive trades.

Unfortunately, the Act had limited results. In the first place London, which was very jealous of outside control, was allowed to have its own separate scheme, and several of the larger cities followed suit. Secondly, the adoption of the Act was largely voluntary, and ratepayers in many areas did not want to spend money on these necessary services. Finally, no effective administrative machinery existed to carry out the Act. Chadwick wanted to make the Poor Law Guardians responsible for the public health because they were the only national form of administration under parliamentary control. There was at the time, however, great opposition to any kind of centralized control. Chadwick's critics did not fail to point out that Chadwick himself was Secretary to the Poor Law Commissioners, and his proposal was rejected. Thus the carrying out of the Act fell to a variety of bodies such as town corporations, Improvement Commissioners, local health boards, and parish vestries, which were often ill-equipped to do so. The weakness of the system was highlighted by the example of Stafford in 1869.

Stafford shows a confusion of old jurisdictions. The old borough is under Improvement Commissioners, while a district within the present municipality, called Newtown, remains without local government. The inhabitants outside the old borough are very desirous of obtaining the benefit of the Local Government Acts, but every attempt has been frustrated upon a division of the council. The Corporation and the Commissioners work separately and often clash. Neither body has power to borrow money for improvements.[6]

The Board of Health did not survive long.

In 1854 Chadwick, whose haughty manner made him many enemies, was retired on a pension, and four years later the Board itself was abolished. Like Florence Nightingale, whose work was about to begin, Chadwick fought unceasingly against ignorance and indifference. He was convinced that many thousands of deaths every year were caused not so much by medical ignorance, as by insanitary conditions which could be put right. Yet despite the difficulties many towns were improved, for public concern had been aroused by the terrible outbreak of cholera in 1848. Bristol was a good example of what an enlightened local government could accomplish. In addition to providing efficient sewerage and drainage, steps were taken to prevent disease. Every morning 'A very able and energetic health officer attends at the board of health, where he meets a staff of inspectors, each having a district under his charge. They furnish reports, and the health officer proceeds to the infected localities', where measures were taken to stamp out the epidemic. The death rate in Bristol was lowered from 31 to 22 per 1,000, with noticeable relief on the poor rates.

Town improvement gained added momentum when the town worker was given the vote in 1867. By this date a majority of Englishmen lived in towns, and M.P.s could not afford to ignore the needs of their constituencies. Thus numerous laws were passed to encourage local authorities to make town improvements. The Torrens Act (1868) enabled them to compel owners of slum houses to make repairs. In 1872 municipal councils were given charge of all matters of urban local government, and the Local Government Board (which replaced the Poor Law Board) could set up health authorities where none existed. Benjamin Disraeli's second ministry (1874–80) saw a good deal of public health legislation. A Public Health Act of 1875 compelled landlords to conform to certain standards of sanitation. Every local council had to appoint a medical officer of health and a

sanitary inspector, who were responsible for public health in their area. The same year saw the passage of the Sale of Food and Drugs Act, and an Artisans Dwellings Act, the work of Richard Cross, the Home Secretary. The former tried to check the adulteration of food with harmful ingredients, such as alum in bread, and empowered local authorities to appoint analysts and prosecute offenders. The latter gave local authorities the right to demolish slum housing and redevelop. In London the Metropolitan Board of Works began to attack its worst slums, Leeds began to pull down its back-to-back houses, and Liverpool to clear its cellar dwellings, all as a result of the Act. The most remarkable achievement was that of Birmingham which, during the term of its famous mayor, Joseph Chamberlain, was, in his own words, 'parked, paved, assized, marketed, Gas-and-watered— and *improved*—all as a result of three years' active work'.

Industrial developments and changes in social life also contributed to better health. The use of iron pipes for water supplies enabled cities to obtain their water supplies from a distance, so that Manchester got its supply from Thirlmere in the Lake District, and Liverpool from Vyrnwy in Central Wales. Transport improvements solved the problem of feeding town populations, and enabled people to get away from the towns into the countryside. The inventions of the bicycle, and to a lesser extent the motor car, did much to encourage a cult of the open air, which was reflected in the change in women's clothes. The building boom of 1900–10 in nearly all towns, and especially London, was closely related to developments in urban transport which allowed people to live farther from their work. Thus overcrowding, one of the worst features of life in industrial areas, was relieved. Unfortunately, the backlog of slum and substandard housing was so great that the problem of what is now called urban renewal was a permanent one, and is still with us. The most that could be achieved was a gradual improvement in the quality of the nation's housing.

Local government

As we have seen, one of the greatest obstacles to the improvement of health in towns was the lack of efficient local government, essential to a developing industrial community. At the beginning of the nineteenth century local government was based upon a chaotic system inherited from the past. Local government and parliamentary government existed separately and with little contact with each other. Local matters such as turnpikes, enclosures, and town improvements were usually attended to by private individuals or groups of people, whose schemes had to be approved by private Act of Parliament. In rural areas the justice of the peace was the chief agent of government. In chartered boroughs the town's business was conducted by corporations which were often self-elected and corrupt. Many new industrial towns such as Bradford, Leeds and Birmingham still retained the old parish system.

Town government was partially reformed in 1835 by the Municipal Corporations Act which practically abolished the old system in 178 chartered boroughs. In these towns the corporations were replaced by town councils elected by all ratepayers who had lived there for three years. Each council had to appoint a paid town clerk and a borough treasurer, and the town's income and expenditure was to be officially audited each year. The new councils were given powers to levy a rate, and to take over if they wished, the duties hitherto assigned to Improvement Commissioners. Unincorporated towns could apply for charters, as Birmingham and Manchester did in 1838. However, few town improvements resulted from the Act until after 1870. This was for a number of reasons. The powers of the new councils were narrowly restricted. Secondly, many towns found it difficult to maintain even existing standards in the face of a rapidly

growing population. Thirdly, by no means all towns had councils; in 1848 there were sixty-two towns which did not possess borough status.

Yet the administrative machinery whereby towns could be improved had been created. It remained to give town councils the necessary powers, such as the right to demolish slums, and to compel backward councils to maintain certain minimum standards of public health and housing. From about the middle of the century the activities of town councils were considerably extended by a series of housing and public health Acts, some of which have been described above (see pp. 170–1). Thus in 1890 local authorities were given the right not only to pull down condemned dwellings but to replace them with council houses, whose occupiers rented them from the council. Little advantage, however, was taken of this power until the Addison Act of 1919.

Where new problems of local government arose, Parliament tended to create 'ad hoc' bodies, i.e. special authorities to deal with particular problems, instead of making a clean sweep of an out-of-date system. Thus in 1847 local boards of health were established, in 1870 locally elected school boards were created by Forster's Education Act (see pp. 139–41), and in 1872 the whole country was divided into urban and rural sanitary districts. This multiplicity of administrative units led to one MP declaring: 'We have a chaos as regards authorities, a chaos as regards rates, and worse chaos as regards areas.'

By the time the Local Government Act was passed in 1888 reform was long overdue. The counties were treated as large boroughs, and were given elected councils, which took over the administrative duties of the overburdened justices of the peace. Some counties which were considered too large to form a single administrative unit were divided, so that there were sixty-two administrative counties (including London County Council) for fifty-two geographical counties. Sixty-one of the larger towns (those with populations of at least 50,000) were withdrawn from the control of the county councils, and given county borough councils. As other boroughs reached that population they could apply for county borough status, though today the population of a county borough is usually over 100,000.

Six years later the scheme of local government was completed. The urban and rural sanitary districts were renamed urban and rural districts, each with an elected council. In urban areas poor relief was kept in the hands of the Guardians, but in rural areas it was administered by the councils. In addition, some seven thousand parish councils were created, so that the entire structure of local government in England and Wales rested upon popular election. Both parish and district councils remained subordinate to the county councils. Unfortunately, the high hopes of a flourishing 'village democracy' which the 1894 Act inspired were soon dashed, since the councils could only raise the proceeds of a 3d rate, so that their activities were severely cramped by lack of finance.

Throughout the reorganization of local government London retained its unique position. In the early years of the nineteenth century London was administered by over three hundred different local authorities, each confined to a small area and working independently of the rest. In 1855 the Metropolis Management Act created a Board of Works for the whole area, with powers to provide the main sewers, street improvements, and the London Fire Brigade. The twenty-three larger parishes were given vestries, and the smaller parishes were grouped into fifteen districts, each with its own board. The 1888 Local Government Act transformed the Metropolitan Board of Works into the London County Council. Finally, in 1899, the London Government Act replaced the vestries and district boards by twenty-eight metropolitan boroughs which acted as public health and housing authorities under the general supervision of the LCC. The square mile of the City of London, with its Lord Mayor and Corporation, was left untouched.

REFERENCES

1   Edwin Chadwick, *Report on the Sanitary Conditions of the Labouring Population* (1842).
2   Edwin Chadwick, op. cit.
3   Report of Commissioners appointed under the Poor Law Act: *Parliamentary Papers*, 1838/ XXVIII, p. 3.
4   Lord Beaconsfield, *Sybil or Two Nations* (1895 ed.), p. 179.
5   Report of the Poor Law Commissioners to Lord John Russell, *Parliamentary Papers*, 1837–8/ XXXVIII, p. 2.
6   Report of the Adderley Commission on the Sanitary Laws (1869–71), *Parliamentary Papers* 1871/XXXV, p. 372.

Life for most people certainly became better during the nineteenth century. Social reform, progress in public health, the development of communications, trade unions, and education, and the wealth and employment generated by the growth of trade and industry, all helped to improve the standard of living. Yet the benefits of the Industrial Revolution passed many people by, and for them life was still a wretched existence. There was much distress among skilled craftsmen (such as handloom weavers), when machines took away their work. Workers in declining occupations suffered falling wages and unemployment. Periodic bouts of unemployment also resulted from fluctuations in the volume of trade, to which Britain as an industrial nation was particularly prone. As time went on, more and more people realized that unemployed workers could hardly be held responsible for their misfortune, and gradually the state assumed responsibility for their welfare.

Until 1834 poor relief was largely based on the Elizabethan statute of 1601. This placed the duty of looking after the poor on the parish, the only form of regional organization which covered the whole country. A poor rate was levied on all landowners, and the money collected went towards building Houses of Correction, where the *idle* poor were subjected to a regime of hard work and a strict diet, and Workhouses, where the 'deserving poor' were housed. It was intended that the inmates of workhouses be given useful work, using raw materials bought out of the proceeds of the poor rate, so that they might be self-supporting. But this idea proved impractical, and the only form of work done was usually of an unpleasant nature, such as bone crushing.

Each parish was responsible for its own poor, and an Act of Settlement (1662) enabled a newcomer to a district to be removed within forty days unless he had a certificate acknowledging the responsibility of his own parish for his support if he became destitute. This made it difficult for an unemployed man and his family to leave their home parish and find work elsewhere. Under a Workhouse Act of 1722 every parish was technically responsible for providing a workhouse in which paupers might be lodged. Anyone who refused to enter a workhouse was to be refused relief of any sort, since it was assumed he was able to support himself, and his family. This was known as the 'workhouse test'. But there were some 15,000 parishes and townships in England and Wales, and it was uneconomic for each parish to maintain its own workhouse. Thus outdoor relief was fairly common.

It was to remedy this deficiency that Gilbert's Act (1782) was passed. Parishes were allowed to combine into Unions for more efficient administration of the Poor Law, and each Union was to provide its own workhouse. The severity of the system was relaxed, and workhouses were to be limited to the old, the sick and infirm, and children. Paid Guardians of the Poor were appointed by J.P.s to provide work for the able bodied, and grant outdoor relief if none was available. Gilbert's Act, however, had limited success. Because wages were supplemented by relief the cost of the Poor Law was increased without at the same time reducing the number of paupers. Furthermore, the Act was optional, and few parishes joined together into Unions, since this generally involved the expense of building a new workhouse.

The outbreak of the French Revolutionary

War put an intolerable strain on the system. Food prices soared, while wages lagged behind. Moreover, it was not easy to find sufficient work for a rapidly growing population. The decline of domestic industry and the spread of enclosures, which involved the loss of common pasture rights, meant reduced earnings for the poor. Except for parts of northern England, where farmers had to compete with millowners for labour, the standard of living of agricultural labourers declined. In the South of England, where there was little employment other than farm labouring, the plight of the poor became so desperate that something had to be done.

In 1795 a group of magistrates met at the Pelican Inn in the Berkshire village of Speen, where they decided to grant relief to the poor even while they were still working. Relief was to be given according to a sliding scale of allowances, based on the number of dependants in the labourer's family, and the price of bread:

When the Gallon Loaf of Second Flour, weighing 8 lb 11 oz shall cost 1s.

Then every poor and industrious man shall have for his own support 3s weekly, either produced by his own or his family's labour, or an allowance from the poor rates, and for the support of his wife and every other of his family, 1/6.

When the Gallon Loaf shall cost 1s 4d.

Then every poor and industrious man shall have 4s weekly for his own, and 1s and 10d for the support of every other of his family.

And so in proportion, as the price of bread rise or falls (that is to say) 3d to the man, and 1d to every other of the family, on every 1d which the loaf rise above 1s.[1]

The Speenhamland system spread rapidly throughout the South. In some areas the allowance system was modified by the adoption of the 'Roundsman' system. Paupers were given work tickets by the Guardians, and sent on the rounds of the parish asking for work. The parish paid part of the man's wages, the employer the rest.

Though it has been argued that the Speenhamland system saved England from a revolutionary upheaval in the early nineteenth century, the system had some unfortunate results. It degraded the poor, and took away their incentive to work harder. It encouraged farmers to pay low wages, since they already had to pay the poor rate. Farm labourers were encouraged to marry before they were able to support a wife and family, since every child was worth 1/6 a week in relief. The cost of supporting the poor soared. Poor Law expenditure in 1750 was £600,000; in 1818 it was £8 million, or 13/3 per head of the population.

In 1832 a Royal Commission was set up to investigate the operation of the Poor Law and to recommend changes. The report issued in 1834 condemned outright the allowance system. In reaching this view the Commissioners were influenced by Malthus's thesis that subsidizing wages according to the number of dependants in a labourer's family encouraged a high birth rate. Secondly, they took notice of the fact that the agricultural riots of 1830 had been most severe in areas where the greatest amounts of outdoor relief had been paid. The allowance system, they argued, made the poor lazy, thriftless and insubordinate.

Every penny bestowed, that tends to render the position of the pauper more eligible than that of the independent labourer, is a bounty on indolence and vice. We have found that, as the poor rates are at present administered, they operate as bounties of this description, to the amount of several millions annually.[2]

The Commissioners also concluded (wrongly as it turned out in the case of wages), that the withdrawal of relief would have the following effects.

First, the labourer becomes more steady and diligent; next, the more efficient labour makes the return to the farmer's capital larger, and the consequent increase of the fund for the employment of labour enables and induces the capitalist to give better wages.

The Poor Law Amendment Act of 1834 accepted the main principles of the Report, and established a new form of authority to replace the local overseers of the poor, who were often corrupt as well as inefficient. A Board of three salaried Commissioners, with Edwin Chadwick as Secretary, was set up to superintend the operation of the Act, which applied to the whole of England and Wales. Parishes were to be grouped into Unions, and a central workhouse was to be built in each Union. Local Boards of Guardians, elected by all ratepayers, including women, were to supervise the work of paid officials in the Union workhouses. The Report also recommended that outdoor relief should be abolished for all able-bodied persons and their families. After 1834 therefore, except for the sick and the aged, the poor could only obtain relief by entering a workhouse, though until the new workhouses were organized, outdoor relief continued as a temporary measure. Life in a workhouse was made so unattractive that it was less 'eligible', i.e. less likely to be chosen, than the lowest paid employment. Thus the relief of the poor was based on two main principles, the 'Workhouse Test', and 'Less Eligibility'.

The new system of poor relief was quickly brought into being. By 1839 some seven hundred Unions had been organized, covering most of the country. The Act also succeeded in reducing the poor rates, which had fallen by one-third in 1850. One example may be quoted as an illustration. 'In the parish of Hitchin, in Hertfordshire, a well-managed parish, where an increase was confidently predicted, the poor rates in 1835, before the formation of the Union, amounted to £1,716; after the Union, they were reduced to £496.'[3] The new system also restored the self-respect of the labourer, for it compelled him to work harder in order to avoid the misery and 'badge of shame' which entry into the workhouse involved.

But all this was achieved at a high price. The workhouses were bitterly, and with some justification, called 'bastilles' by the poor. For it was the calculated intention of the Act to make parish relief the last resort for a pauper, and the person who administered it 'the hardest taskmaster and the worst paymaster that the idle and dissolute can apply to'. A typical workhouse dietary consisted of

Breakfasts—6 oz of bread and 1½ oz of cheese. Dinners—Sundays 5 oz of meat and ½ lb potatoes. Tuesday and Thursday ditto. Other days 1½ pints of soup. Supper—days on which there was meat for dinner, 6 oz of bread and 1½ pints of broth; other days 6 oz of bread and 2 oz of cheese.[4]

Until 1842, when the early rigours of the workhouse regime were relaxed, all meals were eaten in silence. Families were broken up, the men and the women being housed in separate blocks, while parents were not allowed to see their children even once a day without permission. No books were provided, furniture was scanty and uncomfortable, and the cheapest medicines were provided for the sick. Vagrants and the mentally sick were housed with the ordinary paupers. Thus children and old people, who were least responsible for their misfortunes, suffered most.

Nor did the expected rise in the labourer's wages come about until much later. Employers did not feel obliged to pay a living wage if they could obtain labour for less, and a labourer, with the threat of the workhouse hanging over him, could not risk losing his job by demanding more money. It was not always the fault of the labourer if he was not paid a wage sufficient to keep himself and his family. The Commissioners and Guardians were not cruel men, but in treating poverty as a crime they lacked sympathy for those who were unable to help themselves. The administration of the New Poor Law would have been more humane if notice had been taken of William Cobbett's question and answer: 'What is a pauper? Only a very poor man.'

65 *'The Poor Laws Past and Present'*
Workhouse conditions in 1836 are contrasted with those which existed
before the Poor Law Amendment Act of 1834

In Wales and the North of England especially, there was fierce opposition to the New Poor Law, and its operation was one of the reasons for Chartism (see Chapter 23). Gradually, however, its worst features disappeared, though the workhouses, with their high, barrack-like buildings, always remained forbidding places. Railway construction provided work for thousands of labourers, and the numbers in workhouses fell. In 1847 the 'three Bashaws of Somerset House', as the hated Commissioners were known, were replaced by a Poor Law Board under the control of a minister in Parliament. Conditions inside **workhouses were improved**—in 1865 for instance, Guardians were instructed to provide 'expensive' medicines such as cod liver oil and quinine for the sick. After 1868 workhouses had to conform to certain standards of lighting and air space which were laid down in government regulations.

The Poor Law Amendment Act set the pattern of poor relief for nearly a century. In 1871 the Poor Law Board disappeared, and the Local Government Board assumed responsibility for poor relief. Though a Royal Commission in 1905 recommended that the Boards of Guardians be abolished, this was not carried out until 1929. By that time the administration of poor relief and the system of national health and unemployment insurance created by Lloyd George in 1911 had become hopelessly entangled. Neville Chamberlain's Act of 1929 swept away the locally elected Boards of Guardians, and their functions were taken over by the county and county borough councils, which by that time occupied a most important place in the structure of local government.

Long before this, the state's attitude to poverty and unemployment had altered greatly. Adam Smith, in the *Wealth of Nations*, had talked about the state's duty of 'protecting every member of society from the injustice or oppression of every other member in it'. Once it was accepted (as it was in the second half of the nineteenth century), that poverty was an *economic* rather than a *moral* problem, the morality of the system itself which created and tolerated poverty was

questioned. Thus many people were shocked by the revelations of Charles Booth, a wealthy shipowner, who in 1889 published the *Life and Labour of the People of London*, based upon his researches into the lives of the labouring poor. He proved that almost one-third of the capital's population lived below the poverty line, that is to say, they did not earn enough to maintain themselves in proper health. Nor was London exceptional. Seebohm Rowntree conducted similar investigations in York, and in his survey *Poverty: A Study of Town Life*, produced a comparable figure of 28 per cent. (See table below.)

This clear evidence that more than one quarter of the population lived substandard lives made obsolete the Victorian 'laissez-faire' attitudes whereby the state had provided, within fairly prescribed limits, the freedom for each individual to improve his own standards of life. It was now realized that the state had a duty to protect the whole community from desperate need, and, as far as its resources allowed, to guarantee all its members the opportunity to live reasonable lives. After 1890, with industrial unrest on the increase, both the Liberal and the Conservative parties competed for working-class votes by urging measures of social and economic reform. The

This table[5] is based upon the findings of Rowntree's survey of York in 1898. It relates to the occupants of one particular street in York. Families were classified according to weekly income; Class A earning under 18/-, Class B 18/- to 21/-, Class C 21/- to 30/-, Class D over 30/-.

Note that unemployment was not the only reason for poverty; the death of the wage earner, too many children, and poor health were all important causes.

Class	Rent	Inmates	Rooms	Age	Occupation of Head of family	Remarks
B	2/3	5	2	old	Unable to work	Two sons work as labourers
B	3/3	7	2	33	Railway labourer	4 boys, 1 girl. House dirty
B	3/3	7	3		Waterman	4 boys, 1 girl. House dirty and untidy
A	3/3	9	3		Shoemaker	4 boys, 3 girls. House dirty. Very little furniture
A	3/3	7	5		Labourer	3 boys, 2 girls. Wife not very strong. House dirty
B	3/3	2	3		Widowed shopkeeper	Very respectable
D	6/0	12	5	47	Painter	Takes in lodgers at 2/6 per week
D	3/3	5	3	50	Widow, washerwoman	2 sons labourers, daughter works at laundry
D	3/3	6	5		Widower, joiner	4 boys, 1 girl
D	3/3	7	3		Hawker	2 married daughters at the confectionery works
D	7/0	10	6	55	Widow	Keeps lodging house. Two daughters help with housework
D	2/3	2	2	24	Labourer	Wife at confectionery works. House clean
D	2/3	2	2	48	Widow, French polisher	Daughter 26 years old, also French polisher
D	2/3	2	2	40	Labourer	Brother is a labourer
C	2/3	3	2	50	Widow, out to work	Daughter 28 years old goes out to work. Very poor, untidy
D	2/3	2	2		Hawker	
A	2/3	2	1		Widow	Disreputable old woman. Ill. Ought to be in a workhouse
D	2/3	3	2	48	Widow, chars	Son labourer. Daughter chars. Mother poor. Daughter's husband is out of work
A	2/3	1	2		Widow	Has very little to live on. Her three married sons have left her. She has parish relief

Liberal party in particular was conscious of the growth of the Labour party, with its programme of radical social reform, though the latter's strength in the country was not reflected in terms of parliamentary members until 1906, when Labour won twenty-nine seats.

When the Liberals were swept into office in 1906 with a huge majority they embarked upon a remarkable series of social reforms. One of their first measures in 1906 gave many workers greater security against accidents at work. An Act of 1891 had applied safety regulations to a number of dangerous trades. This was consolidated by Joseph Chamberlain's Workmen's Compensation Act of 1897 which made employers responsible for the cost of compensating and providing medical care for workers injured in these industries. The Liberals extended the terms of this Act to six million workers, including domestic servants. An attempt to reduce the incidence of unemployment was made by the creation of Labour Exchanges in 1909. William Beveridge's Report *Unemployment* had demonstrated that much unemployment was of a casual nature and avoidable. When a worker was laid off, or made redundant, it was hard for him to find another job, for he had to tramp the rounds of employers in search of a suitable vacancy. Labour Exchanges provided centres where employers could make known their needs for labour, and where the unemployed could be given information on jobs available. Beveridge was given the task of organizing the Exchanges. Talk of a minimum standard of living for all was again translated into action by the Trade Boards Act of the same year, which laid down a legal minimum wage in a number of the lowest paid women's trades, the infamous 'sweated trades', such as cheap tailoring, and box and chain making. The list of industries covered by the Act was soon extended. A Shops Act (1911) gave shop assistants regular mealtimes, and a weekly half day's holiday, though it failed to touch the major question of working hours. Trade

Union Acts of 1906 and 1913 (see Chapter 22) also helped the working classes in their efforts to push up their standard of living.

Two great achievements of Lloyd George, Chancellor of the Exchequer after 1908, laid the beginnings of the modern Welfare State. The first aided the most needy section of the population—the aged poor—who had been unable to save from their earnings against the time when they would no longer be able to work. Unless they had a family able and willing to support them, these unfortunate people ended their days in the misery of a workhouse. The Old Age Pensions Act of 1908 provided a small, non-contributory pension varying from 1/- to 5/- for a person over seventy earning less than 12/- per week. A married couple received 7/6. To support the scheme, the sum of £1,200,000 was set aside in the 1909 budget. The cost of the new social services (and also the naval armaments race with Germany, which was hotting up), was borne by extra taxation. Lloyd George raised income tax from 1/- to 1/2, and introduced several new taxes; super tax, which became payable on incomes over £3,000 per annum, a tax of 20 per cent on the unearned increment of land when it was sold, i.e. in cases where the increased value of the land had not been due to the landowner, but to independent factors such as town or industrial development, and taxes on petrol and car licences, whose proceeds were to be paid into a Road Fund for the improvement of the nation's roads.

All these taxes hit the pockets of the wealthy, and the so called *People's Budget* appeared at the time to be so revolutionary, that the House of Lords took the unprecedented step of rejecting it, thus laying itself open to the charges of acting undemocratically, and of flouting a constitutional convention that the Lords should not tamper with a money bill. Parliament was dissolved, and in the ensuing election the Liberals were again returned, albeit with a greatly reduced majority, and the Lords passed the budget. One important consequence of the crisis was the determination of the Liberal government to prevent the House of Lords from ever again frustrating important bills passed through the Commons, and a bill to reform the Upper Chamber was introduced. The Parliament Act, eventually passed in 1911 under the threat of the creation of sufficient peers to force its passage through the Lords, cut down the life of Parliament from seven years to five, thus making it more dependent upon the electoral will of the people, and abolished the Lords' power of the veto. The Lords could not withhold consent to a money bill, nor prevent any bill passed by the Commons in three consecutive sessions from becoming law, so that the Upper House merely retained the power to delay a bill for two years.

Lloyd George's second great measure was the National Insurance Act of 1911. Few workers had the financial resources to tide them over a period of unemployment or sickness, so that they were often forced to apply for poor relief. To begin with, the Act only applied to a few industries notorious for fluctuating unemployment, such as engineering, shipbuilding, building, and iron founding, but by 1920 nearly all wage earners except domestic servants and agricultural labourers had been brought into the scheme. A weekly stamp of 9d, fixed to the employee's insurance card, entitled the worker to a limited amount of sickness and unemployment benefit, which was drawn through friendly societies approved by the government to administer the scheme. The weekly stamp was made up by compulsory contributions of 4d from the worker, 3d from the employer, and 2d from the state. Workers in these industries were also placed on a doctor's 'panel' of patients, where they could receive free medical attention. Combined with the schemes for school meals for needy children (1906), and free medical inspection of school children (1907), it did much to raise the general level of the nation's health.

Lloyd George's pioneer scheme of social insurance was a practical expression of the state's wish to protect the welfare of all its citizens from birth till death. The use of taxation as an instrument to redistribute the nation's wealth, which Lloyd George envisaged in order to improve the living standards of the great mass of the people, became an accepted fact of politics. But when Lloyd George in one of his speeches asked:

Who made ten thousand people owners of the soil and the rest of us trespassers on the land of our birth? Who is responsible for the scheme of things whereby one man is engaged through life in grinding labour to win a bare and precarious subsistence . . . and another man who does not toil receives every hour of the day, every hour of the night, whilst he slumbers, more than his poor neighbour receives in a whole year of toil?[6]

he shocked many of his listeners with the violence of his attack upon privileged wealth. For, though the principle of social services according to need rather than ability to pay is commonplace today, in the very early 1900s it appeared revolutionary; fifty years earlier, however, such a proposal would have been unthinkable.

REFERENCES

1   Sir Frederick Eden, *The State of the Poor in 1797*, Vol. I, p. 577.
2   *Report of Royal Commission on the Operation of the Poor Laws* (1834).
3   Second Annual Report of the Poor Law Commission, *Parliamentary Papers*, 1836/XXIX, p. 29.
4   Second Annual Report of the Poor Law Commission, op. cit.
5   From B. Seebohm Rowntree, *Poverty: A Study in Town Life* (Longmans).
6   *The Times*, 11 October 1909.

Compared with her predecessor of two or even one hundred years ago, the woman of today enjoys a great deal of liberty. To nearly all intents and purposes she is on an equal footing with men. This state of affairs was not achieved without a struggle; it has come about both through economic and social changes affecting all society, and through the efforts of courageous and enlightened women and men.

In 1792 Mary Wollstonecraft in her *Vindication of the Rights of Women* said that women should have the same educational opportunities as men, and that middle-class women should be permitted to earn their own living. But she was far in advance of her time, and in 1825 William Thompson wrote of a man's circumstances at that date: 'The house is his house with everything in it, and of all fixtures the most abjectly his is his breeding machine, the wife.' Very few women in the eighteenth and early nineteenth centuries had any say in matters regarding their own destinies. When a woman married all her property was transferred to her husband, as was anything she inherited after her marriage. Middle and upper-class women usually led lives of enforced idleness. It was considered important for them to get married, and if they failed to secure husbands they became dependent on male relatives. The idea of a young woman earning her own living or qualifying for a profession was hardly considered. Practically the only employment open to a girl of this class was that of governess, in which case it was assumed that her family could not support her. Paid employment outside the home was 'unladylike', so that the usual status of the middle and upper-class female was complete dependence on her 'lord and master'.

The case of the working-class woman, however, had always been different, in that no life of ease was ever possible for her. Under the domestic system of industry women had always had to work hard and for very little reward, both in the home, and on the land at busy times such as harvesting and haymaking. The decline of cottage-based industries altered their position without necessarily improving it. In country areas the standard of living in many households, which had come to rely on the earnings of wives and children, went down and, though many women were then employed in gangs hoeing and weeding in the fields, they tended to depress agricultural wages even lower. Women were extensively employed in industry, not only as textile operatives, but in many arduous, unpleasant tasks such as slate quarrying, and the metal-working trades. Until the Mines Act of 1842 women worked underground in coalmines, and even after that date they were still employed at the pithead. Many working-class girls went into domestic service. The most desirable job a labourer's daughter could hope for was service with a good family, and her parents would try to place the child when she was between ten and fifteen years old. In the nineteenth century this practice was so widespread that nearly one-third of all girls between the ages of fifteen and twenty were in service, and the Census Report of 1891 remarked on how few girls there were in country districts, for there were virtually no other openings for country girls. If they married they went back to the tedium of cottage life, where they were worn out by too much work and child-bearing—though matters gradually improved.

Nonetheless, working-class women, by earning their own living, achieved some sort

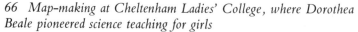

66   *Map-making at Cheltenham Ladies' College, where Dorothea Beale pioneered science teaching for girls*

of independence, a fact which did not pass unnoticed by their social superiors. Some intelligent women began to press for the opportunity to support themselves and be of use to the community. Outstanding among these was Florence Nightingale (1820–1910) who, in spite of coming from a good home, insisted upon entering the nursing profession, which at that time was not thought to be a suitable occupation for a respectable woman. The low calibre of its recruits had prompted Dr Southwood Smith's judgment that 'The generality of nurses in hospitals are not such as the medical men can place much confidence in'. Florence Nightingale organized a nursing service to relieve the sufferings of British soldiers during the Crimean War (1854–6). By her determination she forced the army authorities in the Crimea to accept her modern methods of hospital management, and

brought about a new era in medical practice. Florence Nightingale flew in the face of tradition by training women for nursing, but the idea of women being trained for an occupation spread.

The first steps towards improving the education of girls and young women had already been taken. Until 1840 girls of poor parents, if they received any education at all, usually went to a dame school, or similar institution. Middle-class girls had home governesses, or attended a private school where they learned little apart from deportment, music, dancing and needlework. In 1847, however, a Mrs Elizabeth Reid started classes for girls in her own home, and in 1860 this became known as Bedford College, the first college of higher education for women in the country. Queen's College, London, was opened in 1848 by two Christian Socialists, Charles Kingsley and

F. D. Maurice, as a training college for women teachers. Two women who studied there, Frances Mary Buss (who in 1850 became headmistress of the North London Collegiate School), and Dorothea Beale (later Principal of Cheltenham Ladies' College), set new standards in girls' education. In 1872 the Girls' Public Day School Trust was formed, and by the end of the century thirty-three secondary schools modelled on the Collegiate School had been built, providing secondary education for over seven thousand girls. After the Balfour Education Act of 1902 more girls' schools were built, and from about 1910 grammar-school education for girls had achieved parity with that for boys. As the demand for higher education for women grew, university extension lectures were started in some northern cities during the 1860s. In 1869 Emily Davies opened a hall of residence for women students at Hitchin. In 1873 Girton College, Cambridge, was founded when the women moved into new premises in the village of Girton, two miles from the centre of Cambridge. In 1871 Anne Clough provided a house of residence for women students at Cambridge, which in 1880 became Newnham College. By 1879 Oxford University also had two halls of residence for women, Somerville and Lady Margaret Hall.

As more women were educated, so their demand that the professions be open to them grew. The Census Report of 1871 stated: 'They are excluded wholly or in great part from the Church, the Law, and Medicine. Whether they should be rigidly excluded from these professions or be allowed—on the principle of freedom of trade—to compete with men, is one of the questions of the day.'[1] The first of these male preserves to admit women was the medical profession. The pioneer of women's entry into it was Elizabeth Garrett Anderson, who studied medicine in England, but had to take her degree in Paris. In 1874, however, the London School of Medicine for Women was opened, and by 1901 there were 335 practising women doctors.

Women's entry into the legal profession was more difficult, and was only achieved after an Act of 1919 removed any kind of discrimination against women. Few women have been successful at the Bar, but notable exceptions have been Helena Normanton and Rose Heilbron. The Church on the other hand has opposed the entry of women to this day.

Two inventions, the telephone and the typewriter, perhaps did more than anything else to create jobs for women outside the home. From its beginning women were employed in the telegraph service, and by the end of the century 40 per cent of those employed in the telegraph and telephone services were women. The invention of the typewriter led to a minor social revolution. Before the 1880s it was practically unheard of for women to be employed in an office, but by 1901 there were over 55,000, which was nearly three-quarters of all business and commercial clerks. Furthermore, the increase in the number of retail shops in the late nineteenth century meant that more female shop assistants were needed.

Women were becoming emancipated in other ways too. The Married Women's Property Acts of 1870, 1882 and 1893 altered the unfair financial situation of married women. They were given full legal control of all property they owned at the time of their marriage, and which they acquired after marriage, either through inheritance or by their earnings. In this atmosphere of greater freedom dress became less cumbersome, and the crinoline, and long, sweeping dresses were replaced by less awkward skirts. In the eighties lawn tennis became popular, and in the nineties cycling. Thus the young lady of 1900 was achieving independence; great inequalities still existed, but she was articulate in pressing for their removal. It is with this background in mind that we turn now to trace the history of the movement which demanded the vote for women.

The first petition for female suffrage to be laid before the House of Commons was in 1833, when 'Orator' Hunt presented a bill stating that 'every unmarried female, possessing the necessary pecuniary qualification should be allowed to vote'. No action followed this request, but at least the question had been brought before the public's notice. In 1847 a Quaker, Ann Knight, published the first leaflet issued on women's suffrage, and four years later she formed the Sheffield Association for Female Franchise. In 1865 J. S. Mill was elected Liberal M.P. for Westminster. His wife had been an enthusiastic believer in votes for women, and his election address had included a statement that he was in favour of it. Shortly after entering the Commons he introduced a petition calling for the enfranchisement of women, which had been taken to Westminster by Emily Davies and Elizabeth Garrett, while in May 1867 he moved an amendment to the Reform Bill proposing the inclusion of women. It was defeated by 194 votes to 73, but this was a sizeable minority, and it encouraged the formation of women's suffrage societies in London, Manchester and Edinburgh. The first public meeting held in support of votes for women took place in Manchester in April 1868. Similar meetings were held in other parts of the country, but public opinion in general did not react favourably to such 'unladylike' behaviour. Queen Victoria herself was unsympathetic towards the whole question, and in 1870 she wrote: 'The Queen is most anxious to enlist everyone who can speak or write or join in checking this mad, wicked folly of "Woman's Rights", with all its attendant horrors, on which her poor feeble sex is bent, forgetting every sense of womanly feeling or propriety.'

One woman who stayed unshaken in her devotion to the cause was Lydia Becker. From 1870 until her death in 1890 she edited a magazine called *The Woman's Suffrage Journal*. She also supervised all the parliamentary work on female suffrage that took place during these years. Private members' bills on this subject were introduced every year in the 1870s, except 1874. Nearly all were defeated,

and even when, as once in the 1880s, and again in 1897, there were majorities in favour, the bills were shelved, either through lack of parliamentary time, or because no political party was willing to adopt them. It is important to realize that all these proposals were not for universal female suffrage (after all, not all men could vote at this time), but for enfranchising women who owned property, because it explains why the Liberals, many of whom favoured, in principle, the idea of votes for women, did not want to enfranchise just the Tory section of the female population, as women of property usually were. Some small concessions to the right of women to vote were made. After 1869 women ratepayers could vote in local municipal elections, and, after 1888, in county council elections, but these were not at the time considered very important. Under the 1870 Education Act women ratepayers could also vote for, and be members of, school boards. Yet the real prize, the National Vote, was still as distant as ever.

With the passage of the Third Reform Act in 1884, which gave the vote to agricultural labourers, many of whom were illiterate, the indignation of educated women grew, for they felt this to be an insult to their intellect. Thus by the start of the twentieth century, when there was much more general female emancipation, the demand for the vote had become insistent. Nor was the suffrage movement confined to middle and upper-class women. In 1901 and 1902 Eva Gore-Booth organized petitions to Parliament demanding votes for women which were signed by 67,000 textile workers in the North. In October 1903 Mrs Emmeline Pankhurst founded the *Women's Social and Political Union*, whose activities brought the suffrage question very much to the fore in the next few years. She and her supporters were called suffragettes, a word coined by the *Daily Mail* to distinguish them from the more law-abiding suffragists.

Suffragettes interrupted election meetings, and in 1906 created a disturbance outside Asquith's house. They were dispersed forcibly by mounted police, who reared their horses over women who had fallen, and several suffragettes were arrested and imprisoned in Holloway Gaol. In 1908 Edith New addressed bystanders in Downing Street and, to prevent the police from moving her on, she chained herself to the railings. This was the first example of what became a common practice. She was sent to prison for three weeks. In October of the same year Mrs Pankhurst and her daughter Christabel, and Flora Drummond, known as the 'General', were arrested for inciting the public to 'help the suffragettes to rush the House of Commons', and sent to prison. Even in prison, however, suffragettes continued their campaign. In July 1909 Marion Wallace-Dunlop told the Governor of Holloway that unless she was given better treatment in prison she would go on hunger-strike. She carried out her threat, and was eventually released, faint and starving, but triumphant. When other

67 Women voted in a General Election for the first time in December 1918

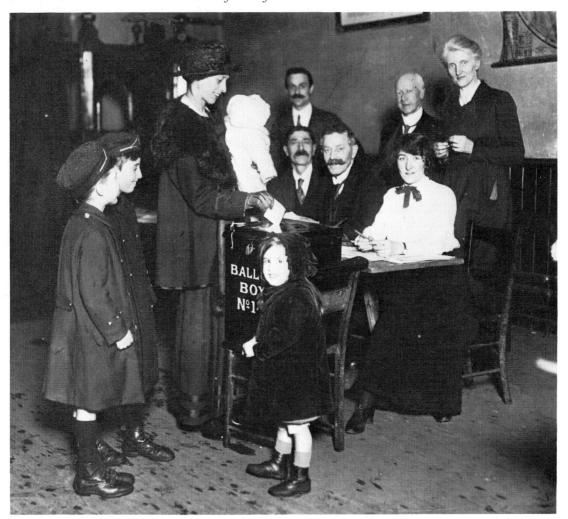

suffragettes copied her example the Government introduced the drastic measure of forcible feeding. This led to a good deal of public sympathy for the suffragettes, but it was due more to their sufferings in prison than agreement with their aims.

Yet when Asquith announced in November 1911 that the Government intended to introduce a bill for universal manhood suffrage which could be amended to include women, the militant suffragettes were furious, for they wanted the vote to be given to qualified women as a right, and not as an appendage to the male suffrage question. Outbursts of violence followed; stones were thrown at windows in the houses of prominent people, and shop windows were smashed in London's West End. One jeweller stuck a placard in his shop front which read: 'Ladies, if we had the power to grant it, you should have the vote right away. Please do not smash these windows, they are not insured.' Many suffragettes were imprisoned, and Christabel Pankhurst went to Paris where she continued the campaign. Meanwhile the Conciliation Bill of 1912 was defeated. The violence of the militants had alienated many former supporters.

The year 1913 was a disheartening one for the suffragette movement, for in January the promised Franchise Reform Bill was withdrawn, and a private member's bill was defeated by forty-eight votes in May. The frustration and anger of the suffragettes found its outlet in increased militancy. Public buildings and pillar boxes were set on fire, bombs were placed in offices and warehouses, telephone wires were cut, and valuable paintings in art galleries were slashed. The Government passed the 'Cat and Mouse' Act which enabled the authorities to release hunger strikers instead of forcibly feeding them (which gained the suffragettes much public sympathy), and to re-arrest them if they

wished at a later date. On 4 June Emily Wilding Davison was killed when she threw herself in front of the last group of horses in the Derby. A great procession of women attended her funeral. The campaign of violence continued until the outbreak of war in 1914, when the suffragettes joined enthusiastically in the war effort. All suffragette prisoners were released, and the Pankhursts used their talents for public speaking by addressing recruiting meetings. During the war women worked in a multitude of jobs formerly done by men, and so ensured that after the war women would be given the vote. The Electoral Reform Act, which became law in January 1918 was passed with a huge majority. It gave the vote to all women over 30 who were ratepayers, or married to ratepayers. In 1928 women were finally given the vote on equal terms with men, that is to say, at the age of 21.

It has sometimes been said that women got the vote as a result of their work during the war but, although this was certainly a more important factor than the activities of the suffragettes, it was not the only one. Millicent Garrett Fawcett, a constitutional suffragist, spoke more truly than she realized when she wrote in 1886:

Women's suffrage will not come, when it does come, as an isolated phenomenon; it will come as a necessary corollary of other changes which have been gradually and steadily modifying during the century the social history of our country. It will be a political change . . . based upon social, educational and economic changes which have already taken place.[2]

REFERENCES

1   *Report on the Census*, 1871.
2   *The Nineteenth Century* (May 1886).

PART III

CHAPTER 29
The Challenge to Britain's Industrial Lead

The nature of the challenge

The description of Britain in 1870 as the 'workshop of the world' was not a fanciful expression, but a straightforward fact. Britain's lead in the value of her exports was astonishing. The total fell not far short of that of Germany, France and the United States put together while, if the trade of Britain's colonies was added to that of the mother country, the figure was greatly in excess. This is all the more surprising when it is realized that nearly all Britain's exports were manufactures.

Yet by the close of the nineteenth century British manufacturers no longer enjoyed unquestioned supremacy in home and foreign markets, and it was becoming more difficult for Britain to sell her goods abroad. Even in the colonies, and especially in the Far East, where British manufacturers formerly had a practical monopoly, the effects of foreign competition were increasingly felt. This had been inevitable once industrialization spread to other parts of the world, but few Englishmen living at the time of the Great Exhibition expected the foreign challenge to be so severe, or for it to come about so soon.

The unprecedented boom years of the 1850s and 1860s, when England's economy for a brief period was the fastest growing in the world, had been due largely to a combination of circumstances which could never recur. World trade was expanding rapidly, and manufacturers could hardly avoid making profits. Plentiful supplies of capital had been accumulated, much of which was invested abroad. A high proportion of this investment returned to Britain in the shape of orders for machinery, locomotives, civil engineering projects, and ships. Just as important was the fact that the interest alone on these vast sums invested abroad was usually sufficient to convert an annual trade deficit into a healthy balance of payments surplus. Moreover, because Britain was the first industrial nation, she was in a favourable position to supply the manufactures other growing countries needed. At home industrial growth was especially rapid as mechanization spread from the cotton industry to others. The flow of people from the countryside to the towns, where higher wages could be earned, meant that labour supplies kept pace with industrial expansion. But from the early 1870s industrial production, though it continued to rise, increased much more slowly than in the previous half-century. What was far more ominous, industrial growth in England proceeded much more slowly than in Germany or the United States. By 1914 these two nations, in several respects, had overtaken Britain. Why was this so?

The rate of expansion of the United States was remarkable. America's population in 1860 stood at 31 million; by 1910, largely as a result of immigration, it had soared to 91 million. The flood of immigrants brought with them a wide range of mechanical skills and knowledge, combined with a readiness to work hard in the new land of their choice. After the Civil War (1861–5) America concentrated on internal development. Railways were built across the continent. In the seven years from 1866 to 1872 53,000 kilometres (33,000 miles) of track were laid, more than doubling the existing length, and in the 1880s an additional 120,000 kilometres (75,000 miles) of track were constructed. Homestead Acts which enabled immigrants to obtain land cheaply encouraged the further development of the West. It was the vast quantities of grain produced by the prairie farmers, and the cattle ranching of the Mid-Western States, which depressed British farming. America also had huge resources of timber and coal, rich iron-ore fields in the Appalachians and Alleghenies, and oil in Pennsylvania and the South-West. American manufacturers took full advantage of a rapidly expanding home market, eagerly adopting more efficient new machinery and industrial processes as soon as they appeared. Even in 1860 America was already the second most important manufacturing nation in the world, and was catching up Britain rapidly.

Germany also had greater natural resources than Britain, and her economic growth after 1871 was startling. In 1871 the unification of Germany had transformed the thirty-nine states which formed Germany in 1815 into two, Germany and Austria–Hungary. After Prussia's victory in the Franco-Prussian War (1870–1), Germany, the 'enlarged Prussia', annexed Alsace–Lorraine, which had the richest iron-ore field in Europe, as well as being an important textile manufacturing area. In addition, Germany had rich coal and iron deposits in the Rhineland, Saar, Silesia, and Saxony. This combination of coal and iron produced the most powerful iron and steel industry in Europe.

The Gilchrist–Thomas adaptation of the open hearth process (see p. 116) made possible the exploitation of the phosphoric iron-ore deposits of Lorraine and Pennsylvania, enabling both the German and American iron and steel industries to forge ahead. The following table shows how rapidly their production of pig iron overtook that of Britain.

Pig Iron Output (in millions of metric tons) 1871–1910

	Germany	United States	Great Britain
1871	1·5	3·9	6·5
1880	2·7	3·9	7·8
1890	4·6	9·3	8·0
1900	8·5	14·0	9·0
1910	14·8	27·7	10·0

In steel production a similar picture emerges. Britain was overtaken by the United States in 1890, by Germany in 1893. German steel plant was much larger than British; even in 1900 new British steel plants were only one-third as big as their German competitors. In the period 1910–14 Germany made more than twice as much steel as Britain. Steel was the most important industrial metal in the world, vital not only to armaments, but in all heavy engineering and a host of other industries. The fact that Britain had dropped to third place in steel production by 1893 was a clear sign of the growing competition between the industrial nations.

Britain's lost leadership in steel production was only one element, though a very important one, in the challenge to her industrial supremacy. It was natural that many nations should wish to develop their own industries in order to raise the standard of living of their own people. At least in the early stages of their growth, these infant industries needed protection, and so high tariff barriers were erected against British manufactures. In 1879 Bismarck, the German Chancellor, introduced Protection, partly in response to demands from landowners and industrialists alike that the state should protect their interests, partly because he saw a source of revenue which would make him independent of parliamentary control. France and several other European countries also put up tariff barriers, and in America too, tariffs became increasingly protective after the Civil War.

For a long time British costs of production were so low, and her manufactures so superior in quality, that firms had little difficulty in exporting their surplus goods. But as other nations improved the efficiency of their industries competition became more severe. Furthermore, Britain was alone in being a Free Trade nation. Although this meant that raw materials and foodstuffs could be imported cheaply, it also meant that foreign manufactures were freely allowed into the country, so that foreign manufacturers could compete with British firms without having to pay import duties. This competition was most intense when trade was slack, and the practice of many continental firms of selling steel more cheaply in foreign markets than at home was strongly resented as unfair competition. Foreign manufacturers were able to 'dump' their goods on the British market, thus depressing home prices, while British manufacturers were unable to retaliate owing to the presence of tariff barriers.

Thus it was more difficult for British manufacturers to sell their goods abroad. In 1886 a Royal Commission reported that even

in neutral markets, such as our own colonies and dependencies, and especially in the East, we are beginning to feel the effects of foreign competition in quarters where our trade formerly enjoyed a practical monopoly. . . . The increasing severity of this competition both in our home and in neutral markets is especially noticeable in the case of Germany. . . . In actual production of commodities we have few, if any, advantages over them; and in a knowledge of the markets of the world, and determination to obtain a footing wherever they can, and a tenacity in maintaining it, they appear to be gaining ground on us.[1]

One reason for Britain's declining rate of industrial growth was her backwardness in technical and scientific education. Many of the newer industries, such as electrical engineering, motor cars, chemicals, plastics, and synthetic fibres, which were to become pacemakers in the twentieth century, were much more science-based than the established industries. They needed specially trained management and staff if they were to realize rapidly their full potential. Yet it was precisely in the field of scientific and technical education that Britain lagged behind her competitors. Germany's technical education was far superior to Britain's, but it was not until 1889 that the first Technical Instruction Act was passed in an effort to make up the leeway. The result was a shortage of chemists. According to Lord Haldane, 'there were only 1,500 trained

chemists in this country altogether. . . . On the other hand, four large German chemical firms, which have played havoc with certain departments of our trade, employ 1,000 highly trained chemists between them.'[2]

Britain also lagged behind in technical innovation in industry. Thus the English steel industry was slow to adopt new methods, whereas the American steel industry eagerly introduced labour-saving techniques. 'Most English engineers', the Tariff Commission reported in 1904 'on visiting American workshops, have been greatly surprised to see so few men about. Automatic machinery is much more largely used there than in this country.'[3] There were a number of reasons for this. Firstly, American labour was highly paid, and this provided an incentive to cut down on labour costs wherever possible. Secondly, American society was a very open one, and there were many opportunities in a rich, expanding continent for men with the ability to work hard to make a fortune. In Britain most firms were family businesses, and the flair of their founders was not always inherited by their descendants. Thirdly, factory machinery and premises were expensive to replace, and so long as profits were made there was a reluctance to change to more efficient methods of production. Thus many factory owners made do with steam-driven machines when their competitors abroad were converting their plant to electrical power.

In a very real sense Britain was trapped by the success of her Industrial Revolution. Much of her capital equipment was obsolete and difficult to replace. The newer industrial nations were able to adopt the most modern machinery and methods. Their factories, mines, and industrial premises were better planned and more efficient. As a pioneer of industrialization Britain made many costly mistakes. Her rivals were often in a position to learn how to avoid them. Perhaps most important of all, Britain's prosperity was based largely on a narrow range of industries. These were textiles, engineering, iron and steel manufacturing, shipbuilding and coalmining. But in a world that was industrializing fast these were the industries where competition was bound to be most severe. Britain's reliance on them was one reason why her rate of economic expansion began to slow down after 1873. By 1914 these industries had almost reached the limits of their usefulness, though this fact was not readily appreciated until the depressed 1920s and 1930s.

It was significant too that after about 1870 costs of production no longer fell, and in many cases were actually rising. The willingness of people to move from the land to the towns in search of better paid jobs had provided mid-Victorian manufacturers with plentiful and cheap labour. After 1880 the rural exodus virtually dried up, and after 1900 the only major population shifts in Great Britain were from one industrial area to another. Finally, the great age of steam power had done its work in forcing down costs of production, and further economies were to be marginal.

New forms of power

By the 1880s the technological possibilities of the steam engine had been exhausted, though it was to retain its supremacy over other forms of power for many years to come. But in the latter decades of the nineteenth century two new forms of power, the internal combustion engine, and electrical power, each with enormous potential, were developed.

The first practical internal combustion engine was produced in 1859 by a Frenchman, Etienne Lenoir. It was fired by a mixture of gas and air. Shortly afterwards, in 1863, he designed a self-propelled carriage which he drove down the Paris boulevards at 8 k.p.h. (5 m.p.h.) to the consternation of pedestrians. But his two-stroke engine was very noisy, and it consumed too much fuel for it to be a commercial proposition. In 1862 Beau de Rochas hit upon the principle of the four-stroke engine, which was much smoother

running than a two-stroke. In 1876 a German engineer, Nikolaus Otto, built the first commercially effective gas engine along the lines suggested by Rochas. Relatively silent in operation, the engine was called *Silent Otto*.

Internal combustion engines were more efficient than steam engines. Unlike the latter, which needed constant stoking (sometimes half the crew of a steamship were stokers), the flow of fuel could be regulated automatically, and labour costs were slashed. Often gas was a wasted by-product of industrial processes, for example in coking and smelting, in which case it was cheaper to use than coal. In addition, the internal combustion engine was cleaner and needed less maintenance.

But the internal combustion engine could not be used for transportation until petroleum had been substituted for gas as fuel. This was the achievement of two German engineers, formerly Otto's assistants, Carl Benz (1844–1929) and Gottlieb Daimler (1834–1900). In 1884 they both built petrol-driven 'horseless carriages'. Elsewhere on the Continent, and in the United States, there was great enthusiasm for the new invention, but in England development was retarded by the Red Flag Act of 1861, which limited horseless carriages to a maximum speed of 4 m.p.h. (6 k.p.h.), and laid down that each one should be preceded by a man carrying a red flag to warn other road users. It was not until 1896 that the Act was repealed, and the speed limit raised to 14 m.p.h. (23 k.p.h.). This step was commemorated by a London to Brighton race for automobiles, which became an annual event. The repeal took the brake off the development of the motor car, and within ten years over 20,000 cars had been built in Britain.

The early motor cars were hand-made and expensive, and for many years remained a luxury afforded only by the very rich. By modern standards of travel comfort they were very uncomfortable. The motor cars were open to the weather, and driver and passengers wore goggles and specially warm clothing. The ride was a bumpy one, for the roads had been neglected since the coming of the railways, and it was not until just after the First World War that pneumatic tyres were substituted for solid rubber ones for heavy transport. Consequently, the motor car was not universally desired even by the rich who could afford one. In Queen Victoria's view, motor cars 'smell exceedingly nasty, and are very shaky and disagreeable conveyances altogether'—though the Prince of Wales enjoyed a ride in a Daimler in 1899.

Progress in the motor-car industry was slow until the arrival of assembly-line construction and mass production in the 1920s. In England the lead in making cheaper cars was taken by William Morris (later Lord Nuffield), and Herbert Austin. Morris began the production of cars at Cowley, near Oxford, and by 1922 he had, after starting almost from nothing, built up Morris Motors. In the same year Austin began mass production of one of the most famous cars of the past, the Austin Seven, or 'Baby Austin'. But the outstanding name in the field of mass production of motor cars was an American, Henry Ford, who founded the Ford Motor Company in 1903. His aim was to mass-produce a cheap, reliable, standard motor car, whose design need not be changed for a long time. The result was the Ford Model T, which could be bought in almost any colour, as long as 'it was black'. More than any other individual, Henry Ford was responsible for the motor car becoming the means of mass transportation.

The internal combustion engine revolutionized town transport. By the end of the nineteenth century the horse-drawn omnibuses in towns were being rapidly replaced by motor buses and electrically driven trams. By 1910 there were one thousand motor buses operating in London alone. The electric tram was first introduced at Portrush, in Northern Ireland, in 1883. The first regular tram service was at Blackpool. In 1891 Leeds replaced its horse-drawn trams with electric ones, and several other large cities followed suit. By 1914 there were over 2,500 miles of tramlines

in British cities. By that time horse-drawn buses had almost disappeared, and the picturesque cab had given way to the taxi.

In sea transport, the efficiency of the steamship was further improved by the invention of the diesel engine. In 1897 a German engineer, Rudolf Diesel (1858–1913) patented a new type of internal combustion engine which used diesel, or crude oil, as fuel, so that it was extremely cheap to run. Oil had many advantages over coal. It was a more efficient fuel, and enabled a ship to sail 40 per cent farther than it could for the same weight of coal. Refuelling was a simple matter of connecting pipes to the shore supplies or oil tanker, and sucking the fuel into the ship. Oil-burning ships needed fewer stokers. In conventional steamships the coal had to be shovelled from bunker to bunker nearer the furnaces as the voyage progressed, a tedious and exhausting process. By the First World War many steamship companies had followed the lead of the Hamburg–Amerika Line and had converted their liners from coal-fired to oil-burning ships. The British Admiralty, too, was quick to grasp the advantages of oil-burning warships. Not only could steam be raised much more quickly, an important factor in naval warfare, but greater speeds and radius of action could be achieved. Fleets could be refuelled at sea, and not weakened by having to detach part of the fleet periodically for coaling in the nearest harbour.

Diesel engines were ideal for heavy duty work, such as driving locomotives, bulldozers, lorries and coaches. The development of diesel-driven transport was yet another aspect of the challenge to Britain's economic supremacy, which had been largely based upon abundant supplies of coal. All Britain's oil had to be imported, while at the same time foreign demand for coal, which was a major export, declined as diesel transport spread.

The development of the internal combustion engine came at a very convenient moment for the oil companies. The earliest use of oil had been as a substitute for whale oil as a

*68   Demonstration of electric lighting in
Trafalgar Square in 1848*

source of lighting. In 1857 an American called
Ferris had succeeded in refining the vile-
smelling crude oil, and producing kerosene.
As demand increased, a hunt for underground
oil began, and its discovery in Pennsylvania in
1859 started a boom in 'black gold'. But for
many years petrol was a useless by-product of
refining oil, and a nuisance because of its
inflammability. With the growth of the motor
car industry, however, the oil industry became
an immensely important international business. As new oil-fields were developed in
Russia, Mexico, Borneo and Texas about the
turn of the century, the price of petrol fell
and demand rose. When the Anglo-Persian
Oil Company was founded in 1909 the British
Government was a major shareholder.

Today, there is hardly anyone in Britain who
is not in some way dependent upon electricity.
Without electricity industry would grind to a
halt, and life would be without many comforts usually taken for granted. Electricity has
several important advantages over other forms
of power. It can easily be converted into heat,
light and motion. It can be stored and trans-

mitted without serious loss, and the consumer
need only pay for the actual amount used. It
requires no particular location, and it can be
placed within the reach of nearly everybody
at relatively low cost.

But at the beginning of the nineteenth
century electricity was still a scientific curiosity. Its first practical applications were in the
electric telegraph by Wheatstone and Cooke
in 1839, and in electroplating, pioneered by
John Wright of Birmingham, in 1840. The
widespread use of electrical power, however,
was not possible until the improvement of the
dynamo by William Siemens in the late 1860s.
This made possible the generation of electricity
for industrial use, and stimulated further
research. The next major development was the
invention of the telephone in 1876 by Graham
Bell, a Scotsman living in America. Two years
later great interest was aroused when 30,000
spectators at Bramhall Lane, Sheffield, watched
a football match played under the light of four
electric arc lamps. The players could be seen
'almost as clearly as at noonday. The brilliancy
of the light, however, dazzled the players, and
sometimes caused strange blunders.'[4]

Arc lamps, however, were only suitable for
illuminating large spaces. But it was not very
long before the development of an electric
lighting industry was born with the invention
of the incandescent lamp, using a carbon
filament, by Thomas Edison (1847–1931), an
American, and Joseph Swan (1828–1914), a
Newcastle chemist, in 1879. This was of
tremendous significance because its potential
lay not only in industry, but in providing
artificial light in every home in the land.
Equally important, it generated a demand for
electricity, and it was thus the starting point of
a group of industries, ranging from the
generation and distribution of electricity
itself, to the manufacture of all kinds of
electrical goods and machinery.

The first step towards electricity generation
on a commercial scale was taken by the
Siemens Brothers in 1881, when they built
the first power station at Godalming, in

Surrey. Soon others were built, each supplying a local market, on the principal of the Electric Lighting Act, which declared that each parish should have its own power station. This was a mistake, and it was quickly realized that considerable savings could be made if electrical current could be distributed through cables, using high voltage, alternating current in order to minimize the loss of energy. The first large power station was built by Ferranti at Deptford on the Thames in 1882 to supply London. By 1895 electricity was competing with gas, not only for domestic lighting, but as a source of industrial power. In 1900 the principle of the grid system of electricity supply was firmly established, and many shops, homes, factories and shipyards could now be provided with electrical power.

The demand for electricity from industry and transport grew steadily. Cannon Street Station and the Royal Albert Docks were illuminated by electric lighting. Electrically driven trams date from 1883. Some parts of the railway network were electrified, including the Southport to Liverpool line, and a stretch of line in Tyneside. In London the new underground 'tubes' were driven by electricity, the first one being the City and South London Railway in 1890. The electric arc furnace, yet another invention of Sir William Siemens, was used in the manufacture of steel. Large amounts of electricity were used in the extraction of aluminium from bauxite, and in the caustic soda process. On Tyneside, several engineering firms and shipyards installed electrical plant.

This enterprising step was due chiefly to the personal influence of Sir Charles Parsons (1854–1931), an outstanding British engineer. It was a French engineer, Hippolyte Fontaine, who accidentally discovered in 1873 that a dynamo working in reverse became an electric motor. This discovery made it possible to supply electrical power to industry and transport on a wide scale. In 1884 Parsons patented a steam turbine and applied it to marine engines (see p. 106). Turbines have no pistons

or cylinders. Instead, power is generated by rotors spun at high speeds by jets of high pressure steam. In the 1890s Parsons improved the turbine so that it became possible to generate electricity using steam driven motors. Thus Tyneside's plentiful supplies of coal could be used to produce electricity, and Tyneside as a region pioneered the application of electrical power to industry.

Yet despite this bright start Britain was slower than Germany and the United States to exploit the advantages of electrical power. The gas industry was well established and competitive. An efficient incandescent gas burner was immediately developed to compete with the filament lamp. Moreover, gas lighting was cheaper than electric, which to begin with was bound to be costly. Municipal

69 'What Will He Grow To?' King Steam and King Coal consider their infant rival (Punch, 1881)

"WHAT WILL HE GROW TO?"

gas works strenuously fought the introduction of electric lighting. Again, many industries, such as coalmining and textiles, saw no reason to change over from the well-proven steam engine to a new, and largely untried, form of power. Lastly, Britain had few resources for developing hydro-electric power.

The response of British industry

It can fairly be said that a second industrial revolution began with the development of new forms of power, the internal combustion engine and electrical power, and new materials, such as plastics, which gave birth to a wide range of new industries.

Modern plastics began with the discovery of celluloid in 1868 (still used in the manufacture of table tennis balls). This was followed by artificial silk in 1889, viscose in 1892, bakelite, the 'plastic of a thousand uses', in 1909, and cellophane in 1912. Aluminium, with its properties of lightness combined with strength, was invaluable to the aircraft industry, in its infancy in the early years of this century, but destined to become a giant among industries. The manufacture of bicycles and motor cars created a heavy demand for rubber. By 1914 over 20,000 people were employed in the rubber industry, and the tyre-manufacturing firm of Dunlop was already famous. Petroleum, synthetic dyestuffs, and ferroconcrete, which led to the start of steel-frame building, were all important new industrial materials.

But what struck contemporaries most forcibly was not so much the growth of new industries as the continuous, if uneven, fall in prices, which caused firms' profit margins to shrink, and gave the period 1873–96 the appearance of being depressed. Compared with 1874 the value of exports in 1894 was £40 million down, though the actual volume of goods exported was greater. Fortunately for the manufacturers, the fall in food prices reduced the pressure for wage increases, and most firms continued to make good headway.

But agriculture, a major industry, suffered severe depression. Immense quantities of grain flowed from the great plains of North America and South Russia to Europe, where Britain was alone in her refusal to protect her farmers from the full blast of overseas competition. Large-scale imports of meat came from Argentina, the United States, and New Zealand. Imports of tropical and semi-tropical produce grew yearly. This was due to a combination of factors. As the industrial nations grew more wealthy demand rose, for the ordinary working-class family could afford to spend more money on food. Improvements in transport, such as the steamship and the railway, which linked overseas food-producing areas to the coast and enabled their interiors to be developed, all made for rapid and cheaper carriage of freight. New techniques of food preservation like refrigeration and canning meant that perishable food-stuffs could be transported long distances yet still arrive in fresh condition.

Growing industrial competition forced manufacturers to cut their costs wherever possible, and employ their labour forces more efficiently. The engineering industry in particular witnessed a constant stream of innovations. Machines which could be operated by semi-skilled men 'took the brains out of the job'. Wages based on piece-work, whereby the worker was encouraged to produce more, became more common. This raised fears that one worker might put another out of a job. Towards the end of the century the cult of 'scientific management' grew. Some firms introduced time and motion experts into their factories. They studied the workers at their jobs, and by dividing the work up into its component parts, they calculated how time might be saved, and productivity increased.

Industrial competition also stimulated industrial combination. An amalgamation of firms producing similar or identical goods brought a number of important benefits. It reduced competition and meant that the firm gained a larger share of the market. Costs were reduced. Instead of two sets of offices, marketing and sales promotion, there need only be one.

There were also good reasons for one firm to take over another which produced the raw materials needed by the former, or which carried out the finishing processes. (This process was known as 'vertical integration'.) Thus a steel works might buy up iron-ore mines and collieries, in order to have full control of production from start to finish. Similarly, one firm might amalgamate with another producing different goods, in order to diversify its range of products. This was known as 'horizontal integration'. Any decline in demand for one of its products could be cushioned by rising demand for another. There were many such amalgamations during this period. The Salt Union, formed in 1888, claimed to produce 91 per cent of the salt used in this country. The English Sewing Cotton Company was formed in 1897. Other great industrial combines formed then were Vickers Armstrong, the vast engineering, shipbuilding and armaments firm, Imperial Tobacco Company, and J. and P. Coates of Paisley.

The formation of the United Alkali Company in 1891 not only illustrates why certain firms amalgamated with others, but also the kind of difficulty many British firms faced. It had long been known that soda could be manufactured by treating concentrated solutions of salt and ammonia with carbonic acid. The great difficulty was recovering the ammonia, which was expensive, from the ammonium chloride left after the chemical reaction. Ernest Solvay (1838–1922), a Belgian chemist, perfected a process in 1863 whereby the ammonia could be recovered. After mixing ammoniacal brine and carbon dioxide in a still he was left with ammonia, and calcium chloride, or bleaching powder, used in vast quantities by the textile industries. The Solvay process was far more efficient than the wasteful Leblanc process, which was soon abandoned by most Continental firms. By 1900 well over 90 per cent of the soda produced in France and Germany was by the ammonia process. Only

Britain had a large investment in Leblanc plant and was unwilling to change. By means of various economies, such as the recovery of chlorine by Weldon's process (1870), the British alkali industry remained competitive until 1890. Then the introduction of electrolytic methods of producing chlorine cheaply removed the mainstay of firms using the Leblanc process. The desperate expedient of combining nearly all the Leblanc capacity into the United Alkali Company worked for a short while, but by 1920 the Leblanc industry in Britain was no more.

The steel industry was also having to adjust itself to rapid technological change. The steel age may be said to have begun only in the late 1870s, for steel output using the Bessemer and Siemens–Martin processes was relatively small. Only non-phosphoric ores could be used until the introduction of the Gilchrist–Thomas process in 1879 (see pp. 115–16). British steel firms, however, failed to take full advantage of the new process. Britain was well supplied with haematite iron-ore, and manufacturers were reluctant to scrap the Bessemer plant they had only recently installed. They therefore tended to concentrate on making high grade steels containing nickel and chromium, which made the metal stainless, and it was not until the 1930s that the phosphoric iron-ore fields of Lincolnshire and Northamptonshire were exploited.

At first it was tempting to put down the success of German steel makers to the protection given them by their governments, rather than their more efficient methods. But other industries such as cotton and woollen textiles, chemicals, cutlery, and hardware, were all having some difficulty in maintaining their share of world markets. Farmers too were suffering from the consequences of a Free Trade policy. Especially during times of slack trade, therefore, the cry for some degree of Protection was heard.

In 1881 a Fair Trade League was formed to retaliate against other manufacturing nations' protective measures, on the grounds that

Our manufacturers are more and more excluded from the markets of the civilized world, not by fair competition, but by oppressive tariffs. At home they are met by the unrestricted competition of every article which can be made more cheaply in any country by dint of longer hours of work, lower wages, and a meaner style of living on the part of the workers. They enjoy one advantage, cheap food, it is true; but that is purchased, as they are finding to their cost, by the ruin of those dependent upon agriculture, and the consequent paralysis of the home trade in rural districts.[5]

The League proposed that a 10 per cent duty be put on foreign manufactures and foodstuffs. Foodstuffs from the Empire, however, could enter the country duty-free. In this way it was calculated that food prices would rise only very slightly, and manufacturers would enjoy the benefits of Protection without losing the advantages of cheap food.

The Fair Trade League made little progress, but about the turn of the century there developed another movement against Free Trade: Tariff Reform and Imperial Preference. Its apostle was Joseph Chamberlain, once mayor of Birmingham and a leading Liberal M.P. In 1886 he left the Liberal Party because he violently opposed Gladstone's mission to give Home Rule to Ireland, and he joined the Conservative party. Chamberlain was convinced of the need to encourage the economic growth of the British Empire, which in 1900 covered nearly 20 million square kilometres (8 million square miles—or seventy times the size of the mother country), and contained 300 million people.

In 1895 Chamberlain became Colonial Secretary in Balfour's government. He wanted the Empire to become a trade club, where the members gave preferential treatment to each other. This meant that duties would have to be put on foreign imports. Chamberlain's views were not approved by all his colleagues, and in 1903 he resigned from the government in order that he might campaign for Tariff Reform free from the shackles of ministerial

responsibility. Soon, the idea of a duty on imports in order to give preference to colonial produce was enlarged to embrace the notion of Protection for its own sake. Tariff Reform versus Free Trade became one of the most vital issues in the 1906 General Election. But after eleven years of Conservative rule a reaction had set in, and on the basis of the 'swing of the pendulum' the Liberals were due for a period of office. Moreover, Chamberlain's speeches, while they had succeeded in persuading most of his party to accept the idea of Tariff Reform, had also persuaded the Liberals to close their ranks in defence of Article One of their political platform—Free Trade. Chamberlain's arguments about the impending danger of unemployment and lower wages in those industries facing competition from foreign manufacturers carried less weight with the average voter than the Liberals' slogan 'Do you want a Big Loaf, or a Little Loaf?' As a result of the poll, the Conservatives suffered a crushing defeat, and the Liberals assumed office with an overwhelming majority. Free Trade prevailed until the First World War, when the McKenna Duties were introduced in 1915 to save vital shipping space.

The people's standard of living

For twenty years after 1875 the downward trend in prices, especially of food, combined with an upward trend in wages for most groups of workers, brought about a noticeable improvement in the country's standard of living. Of course there were periods of slack trade and manufacturing activity when many workers were unemployed, and in declining industries, or industries where technological change was rapid, many workers were hard hit. But overall the purchasing power of the working classes rose until about 1900, as the following tables (based on figures taken from the Royal Commission on the *Supply of Food in Time of War 1905*) show.

Even more significant was the fall in the

Consumption per head of Population of Imported Articles of Food and Drink 1887–1901 (in lb)

	1888	1891	1894	1898	1901
Bacon and hams	10	13	13	20	20
Beef	9	15	16	19	21
Mutton	3	5	7	9	10
Butter	5	6	7	9	10
Margarine	3	4	3	2½	2½
Cheese	6	6	6	6	7
Eggs (number)	30	34	37	43	49
Cocoa	0·5	0·6	0·6	1·0	1·2
Sugar	71	80	80	85	89
Tea	5	5·3	5·5	5·8	6

price of bread. In 1870 the 4 lb loaf cost 8d in London, but because of all the year round imports of foreign wheat the price fell (as did the return of the English wheat producer).

Retail Price of Bread per 4 lb in London
Household Seconds (H.S.): bread consumed by lower middle class
Other Qualities (O.Q.): bread consumed practically by working class only

Year	H.S.	O.Q.	Price of home grown wheat per quarter
1876	7·04d	5·06d	46/2
1878	7·50	4·88	46/5
1880	6·62	6·13	44/4
1882	7·33	5·46	45/1
1884	6·63	4·58	35/8
1886	5·50	4·75	31/0
1888	5·17	4·50	31/10
1890	5·50	5·25	31/11
1892	5·50	5·18	30/3
1894	4·98	3·95	22/10
1896	4·67	3·83	26/2
1898	6·00	5·25	34/0
1900	5·21	4·32	26/11
1902	5·17	4·40	28/1

Life for most people was better in many other ways too. More opportunities for organized sport, recreation and entertainment had followed in the wake of greater prosperity and leisure for the working classes. Cricket became a national pastime, and an English side toured Australia for the first time in 1861–2. The county cricket championship began in 1873. Rugby Union was born in 1871. The first F.A. Cup Final was played in 1871, and the Football League, with twelve clubs, was formed in 1888. Boxing had already come under the Queensberry Rules in 1867. Previously boxers had fought each other with bare fists, and contests of fifty rounds were not uncommon. Other recreational activities like bicycling and lawn tennis were very popular by the end of the century.

In the absence of radio and television people were more ready than they are today to create their own entertainment. But the light operas of Gilbert and Sullivan enjoyed a tremendous vogue among the middle classes. Their first opera of note was *H.M.S. Pinafore*, performed for the first time in 1878. Soon after, the *Mikado* enjoyed a run of nearly two years. Over the years many others flowed from their pens and imagination. The serious playgoer was catered for by George Bernard Shaw and W. B. Yeats, both of them outstanding playwrights and authors. The working classes flocked to the music halls, the 'Palace of Varieties', with their free and easy atmosphere. A star music hall artist of the times was Marie Lloyd, who immortalized the song 'My old man, said "Follow the band, and don't dilly dally on the way" '. In 1899 a London audience saw a film of the Grand National only a few hours after the race had been run. But the cinema as a popular medium was in its infancy, and its great days were to come later.

Newspapers were read by all sections of the community. As a result of compulsory education most people could read and write. The existence of a mass market brought about a revolution in journalism. Traditional newspapers like *The Times* catered almost exclusively for the educated, male reader. But the ordinary man in the street was likely to be bored by lengthy parliamentary reports and the unrelieved presentation of facts, on which the reader was intended to formulate his own opinions. The new journalism set out to entertain, and provide the opinions. One of the first new-style papers was the very successful weekly *Tit Bits* founded in 1880 by George Newnes. But the press revolution owed most to the efforts and publicity genius of one man, Alfred Harmsworth, later Lord Northcliffe.

In 1896 he founded the *Daily Mail*. It sold for one halfpenny, and within three years the paper had a circulation of over half a million.

Northcliffe's aim was to convert his readership to his own views. Stories were slanted to bring out the 'human interest' angle (which 'sold' the newspaper), and women's features were introduced. The news was doctored to fit in with Northcliffe's propaganda. In 1904 Northcliffe launched the *Daily Mirror* as a woman's paper. As such it failed completely, so it was altered to become a cheap, daily picture paper, and in its new guise it became a great success. In 1908 Northcliffe bought *The Times* but wisely did not change its format or style of news presentation, so that it kept its old readership. He did, however, reduce its price, and under his guidance *The Times* increased its circulation. The Harmsworth Press was assailed for its vulgar sensationalism, but its readers were being educated while they were entertained, and the cheap newspapers should be given some of the credit for training the British people for self-government.

On the surface Edwardian England was an age of material plenty. The well-to-do acquired weekend cottages as country retreats, attended Ascot and Wimbledon as part of their social round, sent their sons and daughters to public schools, and enjoyed all the trappings of an elegant style of living. But for the submerged section of the community life was still a miserable existence. Half the wage earners in the cities were unskilled, earning less than 20/- per week. In Manchester the rent of a four-roomed slum tenement was 5/- weekly, and in reality a town labourer was worse off than the farm labourer who brought home a mere 13/- or 14/-, but had a cottage and garden at a nominal rent, and at least lived in a healthy atmosphere. More than ever before Disraeli's dictum of *Two Nations* applied. Moreover, after 1900 the rising trend of wages was reversed, and price increases more than cancelled earlier wage gains. The worker found that his earnings could not buy as much as before: 1900–14 consumption per head of population of tobacco, beer, meat, tea, and sugar fell slightly—and these years saw a great increase in the militancy of trade unions and the number of strikes.

The unquestioning confidence of the middle years of the nineteenth century had gone. Religion no longer held its former sway. The consciences of many were torn by the glaring inequalities in the health and wealth of the nation. The Government itself was worried about the possibility of a breakdown of law and order. Not only was it faced with the threat of organized labour on the one hand— the idea of a general strike was seriously canvassed in 1912—and by the suffragette movement on the other, but the passions stirred by the problem of Ulster were so bitter that many people wondered whether Britain was approaching the verge of civil war. Ulster, with its Protestant majority, had no intention of joining the rest of Ireland, which was predominantly Roman Catholic, and it was ready to resist union with armed force. On the Continent the threat of European war was beginning to cloud over the horizon. There were even some doubts as to England's continued prosperity, although it was hard for her people to accept that England as an industrial power had been joined, and in some respects overtaken, by other nations. Yet to suggest that England was in decline, or even stagnating economically, would be to give a completely misleading impression. It took two World Wars and the loss of the greatest Empire the world has ever seen, to erase the image of Britain as she was at the death of Queen Victoria, a proud colossus of naval and industrial strength.

REFERENCES

1   *Final Report of the Royal Commission on the Depression of Industry and Trade 1886*, Parliamentary Papers, 1886/XXIII, paras 74–5.
2   Sir Frederick Maurice, *The Life of Viscount Haldane of Cloan* (1939), Vol. II, p. 31.
3   Sir Frederick Maurice, op. cit., Vol. II, p. 31.
4   *The Electrician*, Vol. I, p. 253.
5   W. Farrer Ecroyd, essay on *Fair Trade* in *The Nineteenth Century*, October 1881, p. 589.

CHAPTER 30
The Social and Economic Effects of the First World War

The century of comparative peace which the British people had enjoyed came to an end when war was declared on Germany and her allies in August 1914. Although Europe's history in the nineteenth century had been punctuated by wars, there had been no general European war since 1815. Britain herself, apart from limited colonial wars, had gone to war on only two occasions—in the Crimean War (1854–6), and the Boer War (1899–1902). In neither war had the general public been greatly affected. Moreover, the experience of European wars seemed to prove that modern wars were short. Those few who remembered how entrenched soldiers had inflicted terrible casualties upon advancing infantry in the American Civil War (1861–5), and prophesied the approaching slaughter, were ignored. The country was united in support of Belgium, whose neutrality had been violated by German armies. Admittedly, the war was an unpleasant interlude, but one great fleet action, it was confidently predicted, and a rapid land campaign, would soon settle the issue. The troops would be back home for Christmas—or so it was thought. Thus the British people, feeling justified in their action, and in a spirit of business as usual, entered upon what soon became known as the Great War.

Yet this war irrevocably changed the Englishman's way of life, for it involved all the people in a way no previous war had done. As A. J. P. Taylor writes in the latest volume of the *Oxford History of England*:

The mass of the people became, for the first time, active citizens. Their lives were shaped by orders from above; they were required to serve the state instead of pursuing exclusively their own affairs. Five million men entered the armed forces, many of them (though a minority) under compulsion. The Englishman's food was limited, and its quality changed, by government order. His freedom of movement was restricted; his conditions of work prescribed. Some industries were reduced or closed, others artificially fostered. The publication of news was fettered. Street lights were dimmed. The sacred freedom of drinking was tampered with: licensed hours were cut down, and the beer watered, by order. The very time on the clocks was changed. From 1916 onwards, every Englishman got up an hour earlier in summer than he would otherwise have done, thanks to an Act of Parliament. The state established a hold over its citizens which, though relaxed in peacetime, was never to be removed and which the Second World War was again to increase.[1]

In 1914, however, the Liberal government was slow to admit that the nation's industry and population would have to be organized for waging war. Plans for taking over the railways, whose strategic role had been realized since the Franco-Prussian War (1870–1), were immediately put into effect. For the duration of the war the 130 separate companies were administered by a Railway Executive Committee consisting of representatives from the ten major companies. Shareholders' dividends were to be maintained at the high 1913 level. A number of merchant ships were requisitioned for transporting the British Expeditionary Force and its supplies to Belgium. Sugar and wheat were stockpiled as soon as war was declared but, apart from these obvious measures, government and business were carried on much as usual. Yet, as Britain was by gradual stages put on to a full war footing, the economic life of the country was distorted.

The munitions industry was quite incapable

of supplying the immense quantities of ammunition, ships, guns, and other equipment used on a vast scale in a modern war. The Government passed a Defence of the Realm Act (DORA), enabling it to take over any factory or workshop making munitions. Even so, the Great Shell Scandal of spring 1915, when it was revealed that British artillery on the Western Front was rationed as to the number of shells it could fire every day, showed that a serious crisis had developed in the industry. Nearly one-fifth of the engineering workers had joined the armed forces by mid-1915, and the industry was desperately short of skilled manpower. A new Ministry of Munitions was created, headed by Lloyd George, with the task of overcoming the munitions' shortage. Lloyd George persuaded the trade unions to abandon restrictive practices and to outlaw the strike for the duration of the war. The unions also agreed to 'dilution' of labour, whereby semi-skilled men and women could be employed in munitions work, doing such jobs as filling shell cases with high explosive (a dangerous occupation), thus leaving highly skilled men to be employed more usefully elsewhere. Munitions workers were exempted from military service so long as they stayed in their jobs. There was some direction of labour, for a worker who wished to leave his firm had to obtain a certificate from his employer. If he did not get one he was liable to be drafted into the army. This meant that workers were unable to obtain higher pay simply by offering their services to another firm at a time of acute labour shortage.

Other industries which contributed directly to the war effort also expanded. Government loans on easy terms were made available to steel manufacturers, and during the war steel production jumped by 50 per cent. The metal industries flourished, and coalmining was kept at full stretch, though there was a shortage of labour in the industry, and output fell below the peak of 1913. The chemical industry could no longer obtain German products, and was forced to manufacture its own. Some infant industries, such as aircraft, became important almost overnight.

Agriculture became a front-line industry. Before 1914 the British farmer had not been expected to feed the population, and 80 per cent of the grain, 40 per cent of the meat, and all the tea and sugar consumed in this country came from abroad. Britain, therefore, was very vulnerable to an enemy submarine blockade, which became a serious threat. Heavy losses of merchant shipping in 1915 forced the Government to take steps to increase home production of food. Farmers were encouraged by a mixture of help and compulsion to put more land under the plough. County Agricultural Committees, composed of farmers, were formed with the task of obtaining the largest possible output of food, and farmers who refused their instructions to plough grasslands were fined or imprisoned. By 1918 some 1·2 million hectares (3 million acres) of pasture had been ploughed up for growing potatoes and grain. Bad farmers had their land taken away and given to more efficient farmers. Farmers were given subsidies to produce certain crops. The Corn Production Act (1917) guaranteed farmers fixed prices for wheat and oats for a period of six years, and also granted agricultural labourers a minimum wage of 25/- a week. A sugar-beet industry was started in order to save imports of sugar. The shortage of farm labourers was overcome by employing prisoners of war, 300,000 part-time female workers, and the Women's Land Army, which recruited 16,000 volunteers, to work on farms.

But, in spite of all the farmers' efforts, Britain depended upon getting a large part of her foodstuffs from abroad. Thus Germany's introduction of unrestricted submarine warfare in 1917 brought Britain to the verge of disaster, for at one stage there was only six weeks' food supply in the country, and food rationing was introduced. Local Food Control Committees were set up to deal with the sale of sugar, tea, fats and meat, which were in very short supply. Yet, with the exception of

70   *Haymaking at Lockinge in Berkshire, 1905*
Up to the First World War, which hastened the introduction of tractors
and other types of farm machinery, all the able-bodied inhabitants of a
village turned out to help bring in the harvest

meat, tea, and butter, which by 1918 were rationed nearly everywhere, there was no comprehensive system of rationing (such as there was in the Second World War), and the items which were rationed varied from district to district.

Germany's unrestricted submarine campaign was only the most ferocious way in which Britain's overseas trade was harmed by the war. Germany herself had been one of Britain's most important customers before the war, but Anglo-German trade ceased the moment war was declared. Trade with Russia was virtually cut off when Turkey entered the war in November 1915, and the Dardanelles were closed. Since so much of Britain's production was geared to the war effort, she was unable to meet the needs of foreign customers for manufactures, particularly textiles, iron and steel goods, and coal.

Many countries, which had relied on Britain, either developed their own industries, or went to another source of supply. Britain's Far Eastern markets for cotton goods were especially vulnerable, and were easily invaded by Japanese competitors. Once lost, many of these markets could never be regained.

Home industries which depended upon imported supplies of raw material also suffered. The cotton industry in particular was badly hit. After 1916 imports of raw cotton from the United States, which took up valuable shipping space, were restricted, and there was a good deal of unemployment in Lancashire. A Cotton Control Board fixed a maximum percentage of machinery each mill could use. Imports of timber were cut, and a system of priorities and controls was set up to ration industries which were not vital to the war effort. In 1915 the McKenna Duties were introduced to save shipping space. Luxury imports such as cameras, film, clocks and watches, motor cars and musical instruments, were taxed. Thus almost unconsciously, the Liberals had breached the principle of Free Trade, for at the end of the war the McKenna Duties were kept for raising revenue, and they soon became openly protective duties.

But the most serious wartime shortage was manpower. Britain began the war with a small, but highly efficient, professional army. This was immediately expanded by a rush of volunteers to join the armed forces. So many men enlisted that they almost became an embarrassment to the Government, since there were insufficient uniforms and equipment for them. By 1916, however, recruitment had slowed down, and compulsory conscription was introduced. At first only single men were recruited, but by the end of the war all males between the ages of 18 and 50 were liable to be called up for military service. Many industries, therefore, found themselves short of labour. In a wide range of jobs women took the place of men. As well as working on farms, women drove trams, delivered the post, and were to be found in increasing numbers in factories, shops and theatres. It was their work during the war, when the female labour force increased by $1\frac{1}{2}$ million, that really won women the vote, rather than the violent activities of the suffragette movement, which had intensified masculine prejudice against the idea.

The substitution of female for male labour reduced the pressure for wage increases, since women were paid a lower rate than men, and this, together with the dilution of labour, kept wages relatively low. Consequently, in the latter stages of the war there was a good deal of industrial unrest. The principle of granting flat-rate wage increases to all grades of workers in an industry meant that differentials between skilled and unskilled workers were reduced. The Government tried to keep industrial peace by controlling the prices of essential goods, and introducing an Excess Profits Tax

in 1915 to meet the workers' complaints of wartime profiteering by some firms. This tax, which was repealed in 1921, was levied on firms not individuals. At first the rate was 50 per cent, but it was raised to 80 per cent in 1917. In spite of evasions it raised about one quarter of the tax revenue while it was in operation. A Rent Restriction Act (1915) fixed council house rents at the prewar level to protect tenants from the effects of inflation. Even so, labour problems became one of the Government's chief worries, and peace brought little improvement. On the contrary, the demobilization of millions of men from the armed services only aggravated the problem, though this was at first concealed by a postwar boom and spending spree.

The cost of the war to the community is difficult to assess. Over $\frac{3}{4}$ million men from the United Kingdom lost their lives. Many more had been wounded, and a large proportion of these were permanently crippled or bedridden. Words alone can hardly describe the human misery wrought by four long years of terrible warfare. But, unlike Belgium, France and Russia, parts of which were devastated in the course of the fighting, Britain suffered little physical damage to her industries and private property. Zeppelins, or huge airships, and later, aeroplanes, bombed London, killing 1,400 people but causing little damage otherwise. Some east coast towns, like Scarborough, were briefly bombarded by German naval units. But no attempt was made to invade Britain and, apart from the tiny amount of aerial warfare, the civilian population experienced no loss of life, homes or livelihood as a result of direct enemy action.

Yet, if the actual physical destruction of property in Britain was very slight, the cost of the war, and the amount of material swallowed by it, was enormous. Government expenditure in 1913–14 was £197 million; in 1917–18 it was £2,696 million. The war was paid for chiefly by increased taxation and large-scale borrowing, which was more popular, since it was felt that the financial burden of the war was being shifted on to the shoulders of future generations. In November 1914 income tax and surtax were doubled, and duties on beer and tea were raised. During the war income tax rose from 1/2 to 6/- in the pound, while the exemption rate was lowered from £160 to £130. The yield from direct taxation rose fivefold, and the number paying income tax from 1 to 3 million. These figures reflect the declining value of the pound as well as a rise in wages, but nevertheless, one result of the war was to accustom the Englishman to accept a high level of taxation as a normal state of affairs. Between the two World Wars income tax hovered around 5/- in the pound. The gap between wartime income and expenditure was closed by borrowing, chiefly from the United States, and from the British people itself, which contributed to the war effort by purchasing savings certificates, or War Loan stock. As a result the National Debt jumped from £650 million in 1914 to £7,435 million in 1919 when the interest alone, amounting to over £300 million, was more than the prewar government revenue. Only a small part, however, of Britain's overseas investments, some 15 per cent, was sold, mainly to buy munitions from America.

The Government had started work on a programme of reconstruction as early as 1916. So many sacrifices had been required of the people that a return to prewar conditions was not only impossible, it was not even contemplated. Long before the armistice was signed, the original war aim of defeating Kaiser Wilhelm's Germany no longer convinced people that all the slaughter on the Western Front was worthwhile. Under the influence of President Wilson's famous Fourteen Points' Peace Plan, the war became a 'war to end all wars'. The world was to be made a better place to live in. The proposed peace settlement, by applying the principle of national self-determination, i.e. allowing national groups to rule themselves, would remove an important cause of war. This, together with other arrangements, such as the

proposal for general disarmament, the creation of a League of Nations would (or so it was hoped) ensure peace between the nations. At home, a better society was to be built, as a token that the sacrifices made by all classes had not been entirely in vain.

In this mood of optimism the Government rashly promised 'Homes fit for Heroes', and Dr Addison, who headed the Ministry of Labour, set up in 1917, made arrangements for a rapid expansion of the housing programme, which had been held back during the war. Three quarters of a million new houses were needed, so Addison urged local authorities to press ahead with building council houses. Any cost in excess of a penny rate would be met by the Government. Unfortunately, this offer encouraged builders to put up their prices. Houses which cost £400 to build one year later (1921), when subsidies were discontinued, cost £900. Even so, Addison's efforts resulted in the construction of over 200,000 houses.

In the hope of creating a better society, all kinds of reforms were considered, and many were put into effect. A Representation of the People Act (1918) accepted the principle of 'one man one vote'. (There were a few exceptions to this rule, for until 1948 university graduates and owners of business premises had two votes.) All men over 21 years, and women over 30 years, who fulfilled a qualification of six months' residence were enfranchised. The Act was passed through Parliament by overwhelming majorities, and so nearly 22 million people (13 million men and 9 million women) had the vote, and the Act added more voters to the electoral lists than all previous parliamentary reform Acts put together.

Fisher's Education Act (1918) raised the school-leaving age to 14 and began a scheme for part-time education for those who wished to continue their education after leaving school. A Trade Boards Act (1918) empowered the existing trade boards to investigate sweated trades where there was no machinery for wage regulation. Whitley councils composed of representatives of management and workers were set up to resolve industrial disputes in a variety of industries. An Unemployment Insurance Act of 1920 extended the prewar insurance scheme to all workers earning less than £250 per annum, except civil servants, farm labourers, and domestic servants. A total of 12 million workers was insured against casual, short-term unemployment. In the meantime, jobs were plentiful as the people entered upon a wild spending spree following the wartime austerity, and demobbed service-men were absorbed into civvy street with surprising ease. Trade unions managed to achieve a general reduction of working hours as well as increases in pay for their members in many industries. An eight-hour working day became general.

Unfortunately, this period of prosperity was short-lived, and the British economy entered the doldrums, from which it never fully recovered until the Second World War. Britain's export trade had been severely damaged as a result of the war, and the demand for her staple products such as ships, iron and steel manufactures, textiles and coal, declined. Competition for markets became much fiercer. The shipyards of many coun-tries, which had enjoyed fat order books as a result of submarine sinkings during the war, soon discovered to their dismay that there was a world surplus of merchant shipping. With the slowdown of shipbuilding, and the halt in armaments production, demand for steel dropped. The wartime expansion of steel works in Britain and the United States, and the replacement of Belgian steel plant, destroyed during the fighting, with the most modern equipment, meant over-capacity after the war.

Moreover, as the Balfour Committee's *Survey of Industries* made quite clear, Lanca-shire had lost its pre-eminence as a world supplier of cotton textiles. A large part of the Chinese and Indian markets had been lost. 'China is approaching self-sufficiency as a result of the enormous development of modern spinning plant which has taken place in recent

years.'[2] Britain's export of yarn into India had also declined. 'Before the war some 88 per cent of the weight of the yarns imported came from Great Britain and 14 per cent from Japan. On the average of the years 1924 to 1926, how-ever, only 36 per cent came from Great Britain and as much as 59 per cent from Japan.' At the same time American exports of yarn had grown elevenfold, to some extent at the expense of British trade. 'American yarns are exported almost entirely to South America and Canada, countries to which British shipments have markedly declined.'

A similar picture emerged from a study of exports of finished textile goods.

The Japanese export trade in piece goods had already begun to grow rapidly before the war, but the war, by making European goods unobtainable in distant markets, gave an immense impetus to the Japanese export trade, and to the Japanese cotton industry. Postwar experience, moreover, has shown that the Japanese industry is based upon solid foundations, and that it is not merely able to hold much of the trade which it gained during the war, but is in a position to push its way still further into many important markets. Japanese competition has become formidable in China, India and other great markets of the Far East, and Japanese goods have begun to appear in East and South Africa, in the Middle and Near East, in South America, and to a small extent in Australasia.[2]

Another important effect of the war was to speed up the substitution of petrol, oil, and electricity for coal as sources of energy. This not only had serious consequences for Britain's coal industry (see Chapter 31), it also in-creased the imports bill. All the oil and petrol had to be imported. Secondly, coal had played an important part in the shipping trade as an outward cargo for ships sailing from this country to bring back the vast quantities of food and raw materials needed. As coal exports declined, so the loss of this cargo increased freight rates, thus pushing up the cost of imported goods.

Thus the war accelerated trends apparent

before the war. Britain's reliance on exports of iron and steel manufactures, textiles, and coal, which had formerly enabled her to dominate world trade, had now become her chief source of economic weakness. The Balfour Committee remarked of the Lancashire cotton industry:

If Lancashire is to succeed, it will be necessary for her to see to it that her methods and organization are capable of adjustment if required to meet changed and changing conditions. Only in this way will it be possible for her to place her products on the world's markets at prices, and under conditions, which will enable them to hold their own.

This passage could very aptly have been applied to Great Britain herself.

REFERENCES

1   A. J. P. Taylor, *English History 1914–1945* (Oxford University Press, 1965), p. 2.
2   Balfour Committee, *Survey of Industries, 1925–9.*

CHAPTER 31
The General Strike

Trade unions were in a strong position when the war ended. Their membership had doubled, and in 1920 reached a total of 8 million. Wages too had risen, particularly during the period 1918–20, and in 1920 the working man was slightly better off than he had been in 1914. This was due more to abnormal conditions, such as the labour shortage in the war, and the short-lived postwar boom in trade, than to the activities of the trade unions. Nevertheless, trade unions were aware of the strength to be found in numbers, and they were also determined to maintain and, if possible, improve, the higher standard of living their members enjoyed.

Several very large, militant unions were formed just after the war. Ten unions joined together to form the Amalgamated Engineering Union in 1920. This was followed in 1922 by the formation of the Transport and General Workers' Union, and in 1924 by the National Union of General and Municipal Workers. Many workers supported the 1917 Revolution in Russia. The refusal of London Dockers in 1920 to load the *Jolly George* with munitions to aid the 'Whites', the anti-Bolshevik forces, in their struggle against the 'Reds', was one reason why the Government called off its military intervention in Russia. A Communist uprising in Germany in 1919, though a failure, seemed to bear out Lenin's belief that Europe was on the verge of socialist revolution. In Britain itself the strength of the unions and their socialist aims worried the Government and the ruling classes. For according to one trade unionist, speaking in 1919 at the Central Hall in London, Labour was challenging 'the whole structure of capitalist industry as it now exists. It is no longer willing to acquiesce in a system under which industry is conducted

for the benefit of a few. It demands a system of industrial control which shall be truly democratic in character.'[1] This demand for public ownership, or nationalization, of essential industries was most clearly voiced by the railwaymen and miners.

During the war both the railways and the mines were taken over by the Government, and the benefits of unified control were obvious. After the war both the railwaymen and the miners demanded nationalization, which they saw as a solution to the problems of their industries. In the case of the railways some amalgamation took place, for they were formed into four separate companies. But nothing was done for the coal industry. The Government merely decided to return the mines to their private owners in 1921. The miners were bitterly disappointed, for they had pinned their hopes on nationalization.

The flash-point of industrial unrest right up to the General Strike in 1926 was in the coal industry, where the number of strikes was greater than in most other industries put together. About 90 million workings days were lost in the coal industry in 1920 and 1921 alone. To explain why the coal industry had such an abnormal record of strikes, and why the grievances of the miners led to the only General Strike in this country, we must first examine conditions within the coal industry itself.

Coalmining was an old-established industry and both the cost and the difficulty of winning the coal had been steadily increasing over a long period of time. Some of its problems were described by the Royal Commission on the Coal Industry in 1925, which contrasted the British coal industry with that of the United States.

In the United States, the deepest bituminous coal mining operation is less than 1,000 feet from the surface, and the average depth of the shafts is about 260 feet. Less than one quarter of all the mines have shafts at all; the rest are approached by horizontal 'drifts', or downward slopes, or are 'strip' mines worked in the open after shovelling off the earth above the coal. In Great Britain more than half the coal now being worked comes from depths greater than 300 yards, and nearly one quarter comes from depths greater than 500 yards. In the United States 40 per cent of the bituminous coal output comes from seams 6 feet or more in thickness, and only 19 per cent from seams of less than 4 feet. In Great Britain half the output comes from seams of less than 4 feet, and 10 per cent only from seams 6 feet thick or over.[1]

As a result the average annual output of coal for each miner had fallen steadily from 319 tons in 1879–83, to 282 tons in 1889–93, to 257 tons in 1909–13. In 1924 the figure stood at 220 tons. Coal production had only been maintained by increasing the labour force from around 900,000 in the 1880s to nearly $1\frac{1}{4}$ million in 1925. Hence labour costs were very high, and reducing wages seemed the only way the owners could save money.

Nor was coal the only important source of industrial power. Coal had to meet the competition of oil and hydro-electric power. Oil fuel was increasingly used by industry and in ocean transport. The world production of crude petroleum was estimated at 47 million tons in 1910, and 98 million tons in 1920. By 1926 production had reached 150 million tons. Moreover, the rising cost of coal encouraged coal users to find ways of cutting down the amounts of coal they required. Steel manufacturers, by using more efficient processes, had more than halved the quantity of coal needed to produce a given amount of steel. Furthermore, Britain had always exported a high proportion of her coal output (about 34 per cent compared with 25 per cent for Germany and only 5 per cent for the United States), so that the postwar decline in coal

exports was a heavy blow to the coal industry.

So far as wages were concerned, it was almost impossible to treat the coal industry as one industry, which was what the miners themselves wanted, so long as the mines were privately owned. The chief reason for this was the great variety of pits in operation. Some mines were over one hundred years old, and it was often very difficult to introduce into the older pits modern methods of transport and coal cutting machinery.

The industry cannot be regarded as a collection of more or less uniform undertakings, employing so many men under conditions fairly similar, producing a single article, the costs of production and the price obtained varying little among them at any time. [Rather it may be imagined] *as not unlike a series of farms in a country of valleys and mountains, varying in their productivity from the fat lands by the rivers, through medium lands on the lower slopes, up, through farms of gradually decreasing fertility, to fields that are half rock at the limit of cultivation on the higher slopes. The question for the agriculturalist is how far up the mountainside it is worthwhile to spend labour. And that depends upon the cost of labour at the time, and the degree of hardship that the cultivator is willing to endure.*[2]

For these reasons the owners stubbornly resisted the miners' demands for a national wage to replace district agreements negotiated individually by the management and miners of each colliery. Yet a price-list, or the rates of pay, was a complicated document which caused much argument and bitterness. A whole series of prices had to be agreed upon, not only for hewing coal at the coal face, but for all the 'deadwork' that had to be done. This ranged from removing useless rock and earth to extending the underground transport.

Once the list had been made it was practically impossible to unmake it. . . . Owners in South Wales had been known to sell their pits rather than face the struggle that was bound to follow the alteration of a price-list and the new buyer reckoned the expense of strike breaking in with his purchase price.

Upon the making or altering of a price-list there might hang a very sordid drama. If the men had not held their own with the management, if the wages for a new pit were low—and variations between neighbouring pits with identical seams had been as high as 20 per cent—then a special kind of labour would be attracted there. High pay brought steady and skilful workers; to low pay came nomads and the ne'er-do-wells of the industry; and the very destiny of each little town of five or six thousand depended upon the quality of its miners. In South Wales, for instance, there was little to be expected from the foreign miners, the unlikely immigrants who drifted in from the old North of England pits, or the unskilled labourers from the pastures and ploughlands of Devon and Somerset; and a cheap price-list, in years of normal employment, meant just such foreign labour; it meant casual lodgers in the cottages, men without families; it meant public houses, and drunkenness, and dirt. A price-list was something more than a matter of pence and shillings—it might be the death warrant for a whole community.[3]

At the end of the war the miners demanded public ownership of the mines, a 6-hour day, and a 30 per cent rise in wages. They threatened to go on strike if the Government did not meet their demands. The Government, headed by Lloyd George, was desperately anxious to avoid a strike at a time when the coal industry, as a result of the coal shortage in Europe, was earning high profits by selling coal to Continental countries. It therefore played for time by appointing a Royal Commission, in which owners and miners were equally represented, under the chairmanship of Sir John Sankey, a high court judge. The Government promised to accept the recommendations of the Sankey Commission. But when the Report came out in favour of nationalizing the mines the Government refused to accept it, on the excuse that the Commission was not unanimous in its recommendations. All it did was to pass the Coal Mines Act of 1919, introducing a 7-hour

working day into the coal industry.

The miners felt they had been cheated. They opened up negotiations with the railwaymen and the transport workers to plan joint strike action in support of the miners' claims. At the last minute, the leaders of the railwaymen and transport workers withdrew their promise of support, but the miners went ahead with their strike, which lasted for three weeks in the October of 1920. In the end the miners got an 11 per cent increase on the minimum wage, though this was made conditional on increased productivity, and the rest of the rates had to be worked out. In the meantime the Government, alarmed by the threat of a general strike, passed the Emergency Powers Act of 1920. This allowed it to declare a 'state of emergency' if it considered that the essential supply and distribution of food, water, light and fuel to the community was liable to be interrupted by strike action.

Unfortunately for the miners coal prices slumped at the beginning of 1921 and the Government, finding its control of the mines a financial burden, suddenly advanced the date of their return to private ownership. The owners, faced with falling demand and falling prices for coal, felt that they could not afford to maintain existing wages, let alone the new rates which were being worked out. They announced their intention to cut wages, and when the miners refused to accept the cuts they were locked out. The failure of the miners' strike became certain when, on 15 April, *Black Friday*, the plans for a Triple Alliance with the transport unions came to nought. As soon as the miners' funds were exhausted they were forced to return to work on the owners' terms. Wages were cut, and wages were to be negotiated at district level, not national level.

By 1924 the coal industry once again enjoyed prosperity, though since it resulted from the French occupation of the Ruhr in 1923, it could not last. But with the German mines paralysed by a general strike as part of a campaign of passive resistance to drive the

French out, Britain's coal exports to Europe boomed. The owners agreed to an increase in wages, only to demand a return to the original rates when profits again turned downwards in 1925. The miners appealed to the General Council of the TUC for support, which was granted. Faced with the threat of a general strike, the Government climbed down. This was on *Red Friday*. It agreed to pay the owners a subsidy for maintaining present wage rates, and it appointed the Samuel Commission to inquire into the coal industry. Their findings were rejected by all parties concerned in the dispute. But rather ominously for the miners the Commission agreed with the owners that it could see no alternative to wage cuts as a means of reducing the costs of the industry. The miners rashly resolved 'Not a penny off the pay, not a minute on the day'. When they were asked how they might help the coal industry the miners replied bluntly 'We've nowt to offer'. Since this was also the attitude of the owners, a strike in the coal industry was certain when the government subsidy ended on 31 April 1926.

On 1 May the miners were locked out. The General Council of the TUC supported the miners, but talks between the General Council and the Government continued, for neither side wished to be held responsible for breaking them off. On 3 May the Cabinet abruptly halted the talks, on the excuse that the printers of the *Daily Mail* had refused to print the editorial, thus violating the industrial truce, and the General Strike began at midnight. All transport and railway workers,

71   *A food convoy escorted by armoured cars passes through Poplar after leaving the East India Dock*

printers, building workers, and gas and electricity employees were called out on strike. The remaining workers were held back in reserve, in 'the second line'. The response of the unions called out was virtually unanimous. On 5 May the *British Worker*, the newsheet published by the General Council, reported:

The workers' response has exceeded all expectations. The first day of the General Strike is over. They have manifested their determination and unity to the whole world. They have resolved that the attempt of the mine owners to starve three million men, women and children into submission shall not succeed.

It went on to say that the greatest difficulty the TUC faced was to prevent the second line of workers from joining the strike.

Unfortunately for the miners there was another side to the picture. The Government was in a strong position. It had already formed an Anti-Strike Organization. England and Wales had been divided into ten Divisions, each Division being subdivided into suitable areas for recruiting volunteers and for administering essential services. Each area had a local Food Officer, Road Officer, Coal Emergency Officer, and a Haulage Committee. Food convoys, guarded by troops, kept London well supplied. Many students and ex-officers seized the chance to drive lorries, buses and trams, or fulfilled childhood dreams of driving steam locomotives. With the development of road transport the day when a national rail strike could paralyse the country had passed.

There was also a good deal of support for the Government in its determination to crush the General Strike. There was sympathy for the miners, but many people felt that the whole country was being held to ransom on their account. A few even accused the trade unions of bringing the country to the brink of civil war. Stanley Baldwin, Prime Minister of the Conservative government, which had taken office on the resignation of Ramsay MacDonald's Labour government in 1924, warned the unions that 'The General Strike is a challenge to Parliament, and is the road to anarchy and ruin', and added that the Government would never tolerate a minority to coerce the whole community. Under the influence of right-wing members like Winston Churchill, who remarked 'Either the country will break the General Strike, or the General Strike will break the country', the Cabinet was determined on a fight to the finish with the trade unions. During the strike itself there was surprisingly little violence, however, and the only place where troops were called upon to restore order was in London Docks. Some trams and buses were wrecked in working-class districts in London and Glasgow, and there was an isolated incident of sabotage on a railway line in County Durham. The number of arrests was very small compared with the numbers on strike. In some places football matches were played between the police and strikers.

Suddenly, just when it seemed that the strikers were winning, the General Strike was called off. Though the rank and file of the trade union movement enthusiastically supported the strike, their leaders had little desire to challenge the Government. Far from being revolutionaries, which the Government tried to make them out to be, they had in fact made few preparations for a massive strike. All along they had assumed that the Government would give way to the threat of general strike action, and their intention from the first had been to reach some form of compromise settlement. Thus, when Herbert Samuel proposed that a national Wages Board for the coal industry be set up, which would reduce wages only when the recommendations of the Samuel Commission had been carried out, the General Council accepted the terms. Samuel himself emphasized that the proposals were his own, and were not necessarily approved by the Government, but the General Council wrongly assumed that public opinion would force the Government

72   *A London bus manned by volunteers*
The policeman is there to prevent attack by strikers

to adopt them. Thus after nine days the General Strike was over.

The miners themselves stayed out on strike, but their cause was hopeless. An Act was passed to prevent miners' families getting poor relief. The unequal struggle lasted eight months. Then the miners, many of them near to starvation, surrendered. They were forced to accept longer hours, cuts in their pay, and the hated district agreements, as well as the pool of unemployed miners created by the longer working day.

The Government reinforced its victory over the unions by passing the Trades Disputes and Trade Union Act of 1927. This made illegal general strikes and any strike 'designed to coerce the Government', forbade civil servants to join a union affiliated to the TUC, and reversed the 1913 Trade Union Act. Trade union members who wished to pay the political levy to the Labour Party had to contract in, i.e. sign a form stating they wished to do so, instead of the payment being made automatically out of the member's subscription, unless he had 'contracted out'. (One of the first actions of the Labour government which took office in 1945 was to restore 'contracting out' for 'contracting in'.) But the failure of the General Strike did not lead to any attempt by employers, except in the coal industry, to reduce wages, which remained stable for the next three years. Nor, except by the railway companies, was there any victimization of the strikers.

Trade union activity died down after 1926. The idea of a general strike was discarded by the unions. Trade union membership dropped to less than 5 million, and union funds, after meeting the expenses of 1926, were very low. But the comparative absence of strikes after 1926 was due more to a permanently high level of unemployment than to acceptance by the more lowly paid workers of their position. With unemployment figures never below the 1-million mark there were too many men ready to take a striker's place. Thus the General Strike failed completely to live up to the expectations of either its supporters or its opponents.

REFERENCES

1   *Report of the Royal Commission on the Coal Industry*, 1925.
2   *Report of the Royal Commission on the Coal Industry*, 1925.
3   George Dangerfield, *The Strange Death of Liberal England* (1966), pp. 231–2.

The relative decline of British industry in the face of foreign competition had been evident since the latter part of the nineteenth century. The immense industrial effort called forth by the First World War, and the short-lived boom which followed it, masked this trend, while at the same time contributing to the conditions which made it more difficult for Britain to earn her living abroad. The under-developed countries, once fine markets for Britain's exports, built up their own industries as a result of having their supplies cut off during the war. In particular, they concentrated on steel manufactures and textiles, two of Britain's chief exports, and within a few years they ceased to be very important markets for British firms. After 1922 the shipping industry suffered from surplus capacity. The wartime losses in merchant ships had been more than replaced, and with the volume of world trade falling there were too many ships for the number of cargoes available. More significant still, Britain's share in the world's tonnage of merchant ships fell. With more and more countries turning to oil and electricity instead of coal as sources of power and fuel, the scene was set for the depression in Britain's staple industries during the interwar period.

Many businessmen expected the postwar boom to last several years. In fact, its collapse in 1920 heralded two decades of depression, broken by brief periods of partial recovery. Economic activity picked up again by 1922, and the recovery lasted, with some sharp interruptions, until 1929. Unfortunately, many national economies were dependent on the financial stability of the United States. When the spectacular boom America enjoyed after the war came to an end in 1929 with the Wall Street Crash, the effects spread through the industrialized countries like a great tidal wave.

Many Americans, believing that their prosperity would last for ever, had invested heavily in stocks and shares, often bought with borrowed money. Share prices were pushed sky-high, with a reckless disregard of the fact that by 1928 the market for certain goods was rapidly becoming saturated, and prices were falling. Panic set in once speculators began to have doubts about the wisdom of holding on to their shares. In the rush to sell, share prices tumbled, banks failed, businesses collapsed overnight, production fell, and unemployment rose. To try to restore the situation, American bankers demanded repayment of their massive loans to European countries, causing unemployment to rise in those countries too.

The bottom of the recession was reached in 1933, after which a fairly steady improvement was evident. The Depression would not have been so serious if it had been superimposed upon a background of growing trade. Unfortunately, this was not so. After the war Britain's exports actually declined to about 80 per cent of her prewar total. The only redeeming feature for Britain was that the prices of primary products—foodstuffs and many raw materials—fell on average even more than manufactures, so that fewer goods had to be exported to pay for imports. But even this was a mixed blessing. Primary producing countries could no longer afford to buy so many of our manufactures. It also reinforced their desire for economic independence by making their own manufactures.

Since the First World War the Lancashire cotton industry had been in difficulty. India,

China, and Japan all produced their own cloth. The Japanese captured a large chunk of the Afro-Asian market, which in the past had been dominated by Britain. There was also strong competition from artificial fibres. Yet it was a long time before Lancashire mill owners accepted the unpleasant truth that the great days of King Cotton had gone for ever. At first short-time working was adopted as a temporary measure until the industry recovered. When it did not, the cotton industry reluctantly decided that the oldest mills, containing obsolete machinery, should be closed down, so that a more profitable future might be assured for the surviving firms. Several combines such as the Lancashire Cotton Corporation were formed to increase the industry's efficiency.

A similar pattern of slump and partial recovery occurred in the iron and steel trades. During the Great Depression steel output was only two-thirds of the 1913 figure. In the 1930s, however, the fortunes of the steel industry slowly improved. The British Iron and Steel Federation was formed in 1934 to streamline the industry by creating larger combines. A measure of protection was afforded by the Government. In 1932 a 33⅓ per cent import duty was placed on imported steel manufactures, and the introduction of import quotas in 1935 largely freed the industry from foreign competition. Recovery came not as a result of rising exports, however, but from a growing demand for steel at home, particularly from the expanding motor-car industry. Equally important was the stimulus of rearmament after 1935. In that year Germany announced that, contrary to the letter of the Versailles Peace Settlement, she was rearming. Soon it became clear to the British government that it could not afford to allow the country to remain in its unarmed state in the face of Hitler's warlike intentions of creating a Greater Germany, which would include most of Central and South-east Europe. Government orders for aircraft, warships, machinery, and munitions of all

kinds, together with the outbreak of the Second World War in September 1939, meant that the steel industry returned once more to full-time production.

Both the coal and the shipbuilding industries experienced great difficulties, though the problems of the coal industry proved to be the more intractable. Between the wars, the demand for coal slackened as other fuels, notably petroleum and electricity, became increasingly competitive. Furthermore, both Germany and the United States stepped up their coal output, and France too, which had relied upon coal imported from British coalfields, began to produce more. Output per man shift in the Ruhr, Belgium and Holland rose steeply, while in Britain the increase was a mere 3 per cent. Britain had far too many small, old mines where it was uneconomic to introduce coal-cutting machinery. The solution was amalgamations, and closures of the least productive mines, in order to reduce overheads. Yet in spite of the recommendations of the Sankey Commission (1919), the Samuel Commission (1925), and the Coal Mines Act (1930), hardly anything was done to solve the problems of the industry until the mines were nationalized in 1946.

Britain's shipyards went through a painful period of readjustment to changed world conditions. Many yards were too small, and relied upon out of date construction methods. Scandinavian and Japanese yards were more efficient. In 1930 the shipping magnates began to shut down the most uneconomic yards, causing much hardship in the process. When Palmer's yard in Jarrow, County Durham, closed down, nearly 70 per cent of the town's male labour force was unemployed and, since no other work was available, Jarrow became 'the town that died'. Only in the later thirties, largely due to government orders for warships, did prosperity return.

The decline of the heavy industries, which were concentrated on the coalfields, created the depressed areas of the 1930s. Workers in the heavy industries bore the brunt of un-

73 *The demoralizing effect of long unemployment*
During the Depression 10 out of Wigan's 15
textile mills closed, and 17 out of 40 pits were idle

employment, which never dropped below the 1 million mark between the Wars. In 1930 28 per cent of the labour force in the coal industry was idle. In that year 31 per cent of the working force in South Wales was unemployed, 29 per cent in South Lancashire, and 24 per cent on Tyneside. This compared with 10 per cent in London, and 18 per cent in the Midlands, where the newer industries, which relied upon electricity, not coal, for power, developed.

Mass unemployment meant mass relief. The 1920 National Insurance Act extended the principle of insurance to a further 8 million workers. With the exception of those in agriculture and domestic service, nearly all

workers were included in the scheme. But the system broke down with the first spell of heavy unemployment. Payment of benefit was limited to 15 weeks, and was intended to tide over the recipient between losing one job and finding another. It had not been designed to cope with prolonged unemployment. The Government decided that, when the 'covenanted benefit' ran out, additional payments, known as the *dole* should be made. The unemployed had to queue outside the labour exchanges to collect their money. After 1934 those who claimed the dole had to answer a questionnaire on their income and expenditure. This was the *Means Test*, which was deeply resented by the working classes.

The Government tried to remedy the nation's ills in a variety of ways. Its first thoughts were the orthodox ones of cutting expenditure. In 1921 world grain prices tumbled, and the Government, uneasy about the huge subsidy it would have to pay the farmers in order to maintain guaranteed prices, went back on its promises. Partly as a result of this decision the British farmer found it difficult to make a decent living between the World Wars, and agriculture sank to the status of a depressed industry. The minimum wage for agricultural labourers was another victim of government policy. In 1922 a parliamentary committee recommended economies in government spending, which was slashed by £64 million. The salaries of civil servants and teachers were cut. These economies were known as the *Geddes Axe*, so called because the chairman of the committee was Sir Eric Geddes. Even the unemployed did not escape, for in 1931 unemployment benefit was cut by 10 per cent.

Britain returned to the gold standard in 1925 in an attempt to restore confidence in the world's monetary system. This decision meant that the pound sterling was equivalent to the purchasing power of a definite weight of gold. It therefore provided a practically fixed rate of exchange for other currencies, which was very desirable from the traders' point of view, since it removed the risk of loss from variations in exchange rates. Until then governments and individuals were naturally reluctant to lend money, on which trade depended, if the value of a debt could be almost entirely wiped out by galloping inflation. Britain's action helped to stabilize the major international currencies, and for four years world trade appeared to be reviving. The pound sterling was overvalued, however, and this added to the problems of British exporters by making British goods more expensive. During the Depression the burden of maintaining the value of the pound became too great, and in 1931 Britain finally abandoned the gold standard. For a short while Britain's exports were cheaper, but soon other countries devalued their currencies, and Britain's competitive advantage was eliminated.

Free Trade was another casualty of the World Depression. It had already been breached by the wartime McKenna Duties and the Safeguarding of Industries Act in 1921 (see Chapter 30). In 1932 an Import Duties Act levied a 10 per cent duty on imported manufactures. This was later in the year raised to 20 per cent, and to $33\frac{1}{3}$ per cent in certain cases. Some raw materials were also taken off the duty-free list. A measure of imperial preference was agreed at the Ottawa Conference in 1932. Higher duties were placed on imported foreign foodstuffs, so that preference could be given, in the form of lower duties, to produce from the Dominions. In return, the Dominions gave preference to British manufactures. The results of the agreements, apart from goodwill, were not very encouraging. They offended countries which were not included. In any case both Australia and Canada had close trading links with the United States, which they had no wish to disturb.

The Government also gave financial and other help to depressed industries. Agricultural Rates Acts of 1923 and 1928 exempted all agricultural lands and buildings from payment of rates. Marketing Boards were set up for bacon, milk, hops, and potatoes in 1931 and 1933. Wheat production was subsidized in 1932, and meat in 1934, as farmers were once again given guaranteed prices. A system of quotas, which restricted imports of foodstuffs, protected farmers from the worst effects of foreign competition. Shipbuilding was given government assistance after 1936. Favourable loans were made available for the construction of the two great Cunarders, the Queen Mary and the Queen Elizabeth. The Special Areas Act (1934) tried to stop the drift of population away from the older industrial areas to London and the Home Counties by encouraging light industry to go to the depressed areas. Finally, the Government encouraged amalgamations in certain industries in order to make them more efficient. In 1926 Britain's chemical industries were concentrated in one vast, industrial giant, Imperial Chemical Industries (ICI). Britain's air transport companies were combined in 1924 with government support, to form Imperial Airways Limited. In 1935 another company, British Airways, was formed, which operated services between this country, and Berlin and Scandinavia. Both companies found it difficult to make profits, and in 1939 the two companies were amalgamated by an Act of Parliament into British Overseas Airways Corporation (BOAC).

The development of aircraft and air transport in the twentieth century was very rapid. John Alcock and Arthur Brown crossed the Atlantic for the first time in an aeroplane in 1919. Charles Lindbergh made the first solo transatlantic flight, from New York to Paris, in 1927. The Pacific was conquered by Kingsford Smith in 1926. Commercial airline services were developed between England and Europe, and shortly before the outbreak of war in 1939 the first transatlantic airline services came into operation. The aircraft industry, although still in its early days, grew vigorously. De Havilland, Handley Page, Rolls-Royce, and the Bristol Aircraft Company became large companies employing thousands of people.

Electrical engineering was another important growth industry, employing over 400,000 men and women in 1939. A Central Electricity Board was set up to distribute electricity by means of a national grid, and by the time of the Second World War 9 million people used electricity, compared with 730,000 twenty years earlier. The number of workers making electrical goods, e.g. radios, vacuum cleaners, electric irons and fires, grew threefold.

Probably the most successful industry between the wars was the motor-car industry. In the thirties Britain became the largest European producer of motor vehicles. The home market was protected by the McKenna Duties and by the British road tax and insurance system. This favoured an engine with a small horse power. The larger, more powerful American cars, designed for fast, long-distance travel, were not very suitable for England's winding roads. American car manufacturers, therefore, made little headway in the English market. Oxford, Dagenham and Luton became important centres of motor-car production. Manufacturers developed mass production into 'flow production', whereby the car was built up piece by piece as it moved slowly down an assembly line. At the end of the line the complete car could be driven away for routine checking, when it was ready for delivery. Home production of motor vehicles grew annually and, as the ownership of a motor car became less of a luxury, the number of cars in the country rose from 300,000 in 1920 to 2 million in 1939.

Between 1919 and 1939 many new industries developed in Britain. Man-made fibres, such as rayon, competed with the traditional textiles. Rayon manufacture was dominated by the long-established firm of Courtaulds, which produced at its Coventry factory 80 per cent of the rayon made in this country. Considerable progress was made in the manufacture of stainless steel, plastics, cellophane, cosmetics, disinfectants, vitamins and foodstuffs. Mass production became the rule in those industries producing standardized articles. There was a shift of workers away from the old industries into the newer ones. But the rise of the new industries did not fully compensate for the shrinkage in the older ones. No new industry developed to take the place of Lancashire cotton in the export markets of the world.

The new industries catered almost exclusively for the home market. A novel feature was packaging and mass advertising of consumer goods. Many consumer goods were manufactured and packaged in factories. The package served to advertise the product. Before the Great War advertising had been chiefly limited to patent medicines and tobacco. Now advertising no longer set out to inform, but to persuade, by building up the brand image of a particular product. Advertising became an important industry in itself, influencing fashion and the consumer habits of the whole nation.

CHAPTER 33
Social Life between the World Wars

Many aspects of social life which are familiar to us today—cinema, radio, football pools, dance halls, youth hostels, women's magazines, and mass advertising—were completely, or relatively unknown in 1919. Twenty years later they were part of a way of life. This chapter will attempt to outline the development of these, and other, features of the day-to-day life of the people.

Motor transport was a powerful agent for social change. In 1914 there were no country bus services and, outside London, no urban bus services. The tram was the usual form of town transport, and for longer journeys people usually travelled by rail. The limited means of travel meant that people lived either in the country or in the towns where they worked. There was very little *suburbia*; houses were built close to the town centre and railway station, or near the tram routes, whose termini marked the edges of the town. But in 1928 the manager of the Manchester transport system began to replace his trams with buses. This example was followed in other cities and, by 1932, more passengers were carried by buses than trams. Some country bus services were also established in the 1930s.

The advent of the motor bus and motor car encouraged more people to live in the country and work in the town. City centres were depopulated as people moved out to the suburbs, where new housing estates and ribbon development along the main roads blurred the distinction between countryside and town. Better public transport brought villagers into the market towns, whose shopping centres were transformed. The number of chain stores grew steadily in the thirties. Most towns by 1939 had a Boots, and a Marks and Spencer's store. The small shop and the corner store still made a good living, however, because they offered a personal service, and because it was convenient for housewives to buy their everyday needs in local shops.

At first, motor transport enjoyed considerable freedom from officialdom. Until 1931, when driving tests were introduced, any healthy person over 17 years could drive a motor car. In 1934 a 30 m.p.h. (50 k.p.h.) speed limit was introduced in built-up areas, and traffic lights appeared for the first time. More people were killed on England's roads in 1934, however, than thirty years later, when the number of motor vehicles had multiplied several times.

Road haulage firms and motor coach companies were able to decide their own charges. Railway freight rates were fixed by law. As a result, the lorry, which offered the advantage of door-to-door delivery, captured much business from the railways. By delivering goods to the shop direct from the factory or warehouse the lorry helped bring about changes in the pattern of retail and wholesale trading, by cutting out the middleman. Buses of rival companies operating on the same route sometimes raced each other to collect passengers. The solution was to give each bus company a monopoly over a particular route, and to restrict fare increases by making them subject to the agreement of the Minister of Transport.

The increase of motor vehicles on Britain's roads forced the highway authorities to pay more attention to the upkeep of roads. Rubber tyres broke up the road surfaces. Spraying the road surface with tar brought a new word into the English language—*tarmac*. A modernization programme was begun in

1924, and trunk roads became the responsibility of the Ministry of Transport. Roads were classified as major and secondary, according to their width and importance. Unfortunately, the road building programme was restricted in the 1930s. This was one reason for Britain's congested roads a generation later.

The boom in house building during the thirties was assisted by the prevailing low interest rates. More people than ever before were given the opportunity of buying their own homes, through building society mortgages. There was very little evidence of town planning, though in 1920 Britain's second garden city was begun at Welwyn. (The first was Letchworth in 1903.) The houses were built mainly in a pleasing Georgian style. Elsewhere, there was a craze for mock Tudor. The uncontrolled sprawl of houses, new factories, and garages, ate steadily into the countryside, and attempts to curb the expansion of the Greater London area were unsuccessful.

The general standard of living rose by about one-third between 1914 and 1937. Prices of foodstuffs and manufactures were low during the depressed thirties, so that those who were fortunate enough to be maintained in full employment found that their wages went further. Though central heating was still virtually unknown except in luxury flats and hotels, electric fires in some households gave heat at the flick of a switch. Electrical appliances such as irons, vacuum cleaners and washing machines came on to the market in steadily increasing numbers. A few households even possessed refrigerators. For many people, especially for those who lived in the South and away from the depressed areas, the period between the wars was one of considerable material progress. Those hit by the Depression might find this hard to believe, and they must certainly be excluded from any comment on general prosperity. But there was less acute poverty in the country, following the advances in health, hygiene, and the social services.

There was a slow, but steady increase in population, from 37,887,000 in England and Wales in 1921 to nearly 40 million in 1939. Both the birth rate and the death rate declined. The birth rate was 16 per thousand in the twenties, and 15 per thousand in the thirties. This was lower than either before the First World War, or after the Second World War. More people practised birth control, perhaps because some people preferred to put material possessions before large families. There was also in the thirties a natural reluctance to bring children into a world where their parents were threatened first by unemployment, and then by thoughts of another world war.

There were no startling changes in the distribution of population. The flight from the countryside to the towns continued, as farm workers left agriculture to find better paid jobs. The town's amenities—cinemas and dance halls, shopping centres, transport services, and council houses with electricity—all served to lure people away from the countryside. Many people left the northern industrial towns during the Depression, while places such as Cambridge, Luton, Coventry, and Bournemouth doubled their populations. But this movement away from the depressed areas should not be exaggerated, since it was difficult for many families to uproot themselves completely and migrate to another part of the country. There was a large surplus ($1\frac{3}{4}$ million) of women. This was partly due to the greater infant mortality among males, and their lower expectation of life, and partly to the fact that $\frac{3}{4}$ million men were killed in the war. Apart from Chinese settlements in Liverpool, Swansea, and the East End of London, there were few foreign immigrants living in Britain.

After 1918 class distinctions were far less marked than in Edwardian days. A more even distribution of wealth, the emancipation of women, and the general comradeship between people of different social standing during the war, all contributed to this. Another important factor was the gradual development of mass entertainment and communication.

74 *Beach wear, late 1920s*

Women took a much more active part in commerce, and social and sporting pastimes than they had before the war. Many young men had been killed in the trenches, so that many girls had little hope of marriage. They had to be able to fend for themselves and lead an independent and self-supporting life. There was much more equality between the sexes, even though there was a long way to go before equal pay for equal work was contemplated.

In the twenties there was a craze for dancing. The dances varied from the Vampire and the Shimmy, to the Blues, introduced in 1923, and the Charleston in 1924. It was the age of the Flapper and the 'Bright Young Things'. There was a new freedom in dress. The hobble skirt of 1911 would not do for the girl of a decade later. Gradually, lines became simpler and

freer, and skirts shorter. Women's hair was bobbed, and thus easy to manage. Artificial silk stockings, produced by the rayon manufacturers, proved very popular. Bathing costumes became brief, and there was an increasing acceptance of girls wearing slacks or shorts. Men's dress did not alter so radically, though the introduction of 'Oxford Bags' in 1925 led to a fashion for wide trouser legs which persisted many years. Later, in keeping with the more serious attitude of the thirties, dresses became longer, and less 'boyish'.

The first decade after the war, especially among young people of the middle classes, was one of gaiety. It was almost as if those who had escaped death in the trenches were determined to enjoy themselves. There was a greater emphasis on personal freedom and innovation. Churchgoing showed a marked decline. Nominally most people still belonged to the Anglican Church but fewer attended its services. The Roman Catholic Church had some success in attracting converts to its doctrines, but the Nonconformist Churches, which relied more on evangelical appeals, found their numbers falling.

The period as a whole was one of great development in the sphere of mass entertainment. Although radio had been used previously on ships, it was not until 1920 that regular broadcasting began in England. Wireless enthusiasts had to listen to their sets by means of headphones. In 1922 the British Broadcasting Company, a private company with a measure of government control, was made responsible for broadcasting. The General Strike of 1926, when most national newspapers were out of action, brought home to the Government the unique value of the radio, or wireless as it was more commonly known, as a medium for transmitting news and information to millions of listeners at the same time. Some members of the Government wished the company to be made the voice of the Government. In the event it retained a considerable measure of independence. The company was given a royal charter with a monopoly of sound broadcasting, and a new name, the British Broadcasting Corporation. Since then the BBC has been controlled by a board of governors appointed by the Government. The wireless increased in popularity. When the BBC's charter was renewed in 1936—the year when television was introduced (in the London area only)—most households possessed a radio. By 1939 there were 9 million licence holders.

The BBC set a high standard with its impartial news bulletins, and its programmes of music, drama, talks and discussions. In 1930 the BBC Symphony Orchestra was founded, and this catered for, and created, a greater audience than ever before for classical music. Local dialects gradually became less pronounced as people became accustomed to hearing announcer's English. The traditional

Christmas Message by the monarch was born in 1932, when George V spoke to the nation over the wireless on Christmas Day.

Side by side with the development of broadcasting came the great boom in films. Silent films had been made since the early years of the century. In 1911 there were 94 cinemas in London. By 1935, however, there were over 4,000. Most of the films shown were American. With a few notable exceptions, such as Alexander Korda's *The Private Life of Henry VIII*, made in 1934, British films were of poor quality. The great film heroes and heroines of the twenties were Rudolph Valentino, Charlie Chaplin, Douglas Fairbanks, Gloria Swanson, and Clara Bow. In *It*, made in 1927, Clara Bow portrayed the flapper girl of her age, smoking, drinking, and dancing till dawn. Charlie Chaplin created the tragi-comical figure of the tramp in baggy trousers and outsize boots.

In 1928 the first *talkie* was shown in England, and soon the silent film was ousted from the screen. More and more people went to the cinema, to enjoy Walt Disney's creations of *Mickey Mouse* and *Donald Duck*, or to enjoy an imaginary world of luxury and excitement. Very popular were the films where gangsters, or cowboys and Indians, massacred each other on the screen. Luxury picture palaces were built, and by 1939 weekly attendances at the cinema reached nearly 20 million. Saturday morning cinema clubs were started for children, so they early developed the film-going habit. The lives and loves of film stars—mostly American—were followed with avid interest.

The cinema destroyed its competitors, which were unable to rival the cheapness and convenience of film entertainment. The old-fashioned music halls nearly all closed down. In the big cities a few provincial theatres survived. Attendance at the old social centres, such as church and chapel, workingmen's clubs and local societies, declined. There was less need for people to provide their own entertainment when it was readily available at the cinema, or on the radio.

Interest in spectator sports, however, was stimulated by the radio. While tens of thousands watched the Cup Final at Wembley, millions listened to a live commentary of the match in the comfort of their armchairs. Cricket was probably more popular between the wars than at any time before or after. Cricket enthusiasts could follow ball-by-ball commentaries of Test Matches, or important county cricket matches. The struggle between England and Australia for the *Ashes* was very keenly contested. The 'bumpers' and legside bowling tactics of England's fast bowlers in the MCC's *bodyline* tour of Australia in 1933 aroused passionate controversy.

New sports such as greyhound racing, speedway, and ice hockey attracted crowds of spectators. Horse racing was also very popular, and gambling had no class barriers. Football pools provided a new outlet for betting. In 1923 the FA Cup Final was played at Wembley for the first time. Bolton beat West Ham 2–0. Lawn tennis clubs sprang up all over the country, and golf no longer remained the preserve of the very rich. There was a growing interest in hiking, and in 1930 the Youth Hostel Association was formed.

With schooling compulsory between the ages of five and fourteen years of age, more people than ever before attained a reasonable standard of literacy. A ready market existed, therefore, for those who had reading material to sell. In the early thirties the popular press had a battle for supremacy. The idea of canvassing for readers began with the *Daily Herald*'s door-to-door campaign. Soon the *Daily Express*, the *News Chronicle*, and the *Daily Mail* joined in. First registered readers were offered free insurance policies. Later, free gifts were offered instead. One could register as a reader for a few weeks, receive free gifts, and then register as a reader of another paper, and so obtain more free gifts.

By the time the papers decided to drop this expensive method of winning readers, both the *Daily Express* and the *Daily Herald* had a circulation of over 2 million. Popular magazines included *Woman* (begun in 1937) and *Picture Post* (1938). In 1935 Allen Lane began to publish Penguin books. The first paperbacks had arrived.

The public libraries increased their membership. The detective stories of Agatha Christie and Dorothy Sayers were very popular. The novels of John Buchan, Dornford Yates, and P. G. Wodehouse were widely read. The more intellectual novelists and poets were rather out of tune with the general mood of the people, particularly in the twenties. They appealed only to a minority. James Joyce originated a form of writing known as the 'stream of consciousness' method. The thoughts and actions of the characters were more important than the plot. Some writers, such as T. S. Eliot in *The Waste Land* were gloomy and despondent. In the thirties the major novelists dwelt on social and political problems. Walter Greenwood's *Love on the Dole* dealt with matters of immediate concern to many of his readers.

The general public was much better informed in 1939 than it had been in 1914. The 'gay twenties' had given way to the 'troubled thirties', and men and women grew accustomed to the notion of another war. Its approach was viewed, however, not with the relief and the patriotic fervour which had greeted the outbreak of war in 1914, but with a steadfast purpose arising from the knowledge that the Government had done its best to avoid war. The unity with which the British people went to war in 1939 reflected the greater cohesion which had been achieved in its social life. It could no longer be said, as it could of Britain in the nineteenth century, that Britain was *Two Nations*.

CHAPTER 34
The Second World War
and After 1939–51

The Second World War, to an even greater extent than the First, was to bring about far-reaching changes in economic and social life. In the Great War most of the fighting had been confined to the European land mass. It had been a soldier's war, and in particular, an infantryman's war. Aerial reconnaissance and bombardment were then in their infancy. The only fleet action after 1914 was the muddled battle of Jutland in 1916. In the Second World War both sides summoned to their aid all the vast resources of the state, industry, science, and technology which they could muster. The war was fought in every ocean, in the skies, and on three continents. It involved every man, woman, and child in the land, either directly or indirectly, because both Britain and Germany could carry the war right into the heart of its opponent's civilian population. Both sides adopted the tactics of terror, trying to bomb their enemy into submission. Germany developed self-propelled flying bombs, the V1s (or *doodlebugs* as they were nicknamed), and their successors the V2 supersonic rockets, which exploded on their target before the sound of their approach was heard. South-east England, and especially London, suffered from their attacks in the summer of 1944. The allies developed colossal 1,000-lb bombs, as well as aircraft capable of delivering them, and carried out massed air attacks on German towns and cities. Finally, they succeeded in manufacturing the atomic bomb. The terrible destruction of the cities of Hiroshima and Nagasaki in August 1945, which brought about an abrupt end to the war against Japan, heralded the start of the atomic age.

Britain declared war on Germany on 3 September 1939, but to the surprise of most

people little war followed. Enemy U-boats operated round the coasts of Britain, and one even penetrated the naval base of Scapa Flow and sank the battleship *Royal Oak* at its moorings. But the Germans concentrated their attack upon Poland, and neither the British nor the French had any desire to carry the war onto German soil. Since no direct assistance could be given to Poland, autumn and winter passed in England almost without incident. London's air-raid shelters were unused, except for a false alarm on the first day of the war. For months people carried their gas masks with them until they tired of doing so. About 3 million people, mostly women and children, were evacuated from probable dangers areas into a safer part of the country, but many soon returned to their homes. The first casualties of the war were the victims of road accidents, as car headlights were banned when a general 'blackout' during the hours of darkness was enforced.

The months of inaction in the West, labelled by the Americans as the *phoney war*, came to an end, and the war took on a new meaning, when the Germans invaded Norway in April 1940, and France in May. The swift collapse of France in the face of the German *Blitzkrieg* left the British army literally with its back to the sea at Dunkirk. The evacuation of 300,000 allied troops from Dunkirk was one of the most heroic episodes in Britain's history. Although it was a defeat, it was hailed at the time as a miracle, and it greatly increased the nation's morale, strengthening its conviction in ultimate victory.

The Battle of Britain began in August 1940, when the German *Luftwaffe* tried to destroy the Royal Air Force, thereby preparing the way for *Operation Sealion*, the invasion of

Britain. When the *Luftwaffe* failed to win mastery of the skies the Germans were forced to change their tactics, and to bomb industrial targets. The *Blitz* of 1940–1, the heavy nightly bombing of major cities and ports, such as London, Liverpool, and Portsmouth, though it caused heavy civilian casualties, had little effect on Britain's capacity to wage war.

The conquest of Britain was now a remote possibility, since invasion was almost out of the question. Nevertheless, Britain, unaided, could hardly hope to defeat Germany. The developing stalemate, however, was broken in 1941. In June, German armies invaded Russia in order to fulfil Hitler's dream of winning 'living space' for Germany in Eastern Europe. In December, Japan decided to consolidate her empire by destroying the American Pacific Fleet which lay at anchor in Pearl Harbor. Hitler then declared war on the United States, hoping that he could prevent supplies of arms and raw materials reaching Britain from the New World. From this point, Germany's defeat was almost inevitable. The enormous resources of Russia and America were too great for Germany to overcome. In January 1943, a German army was overwhelmed in the terrible struggle at Stalingrad. In May, British and American armies seized North Africa. Sicily was invaded and overrun by allied forces in July. The invasion of the Italian mainland followed, and in June 1944, Rome was taken. In the meantime, on 6 June 1944, the allied invasion of Occupied Europe took place. Eleven months later Germany surrendered unconditionally. When Japan did likewise three months later, the Second World War, after almost exactly six years of fighting, was at an end.

When Sir Winston Chirchill (1874–1965) became Prime Minister in May 1940, he promised 'Victory at all costs'. Everything was subordinate to the aim of winning the war against Germany. Thus the Emergency Powers Act (1940) gave the Government unparalleled power over people's lives. Compulsory military service was introduced for all men between the ages of eighteen and fifty, except for those in reserved occupations such as mining and agriculture. Even women between twenty and thirty years old were liable to call-up for non-combatant roles. Clothing and many foodstuffs were rationed. Every man, woman and child was issued with a ration book. Meat, fats, bacon, eggs, confectionery, clothing, and many other items were strictly rationed according to a *points* system—though bread itself was never rationed until after the war. Typical rations were 4 oz bacon, 1 oz cheese, 2 oz cooking fat, 4 oz butter and margarine, and 2 oz tea per person per week. Customers had to give up so many *points* or *coupons* for each purchase. This preserved an element of choice in the system. Clothing and furniture were manufactured to a uniform, though lower, standard, called *utility*, in order to save labour and materials. Income tax was raised to 10/- in the pound, and a new tax, purchase tax, was introduced. Banks were compelled to lend large sums to the Government. Private saving was encouraged. All these measures helped to pay for the cost of the war, and, equally important, reduce people's capacity to purchase goods, so that industry could concentrate its resources on the war effort. Many of these wartime controls were slow to disappear after the war, and some became permanent features in the British way of life. Food rationing persisted until 1954, while present-day governments make much greater use of taxation, bank rate, and interest rates than prewar governments to control national expenditure and regulate the economy.

As in the First World War, Britain was dependent upon imports of food and raw materials. In 1939 70 per cent of the nation's food was imported. Many industries, such as cotton and rubber, were wholly or largely dependent upon overseas supplies. Britain was, therefore, very vulnerable to a submarine blockade. During the Battle of the Atlantic, which continued until the middle of 1943, packs of German U-boats sank hundreds of thousands of tons of merchant shipping. The

Government restricted imports of non-essential goods, and industries not vital to the war effort were starved of supplies. Shipping losses were reduced by the adoption of the convoy system, so that merchant ships sailed in convoys with destroyer escorts instead of separately. But the pace of the convoy was set by the slowest vessel, and this reduced the flow of imports into Britain.

British farmers were encouraged by a mixture of persuasion and compulsion to increase production. Since it was more economical to use land for growing crops, rather than for supporting livestock, pasture farming was discouraged, and farmers were paid a subsidy of £2 for every acre of grassland they put under the plough. 1½ million hectares (nearly 4 million acres) were ploughed

up during the war. Farming became more mechanized, and this, combined with scientific use of artificial fertilizers, resulted in a 10 per cent increase in yield per acre without a corresponding increase in the number of farm workers.

By the summer of 1943, however, the U-boat menace had been overcome. It was also clear that Germany's defeat was only a matter of time. Politicians of all parties, and trade union leaders, began to press schemes for postwar reconstruction. Several commissions produced reports which formed the basis of much important legislation during the latter stages of the war, and the Labour governments of 1945–51. The Scott Commission (1942) on the development of the countryside led to the establishment in 1943 of a ministry

75 Cumbernauld New Town

for town and country planning, and to the Town and Country Planning Acts of 1944 and 1947. These Acts gave both the central government and local authorities greater control over the development of the countryside. The New Towns Act (1946) enabled the Government to choose certain areas for the sites of new towns, and fourteen new towns were established. The first was Stevenage. Others included Crawley, Corby and Hemel Hempstead. A National Parks and Countryside Act (1949) set aside parts of the countryside, which were to be preserved unspoiled for the enjoyment of all.

The great educational debate continued throughout the war. The outcome was the 1944 Education Act, carried through Parliament by R. A. Butler, the minister in charge of education. The Act raised the status of the Board of Education to that of a ministry, and it laid down a plan of education for all children between the ages of 5 and 15 years. The old idea of elementary schooling disappeared. Instead there were to be three progressive, but distinct, stages in education: primary, secondary, and further. The local education authorities were made responsible for providing free primary and secondary education for all children in their areas, and to make available scholarship grants for further education. The public schools, which remained outside the scope of the Act, were still allowed to charge fees. Religious education in state schools was to be compulsory and undenominational, but parents retained the right to withdraw their children, on conscientious grounds, from any form of religious instruction. The school-leaving age was to be raised to 15, and eventually, to 16 years. The former was accomplished in 1947, but the latter had to wait until 1972.

Primary schools were to offer a common curriculum up to the age of eleven. Secondary education was to be provided in three types of school: grammar schools with academic courses, technical schools with a bias towards the practical subjects, and modern schools which offered a general education for the majority of children. Transfer to secondary schools was to be based upon the results of a series of tests at the age of eleven. It was not long, however, before this system of education came under criticism. The selection process was not intended to be an examination which children passed or failed, but it was soon viewed as such by parents and children alike. Secondly, although all three types of secondary school were intended to be equal in status, modern schools were regarded as inferior to grammar schools. Thus those children who went to a grammar school were seen as having passed their eleven plus, while those who transferred to modern schools were 'failures'. Thirdly, the accuracy of the tests themselves was called into question. Many people felt that the system of selection was unfair, and that it was wrong to segregate children at such an early age. Comprehensive schools, which took children from the whole range of ability and from all social classes, were set up in London first, and they later spread into the provinces. In the 1960s there was a strong move towards comprehensive schools.

The development of the modern Welfare State

The social reforms which created the modern Welfare State were passed by the first Attlee government, but they followed naturally from the wartime Coalition. The war forced many people to rethink their ideas about the kind of society they wished to build. Certainly, one important effect of the war was to accustom people to accept a large measure of state planning and control in public affairs.

When the war against Germany ended in May 1945 it was decided that a return to normal party government should not be delayed by the continuing struggle against Japan. In the General Election the Labour Party, led by Clement Attlee (1883–1967), won 393 seats, and gained a majority of 149

Scale:
0 — 100 miles
0 — 100 km

N

Glenrothes □
Cumbernauld □
East Kilbride □   □ Livingston
□ Stonehouse
□ Irvine

Washington □
Peterlee □
Aycliffe □

Central Lancashire
□ New Town
Skelmersdale □
□ Warrington
Runcorn □

Telford □
Newtown □
Peterborough □
Corby □
Redditch □
Northampton □
Milton Keynes □
Stevenage □
□ Welwyn Garden City
Cwmbran □
Hemel Hempstead □   □ Harlow
Hatfield □
Basildon □
Bracknell □
Crawley □

76   New Towns in Britain in 1975

over all other parties. Churchill's dismissal seemed to be an act of ingratitude. But the Conservatives had been in power for twenty years, and they were associated with the lean years and massive unemployment of the 1930s. Thus their defeat was, to some extent, due to the swing of the political pendulum. The most important factor, however, was simply that the principles the Labour Party stood for reflected the mood of the electorate. The Labour Party, whose manifesto demanded *Fair Shares For All*, appealed to the large number of voters who wished to see a great extension of the social services, and a more equal distribution of wealth in society. It seemed logical that the party most deeply committed to the development of the Welfare State should be returned to power rather than the party which had strong leanings towards private enterprise.

The blueprint for the Welfare State was Lord Beveridge's *Report on Social Insurance and Allied Services* (1942). In it he recommended that the entire population should be safe-guarded against unemployment and ill-health. The first steps towards implementing Beveridge's proposals were taken during the war. The hated *Means Test* had already been abolished in 1941, and family resources were no longer taken into account when claims for assistance were assessed. The terms 'dole' and 'workhouse', long associated with the old Poor Law, soon disappeared from popular usage. Politicians of all parties promised that the high level of unemployment associated with the 1930s would never return. Food subsidies, rationing, and welfare foods for young children and expectant mothers, abolished the worst poverty. The Family Allowances Act of June 1945, provided five shillings for every child, after the first in a family. The first allowances were drawn in August 1946.

The keystone of the Welfare State was laid in 1946 with the passage of the National Insurance and National Health Service Acts. Under the first Act the whole adult population was compulsorily insured for unemployment and sickness benefits, pensions, and death grants. The adult population was divided into three categories: the employed, the self-employed, and the non-employed. All were required to pay weekly contributions. Every working man and woman was issued with an insurance card, on which the weekly stamps were fixed. The stamp included contributions from the employer and the State. Payment of benefits was taken out of the hands of the friendly societies, and administered by the State.

The National Health Service was largely the achievement of Aneurin Bevan (1897–1960), who became the first Minister of Health. Bevan piloted the Act through Parliament, and he was in charge of the lengthy and complicated negotiations with the British Medical Association. The Act entitled every-body to free medical, dental, and ophthalmic treatment. Drugs, medicines, spectacles, and dentures were to be issued free of charge. This Act made medical care a public service instead of a matter of private enterprise.

The National Health Service proved very costly. Within one year of its operation 5 million pairs of spectacles, and 200 million prescriptions for drugs and medicines, had been issued. After Defence it was the greatest charge on the Treasury. Nevertheless, the Guillebaud Commission, set up by the Conservative government in 1956 to inquire into the cost of the Health Service, reported that it did not consider the cost excessive. Whether more or less should be spent on matters such as promoting better health or education was a political question. It could be argued that making people pay for the means to better health was wrong. Equally it could be said that doctors, dentists, and others pro-vided a service to other people which should be paid for like any other service. Ultimately, society itself had to decide how much it was prepared to pay for improving the nation's health, and how much it would spend on other things like bombs and military bases, motor cars and television sets.

Nationalization

The Labour Party interpreted its 1945 election victory as a mandate to carry out a large programme of nationalization. State ownership of the means of production and distribution had long been suggested by Socialists as a cure for industrial inefficiency, and as a means of promoting a greater measure of social equality in society. The nationalization of the Bank of England in 1946 made very little difference to its operation, since it already existed virtually as a government department. The coal industry was nationalized in 1947, with very little opposition from the Conservatives. The mines had been run down during the war, and massive injections of capital and equipment were needed if the industry was to become a profitable one. The mine owners, who were given £360 million in compensation for the loss of their property, were replaced by a Coal Board. By the Electricity Act of 1947 the generation, supply, and distribution of electricity was placed in the hands of twelve area boards. Similarly, in 1948, a nationalized Gas Council was set up.

Public transport was nationalized in 1948. The railways had been taken over by the State during the two World Wars, and after the First the number of companies had been reduced to four. The replacement of the old-style companies like the LNER by British Railways seemed only the final logical step in a process which stretched back a hundred and four years, when the question of their State ownership was first raised. The 1948 Transport Act also nationalized all long-distance road haulage firms, with the exception of furniture removers.

The proposal to take over the steel industry, however, aroused fierce opposition. The Conservatives argued that the industry was an expanding and profitable one, with good relations between management and men, so that public ownership was unnecessary. Since the Conservatives controlled the House of Lords, which was certain to reject any steel nationalization bill, a bill to reduce the delaying powers of the Lords was passed first. The Parliament Act of 1949 cut the duration of the Lords' veto from two years to one. The Iron and Steel Bill was finally passed, with the amendment that it would not come into effect until the electorate had pronounced its verdict on the measure. When Labour was returned to office in February 1950, although with a greatly reduced majority, the nationalization of the steel industry became a fact, if short-lived. The Conservatives reversed the decision as soon as they were returned to power in 1951.

Britain's balance of payments

At the same time as it carried out a varied programme of social reform, the Labour government had to repair Britain's economy, and avoid the danger of national bankruptcy. Huge wartime debts had been accumulated. Britain had borrowed £4,000 million from Commonwealth countries. Under the terms of the lend-lease agreement, America had supplied, free of charge during the war, military and civil equipment to the value of another £7,000 million. When this aid ceased one week after the surrender of Japan, a large loan was secured from Canada and America to keep Britain solvent until she could earn her own living abroad.

This was not as simple as it sounds. The normal pattern of trade had been destroyed by the war, and exports in 1945 were only half the figure for 1938. This was a very serious matter, since Britain had sold many of her overseas assets during the war, so that imports had to be paid for by exports to a much greater extent than before. Furthermore, industry was ill-equipped to compete in world markets. Investment in new factory plant and machinery had been held up, and existing plant had deteriorated as a result of continuous use and lack of proper maintenance during the war. The process of re-equipping industry was bound to take some time, and raw materials had to be stockpiled before industry could expand production. In the meantime Britain was paying more for imports of food, raw materials, and capital goods like machinery, than she was earning by selling goods abroad.

The Government did all in its power to promote industrial growth. Hugh Dalton, the Chancellor of the Exchequer, reduced Bank Rate to 2 per cent in order to encourage manufacturers to invest in new factories and equipment, and local authorities to undertake building schemes. The home market was deliberately kept short of consumer goods in order to boost exports. New factory building took priority over private housing and hospitals. As a result of these measures, exports by 1947 were nearly 40 per cent higher than the 1938 figure.

Unfortunately, events conspired to hold back Britain's economic recovery. Exports were still not rising fast enough to convert an adverse trade balance into a favourable one. In particular Britain was unable to earn enough dollars to pay for the goods she imported from America. Since trade unions were in a strong position to bargain with employers, wage increases in general more than kept pace with price rises. This meant that British exports were gradually being priced out of world markets. Even the weather contributed to the country's economic difficulties. The winter of 1946–7 was the coldest for fifty years. For three months a blanket of snow and ice covered much of the country. The transport of goods by road and rail was slowed down. The coal industry could not produce enough coal, and a desperate fuel shortage developed. Many factories had to close down, and in February 2 million people were unemployed.

Sir Stafford Cripps succeeded Dalton in November 1947. Cripps combined tax increases with cuts in food subsidies and spending on the social services to reduce consumer demand. Company dividends were limited. A partial wage freeze limited wage increases to 5 per cent in the period 1948–50. This period of government controls, rationing, and wage restraint was known as *Austerity*. Cripps's 'Productivity Drive', however, led to a resumption of full employment, and to a rise in exports. But, just when it seemed that the balance of payments was improving again, a foreign exchange crisis developed, forcing the government to devalue the pound in September 1949. Instead of the pound being worth $4·03 the rate was fixed at $2·80. This put up the cost of imports but cheapened, and therefore encouraged, exports. Although it was regarded as a national humiliation, devaluation certainly led to an improvement in Britain's trading account and, apart from 1951 and 1955, the 1950s produced trade surpluses.

Labour's popularity, however, was waning. In the 1950 General Election the Government's majority was only 6. In part this was a reaction against the continuing shortage of housing and rationing, and in part disenchantment with some of Labour's policies. In 1947 the Government had introduced peacetime military conscription for all young men for eighteen months, and in 1950 this period was increased to two years. Many national servicemen fought in the Korean War (1950–3). Inflation, and the rising cost of raw materials due to the Korean War placed the economy under severe strain. Labour, too, seemed to have lost some of its zest for government, and was running out of new ideas. Two prominent ministers, Ernest Bevin and Sir Stafford Cripps had died. Another two, Aneurin Bevan and Harold Wilson, resigned in April 1951, when Hugh Gaitskell introduced charges for national health spectacles, an economy measure forced upon the Government by the cost of the Korean War. When Attlee called for a General Election in October 1951, in an effort to increase the Government's majority, the Conservatives were returned to power, though such were the eccentricities of the electoral system, the Labour Party actually polled more votes. Thus began a long period of Conservative rule.

When the Conservatives under Sir Winston Churchill came into power in October 1951, the country was ready for a relaxation of the controls which had been a feature of Labour rule. This was not immediately possible, since the Government faced a severe economic crisis, which endangered the stability of sterling. The trade deficit for the first six months alone was £500 million. The Conservative Chancellor of the Exchequer, R. A. Butler, tightened still further the restrictions imposed recently by the Labour government. The foreign travel allowance was reduced first to £50, and then to £25. The standard rate of income tax was raised by 6d to 9/6 in the pound. Purchase tax on a wide range of manufactured goods, including electrical appliances and cars, was doubled. At the same time the banks were ordered to restrict their lending.

These controls were kept for two years, but in 1954 the Conservatives finally brought food rationing to an end, and gradually removed many other controls. Somewhat to their own surprise, and to the growing discomfiture of their political opponents, they discovered that Conservative freedom worked. The Conservatives had the good fortune to take office shortly before the terms of world trade swung sharply in Britain's favour. World prices of raw materials fell on average by one quarter, so that imports were cheaper. Exports of manufactures, however, were fetching slightly higher prices in overseas markets. All this was accomplished without any effort on the part of the British people, which treated itself to an enjoyable spending spree for two years. Much of the increased output of British industry was absorbed by the home market, instead of being exported.

Unfortunately, a setback occurred in 1955,

when the trend of world trade turned the other way. Imports became dearer, and Britain's rate of economic growth slowed down almost to a standstill. In the meantime, prices had risen, partly as a result of Conservative policies, which aimed at making people pay the 'true economic cost' of articles. Food subsidies had been cut in order to meet the objections of the middle classes, who felt they were bearing the brunt of taxation so that lower-paid workers might enjoy an artificially high standard of living. The rise in prices generated a fierce, and successful, demand from trade unions for higher wages for their members. This caused prices to rise higher still, and made it more difficult for Britain to sell her manufactures and services abroad.

The failure to achieve a satisfactory rate of economic expansion led once more to a balance of payments crisis. In an attempt to check the spiral of inflation the Government cut back on its spending on new building, such as hospitals and schools. Bank Rate was raised, and efforts were made to put a ceiling on rising prices. Savings were encouraged by increasing interest rates on National Savings Certificates and Defence Bonds. Macmillan, who was Chancellor in Sir Anthony Eden's administration (1955–7) also exploited people's gambling instincts by introducing Premium Bonds, which bore no interest, but offered lucky holders a chance of winning a large sum of money.

These measures had some success, but by 1957 the amount of money people were spending on consumer goods was giving the Government cause for concern. Once again further restrictions on public spending were imposed. This was succeeded by a deliberate attempt to expand the economy. Inflation, and a renewed balance of payments crisis followed. The fifties, therefore, described by Macmillan in a memorable phrase when he told the British public 'You've never had it so good', ended with yet another severe dose of deflation. In 1960 Selwyn Lloyd, who had succeeded Heathcote Amory, Chancellor in Macmillan's second administration (1959–63), brought in an unpopular 'wages freeze', clamped down on hire purchase regulations and increased Bank Rate. The 'stop–go' economic policies of the fifties caused the Labour opposition to compare the running of the nation's economy under Conservative rule with a car driver who could only use the accelerator and brake.

Selwyn Lloyd's measures had the required effect, but at the cost of mounting unemployment and industrial unrest. In an effort to find more permanent solutions to some of Britain's recurrent economic problems, the Conservatives placed greater emphasis upon long-term planning. Dr Beeching headed an investigation into the organization of British Railways, and recommended the closing down of many unprofitable branch lines. The Buchanan Report (1963) proposed far-reaching changes in the towns and cities to cope with the rapidly increasing volume of road traffic. A National Economic Development Council was created in 1962. Composed of trade union leaders, employers, and economists, its task was to advise the Government on the development of British industry. A National Incomes Commission, whose purpose was to advise on an incomes policy, was less successful.

The dilemma of trying to expand the economy without creating a balance of payments crisis was not the only one the Conservative governments faced. Britain's military role in a world dominated by the two 'super' powers, the United States and the Soviet Union, had to be decided. It was not easy for any government to accept the fact that Britain could no longer compete with either of them on equal terms. Thus both the Labour and the

77 *A deserted railway station*
One of the many branch line stations closed as a result of Dr Beeching's economy drive

Conservative governments persisted in developing an independent nuclear deterrent. A British atomic bomb was produced in 1952, and a hydrogen bomb was successfully exploded in 1957. But Britain was forced into dependence upon the United States for the means of delivering nuclear warheads. At the Nassau Conference in the Bahamas in 1962 Macmillan persuaded President Kennedy to supply Britain with Polaris missiles, which were fired underwater from submarines. In return, the United States was given certain facilities at Holy Loch, in Scotland, for its fleet of nuclear submarines. Britain's participation in the nuclear arms race aroused some opposition at home. The annual 'Ban the Bomb' march at Easter, organized by the Committee of One Hundred for the Campaign for Nuclear Disarmament (CND) was a rallying point for all those who opposed the use and spread of nuclear weapons.

This period also witnessed the end of a once great empire. A map of the world in 1945 showed large areas shaded red—the British Commonwealth and Empire. This included the Dominions of Canada, Australia, New

Zealand, and South Africa, as well as India, Ceylon, Burma, the British West Indies, British Guiana, and large areas of Africa. In 1947 the Attlee administration had brought to an end British rule in India, which became a republic within the Commonwealth. Ceylon also achieved its independence, as did Burma, which left the Commonwealth. During the fifties and sixties Britain's colonial possessions in Africa achieved self-government. Britain made no attempt to withstand African nationalism, or in Macmillan's words, 'the wind of change which was blowing through Africa'. The Gold Coast became Ghana in 1957, and in 1960 Nigeria achieved statehood. By 1964 all Britain's possessions in Africa, with the exception of Southern Rhodesia, had been granted self-government. In 1965 Rhodesia formally announced its Unilateral Declaration of Independence (UDI), and in early 1970 finally severed its last remaining ties with the Crown.

Some responsibilities of bygone imperialism, however, have remained. Commonwealth people have British citizenship, and many took advantage of this fact to come and settle in Britain. Immigration was especially heavy from the West Indies, India and Pakistan. In the period 1960–2 over 400,000 Commonwealth immigrants entered the country. They were welcomed as they relieved labour shortages in certain sectors of the economy, particularly in the nursing profession, but the rapid influx created social problems. Where immigrants were concentrated in major industrial cities such as Leeds, Bradford, Birmingham, and London, they placed an extra strain on the schools and social services, which were already overburdened. The Commonwealth Immigrants Act (1962) gave the Government power to restrict the number of immigrants entering the country each year. The Race Relations Act (1968) made discrimination on the grounds of race or colour unlawful in the provision of goods, services, employment and housing. A Race Relations Board was also set up to investigate complaints. Immigration became a vexed question in the sixties, but there is little doubt that Britain in the latter part of the twentieth century will become a multiracial society.

To the issues of Imperialism, and Britain's military role in the nuclear age, may be added a third—the debate over Britain's economic and political integration with the rest of Europe. In 1957 six European countries— France, Italy, West Germany, Belgium, Holland, and Luxemburg—formally created themselves into the European Economic Community (EEC), or Common Market, by signing the Treaty of Rome. They formed a closely knit trading community with the intention of developing close political links with each other. Britain did not join.

In 1960 Britain set up a rival organization, the European Free Trade Association (EFTA), under the Stockholm Convention. The EFTA countries comprised Austria, Denmark; Norway, Sweden, Portugal, Switzerland, and Britain. (Finland joined in 1961.) In August 1961, however, Britain applied for membership of the Common Market. The complicated negotiations were suspended in January 1963, with no agreement reached. Negotiations were resumed by the Labour Government in 1967, but again fell through when it became clear that France did not support Britain's application.

Soon after the Conservatives were returned to power in June 1970 under Edward Heath negotiations were reopened. By this time the French Government had become more favourably disposed towards Britain's application, and in July 1971 formal terms of entry were agreed in Brussels. Though they were opposed by many Labour MPs, and by a minority of Conservative MPs, the House of Commons voted in October 1971 in favour of Britain joining the Common Market.

Throughout the long and complicated discussions in Brussels the British public was chiefly concerned about the increased price of food which membership of the EEC would bring, since Britain would be forced to bring her prices in line with those of the Common Market. Britain would not be permitted to enjoy cheap foodstuffs imported from countries such as Argentina and New Zealand, since this would conflict with the Common Market's agricultural policy. This issue overshadowed the more important issue of loss of sovereignty which membership entailed. When Britain joined the EEC on 1 January 1973, Parliament lost its freedom to pass whatever laws it decided, since it had to take into account the regulations and wishes of the other members.

Nevertheless, membership had considerable attractions. British manufacturers gained access to a very large and rich market, responsible for forty per cent of the world's trade which, it was hoped, would make British firms more efficient. Membership of the EEC might even cure Britain's economic weaknesses by stimulating the economy to such an extent that it could escape from the cycle of brief periods of growth, alternating with longer periods of restraint, when the economy had to be held back in order to check inflation.

Although Britain's rate of economic growth during the sixties was faster than in any decade since 1900, it did not compare very favourably with that of most other industrial nations. Imports still tended to grow much faster than exports. The realization that Britain was not paying her way in the world led to a lack of international confidence in sterling. Britain's gold reserves dwindled as they were used by the Bank of England to maintain the pound at its official level. Eventually, in 1967, the Labour Government, led by Harold Wilson (Prime Minister since 1964), was forced to devalue, and the value of the pound sterling in terms of dollars was cut from $2·80 to $2·40. This drastic step, together with measures designed to make devaluation succeed, brought about a marked improvement in the balance of payments by 1969. In that year a small trading deficit was amply covered by a large surplus from invisible earnings.

In the spring of 1970, with Britain's eco-nomic prospects now looking very bright, Wilson called for a General Election in June. Most opinion polls forecast a Labour victory, and it was, therefore, to many people's surprise that the Conservative Party was returned to office. The results of the 1970 General Election, compared with that of 1966, were as follows:

	Seats		Votes (in millions)		% of Votes	
	1970	1966	1970	1966	1970	1966
Conservative	330	253	13·1	11·4	46·4	41·9
Labour	287	363	12·1	13·0	43·0	47·9
Liberal	6	12	2·1	2·3	7·4	8·6
Others	6	1	0·9	0·4	3·2	1·6

There is no doubt that the Conservatives' victory owed much to the conviction of many voters that the Labour Government had failed to curb the power of trade unions, and to check inflation and massive wage claims. Nevertheless, the new Government certainly inherited an improving economic climate, since both 1971 and 1972 produced large trading surpluses.

Yet the Conservative Government soon found itself grappling with unemployment and inflation. To cut down unemployment the Government encouraged business and industry to expand, by reducing taxation and stimulating consumer spending. In June 1972 the pound sterling was allowed to *float* (i.e. the Bank of England ceased to support the pound in order to maintain its fixed rate; instead, the pound was permitted to find its own value in relation to other world currencies). As a result, exports grew by 12 per cent, and by early 1973 the economy was growing rapidly. Living standards improved as workers won large wage increases.

Unfortunately, inflation became a serious problem, for the Government failed to convince the trade unions that wage restraint was necessary. In November 1972 Stage One of a statutory incomes and prices policy was introduced. This meant a six months standstill on increases in most prices and rents, dividends and pay. In April 1973 Stage Two began. A

Price Commission was set up to monitor prices, and a Pay Board was given the task of restraining pay rises.

But the Government found it impossible to cure inflation. Manufacturers and service industries had to raise prices to cover their costs. The introduction of Value Added Tax (VAT) on 1 April 1973 increased the cost of most goods and services. Moreover, the Government had no control over world prices of foodstuffs and raw materials, which rose by 47 per cent in 1973. The oil producing nations doubled the price of oil between June and December, and redoubled it on 1 January 1974. Their policies dislocated the economies of the entire western world, and caused a massive balance of payments crisis for Britain.

Meanwhile, the Government's incomes policy was bitterly opposed by the trade unions, who refused to accept pay restraint while prices were allowed to rise unchecked. When Stage Three of the Counter Inflation Act was introduced in November 1973 the coal miners, in support of their wage claim, banned overtime working. Just ten months previously the miners had gone on strike, and had only returned to work when the Wilberforce Commission, appointed by the Government to consider the miners' claim, recommended large increases in their wage rates. The miners were determined to defend their newly-won position as one of the most highly paid groups of workers.

On 13 November the Government an-

78 Calder Hall, Cumberland

nounced a state of emergency to conserve fuel supplies. On 29 November petrol coupons were issued to motorists in case rationing became necessary, and one week later a 50 m.p.h. speed limit was introduced. On New Year's Day a three day working week for industry came into operation in an effort to make coal stocks last through the winter. When the miners went on strike, Edward Heath decided to appeal to the electorate.

In the General Election the Conservatives gained a narrow margin over the Socialists in the number of votes they received, but won fewer seats. Heath resigned, and Harold Wilson formed a new administration, though he did not have an overall majority in the House of Commons. A second election took place in October, which produced a narrow majority for the Labour Party. The results of the two elections were as follows:

	Seats		Votes (in millions)		% of Votes	
	Feb.	Oct.	Feb.	Oct.	Feb.	Oct.
Labour	301	319	11·6	11·4	37·2	39·3
Conservative	296	276	11·9	10·4	38·2	35·8
Liberals	14	13	6·0	5·3	19·3	18·3
Others	24	24	1·6	1·9	5·3	6·6

One of the features of both elections was the size of the votes for the Liberal Party, and the Scottish Nationalists. This was seen as evidence of public disenchantment with both major political parties, whose share of the vote had dropped sharply.

The Labour Party manifestos of February and October pledged that a Labour Government would end statutory wage restraint, and would seek the voluntary cooperation of the trade unions in curbing wage rises. Thus one of the first actions of Wilson's Government was to abolish the Pay Board. In June the Trade Union Congress suggested guidelines for unions seeking pay increases. This co-operation, however, depended upon the Government being successful in its efforts to keep prices down. Since the retail price index for the twelve months ending in June 1975 showed an increase of 26 per cent, many

unions felt it was their duty to protect their members from the effects of inflation by seeking larger wage increases than those recommended by the TUC. Alarmed by galloping inflation, the Government introduced in August 1975 a £6 a week limit on wage rises.

The Government fulfilled another election promise by renegotiating the terms of Britain's membership of the Common Market. In March 1975 Harold Wilson announced the Cabinet's majority decision to recommend to the nation continued membership. In the referendum on 5 June 1975, the first in Britain's history, there was a two to one vote in favour of Britain remaining in the EEC, with 17,378,000 people voting 'Yes', and 8,470,000 voting 'No'. Only the sparsely populated remote areas of Shetland and the Western Islands of Scotland voted in favour of Britain's withdrawal. Thus the long debate on the Common Market was settled.

In spite of Britain's economic difficulties the period 1953–75 was a very prosperous time for the British people. Compared with previous generations people had far more leisure. The length of the average working week was forty hours, though this could be increased by voluntary overtime. Most employees had at least two weeks' paid holiday, in addition to public holidays. In 1967 over 31 million people could afford to take an annual holiday, and five million went abroad.

More people than ever before were able to enjoy the material things of life. Whereas in 1945 nearly all houses were heated by coal fires many homes today have central heating. The television set is almost universal, and many families have colour television. Much of the drudgery of running a home has been abolished. Non-iron fabrics, frozen foods, refrigerators, electric food-mixers, and washing machines all make the housewife's task easier.

The nation's shopping habits have altered. The number of small shops has declined in the face of competition from multiple stores and supermarkets. Competition between small traders and big stores intensified with the abolition of retail price maintenance in 1963. This enabled shops to fix the price of goods instead of the manufacturer. The most important change was the introduction of decimal currency on 15 February 1971 (D Day), when the pound was divided into 100 new pence instead of 20 shillings, or 240 pennies.

Great changes are taking place in society, communications, and industry. Young people are far more ready to question the *status quo* and the Establishment. Pop music, drug-taking, and greater sexual freedom were all aspects of the so-called 'permissive society' which developed in the late sixties. Mass advertising has a powerful influence in shaping people's opinions and habits. People are also better informed as a result of television. Pictures and commentary can be flashed around the world in a matter of moments. Electronic computers now take over from human beings in many fields, from tracking satellites and space rockets, to operating telephone exchanges. Computers are installed in universities, factories, and offices, where they act as 'memory banks'.

A new form of power, nuclear power, competes with coal. The Atomic Energy Authority was set up in 1954 to develop the peaceful application of nuclear energy. Its chief research establishment is at Harwell, in Essex. The first nuclear power station for the generation of electricity was Calder Hall, in Cumberland, in 1956. Chapelcross, in Dumfriesshire, was opened in 1959. Since then several others have been built, and more are planned. In 1970 Britain generated as much electricity from nuclear energy as the rest of the world put together.

Oil and natural gas play an important part in the nation's industrial life. Nearly 100 million tons of petroleum products were imported in 1973. Since 1945 nineteen oil refineries have been built, the largest being at Fawley, on Southampton Water, Stanlow in Cheshire, and Shellhaven on the Thames Estuary. The first supplies of natural gas reached this country in 1964 from the Sahara, but five major North Sea gasfields are now in production. North Sea oil is being rapidly exploited. New forms of power, perhaps undreamt of at present, may be discovered in our lifetime.

The prospects for material prosperity are very exciting, provided men do not destroy themselves in the process. At the same time greater affluence brings its problems. The task of disposing of the nation's garbage has become a daunting one. Empty plastic containers and tin cans by the million are not easily destroyed. Nuclear waste is dumped in the ocean, at a time when knowledge of the possible effects of contamination is uncertain. Car exhaust fumes pollute the air we breathe in towns. Chemical pesticides may increase the product of agriculture, but some forms of wild life are in danger of extinction as a result of their use. The pollution of the atmosphere, rivers, lakes, and oceans, has become a matter for international concern. Here in Britain the open countryside is steadily disappearing as the demands of society on it increase. Old villages are surrounded by new housing estates as commuters jostle for living space away from the towns where they work. New factories, airports, motorways, reservoirs, new towns and suburbs, eat remorselessly into the remaining countryside. Society must be careful that in the quest for material prosperity it does not despoil its most precious asset of all, the land itself.

INDEX